SPACE ADVENTURE COLLECTIBLES

by T. N. Tumbusch

Edited by Tom Tumbusch

Color Photography by Tom Schwartz

B&W Photography by T.N. Tumbusch and Tom Tumbusch

Wallace-Homestead Book Company
Radnor, Pennsylvania

To Erin

Prices listed are based on the author's experience and are presented as a guide for information purposes only. No one is obligated in any way to buy, sell, or trade according to these prices. Condition, rarity, demand and the reader's desire to own determine the actual price paid. No offer to buy or sell at the prices listed is intended or made. Buying and selling is conducted at the reader's risk. Neither the author nor publisher assumes any liability for any losses suffered for use of, or any typographic errors contained in, this book. The numeric code system used in this book is not consistant with previous collectible guides published by Tomart Publications. All value estimates are presented in U.S. dollars. The dollar sign is omitted to avoid needless repetition.

Notice of Copyright Ownership

The characters and other graphics depicted in this collector's reference guide are copyrighted. The rights are last known to be owned by the companies listed as follows: **Alien/Aliens** © Twentieth Century-Fox Film Corporation; **Battlestar Galactica** © Universal City Studios, Inc.; **The Black Hole** © The Walt Disney Co.; **Buck Rogers** © Robert C. Dille; **Captain Video** © The Dumont TV Network, Inc.; **Close Encounters** © Columbia Pictures Industries, Inc.; **Dune** © Dino De Laurintus, Corporation; **E.T.** © Universal City Studios, Inc.; **Flash Gordon** © King Features Syndicate, Inc.; **Forbidden Planet** © 1956 Loew's Incorporated, renewed 1984 MGM/UA Entertainment Co.; **John Carter of Mars** © Edgar Rice Burroughs, Inc.; **Planet of the Apes** © Twentieth Century-Fox Film Corporation; **Rocky Jones** © Space Ranger Enterprises; **Space 1999** © ATV Licensing Ltd.; **Space Patrol** © Mike Moser; **Star Trek** © Paramount Pictures Corporation; **Star Wars** © Lucasfilm, Ltd.; **Tom Corbett, Space Cadet** © Rockhill Productions; **2001/2010/2061** © MGM/UA Entertainment Co.; **V** © Warner Bros., Inc.

© Copyright 1990, Thomas N. Tumbusch

All rights reserved

Published in Radnor, Pennsylvania, 19089, by Wallace-Homestead Book Company. Published simultaneously by Tomart Publications, Dayton, Ohio, 45429.

No part of this book may be reproduced, transmitted, or stored in any form or by any means, electronic or mechanical, without prior written permission from the publisher.

ISBN: 0-87069-565-7

Library of Congress Catalog Card No. 89-51637

Manufactured in the United States of America

3 4 5 6 7 8 9 0   8 7 6 5 4 3

ACKNOWLEDGEMENTS

Most of the people I know had some influence on this work, and it would be impossible to credit everyone. Numerous collectors, dealers and fans provided items for photography and information, including Theresa Bean, Rob Begley, Hal Blevins, Jim Buchanan, John and Vicki Campbell, Von Crabill, Paul Findsen, Rich Gifford, Dennis Hasty, Jeff Kilian, Robert Lesser, Linda O'Leary, Don Maris, Foster Pollack, Karl Price, Dan Riess, Daniel Rous, Joe Sarno, Charles Sexton, Mike Stannard and Dave VanBenschoten.

Special thanks are in order for the editors who have taken the time to review the manuscript in whole or in part: Bill Bruegman, Robert "Boba" Fisher, Jean Ann Gallagher, Wayne Helton, Ed Osepowicz, Gene Seger, William Sikora, Gary Sohmers, Art and Artie Thomas, Tom E. Tumbusch and David Welch.

As a side note, I would like to express my appreciation to Robert A. Heinlein, Frank Herbert, George Lucas, Gene Roddenberry, Steven Spielberg and many others. These masters of science fiction were the delights of my childhood, and undoubtedly contributed to my interest and knowledge in this field.

The color photography is the work of Tom Schwartz, Fred Boomer, Terry Cavanaugh and Beth Gilbert. May the "Schwartz" be with you! Page imaging was done by Type One Graphics, color separations by Printing Preparations, printing by Central Printing and Carpenter Lithographing Company.

Preparation of the final art was aided by Allan Nester and Rebecca Scott. And special thanks go to Rebecca Trissel who did all the desktop publishing.

I am deeply indebted to several people whose assistance and support falls outside the realm of space adventure: Jason Snow and Susan Trotter (who bent a rule or two to help the author meet deadlines), Doug Nerad (who provided last-minute assistance far beyond the call of duty), and Erin McCain (who listened).

Finally, a special note of appreciation should be made to E. J. Benstock for explaining all the *Planet of the Apes* movies to me, enduring my presence during a difficult year, and giving me her hat (not necessarily in that order).

TABLE OF CONTENTS

Acknowledgements 3
Table of Contents 4
Foreword 5
Space Adventure! 6
To the Stars! 6
Guide to Collecting 12
Alien/Aliens 15
Battlestar Galactica 17
Black Hole, The 23
Buck Rogers 27
Captain Video 43
Close Encounters 45
Dune 45
E.T. 51
Flash Gordon 57
Forbidden Planet 61
John Carter of Mars 62
Planet of the Apes 64
Rocky Jones 77
Space 1999 77
Space Patrol 80
Star Trek 89
Star Wars 130
Tom Corbett 213
2001/2010/2061 218
V 219
Index 221
Bibliography 222
About the Author 224

COLOR PLATES

2001/2010 65
Buck Rogers/Flash Gordon 66
Captain Video/Tom Corbett/Forbidden Planet 67
The Black Hole/Space: 1999 68
E.T. the Extra-Terrestrial 69
Buttons, pins, and rings 70
Space Patrol 71
Dune/Alien/V 72
Star Wars 137
Star Wars 138
The Empire Strikes Back 139
Return of the Jedi 140
Star Trek (film) 141
Star Trek (television) 142
Planet of the Apes 143
Battlestar Galactica/Close Encounters 144

FOREWORD

There has never been, to my knowledge, any attempt to detail the numerous aspects of space adventure memorabilia in a single volume. This book is intended to be a general guide to the field, providing an overview which will be useful to novice and experienced collectors alike.

A great deal of time and research has gone into the production of the work. The final output you are holding is the result of many miles of travel, the input of specialized collectors, and an assimilation of literal piles of information.

It would be illogical of me to claim these listings are complete and free from error. Accuracy has been strived for continuously, but mistakes and exclusions will most likely surface. Comments and suggestions are eagerly encouraged as a means of improving future editions.

This book has been written to serve three functions. 1) As an informative guide to the more popular manifestations of space adventure. 2) To list, as completely and accurately as possible, the various items of merchandise produced, in a format which enables easy identification. 3) To provide an estimate of values. Regarding the last, it should be noted that price guides are out-of-date the day they roll off the press. Prices go up and down, and may vary from one area to another. The price ranges shown in this book are, however, relative to each other at the time of publication. In that context, with condition taken into account, prices can be adjusted for local demand factors and changes in market trends.

Enjoy!

Tom N. Tumbusch

SPACE ADVENTURE!

One of the greatest human achievements of the 20th century was a small beginning -- the first steps in the exploration of outer space. The concept, however, was hardly a new one. Space adventure fascinated humankind hundreds of years before Vostok put the first man in orbit. Men and women have long dreamed of other worlds, of voyages across the cosmos and the strange new creatures they might find. Many of yesterday's fantasies have become reality today.

"Space adventure" is a term used to describe fiction which speculates on the dramatic and dangerous exploration beyond our own planet. It seeks to probe the mysteries of space. Questions like: What's out there? Who (or more often, what) will we encounter? What new advances in technology will accompany space travel? What will be universe be like when interstellar travel is part of everyday life?

Space adventure should not be confused with science fiction. The latter is a much broader category. Nor is it limited to "space heroes" like Buck Rogers or Luke Skywalker. This work deals with space adventure genres where licensed merchandise was produced, from the earliest John Carter novels to "Star Trek: The Next Generation".

There have also been hundreds of space toys not related to a comic strip, book, film or television show. Although many such pieces are interesting and collectible, (especially robots) they are numerous enough to fill a separate book.

TO THE STARS!

Man has been fascinated by outer space since the dawn of recorded time. The Chinese kept detailed records of events they viewed in the heavens. Early civilizations believed the stars and planets were floating palaces in the sky, inhabited by the gods. Many thought the patterns of the stars could be interpreted, predicting the future.

The concept of leaving Earth to explore the vastness of space is centuries old. The noted German astronomer Johannes Kepler wrote a book called *The Dream* in 1609. Having fallen asleep in his chair, he embarked on a fantastic voyage to Levania (the moon). Kepler's vehicle was a sailing ship, capable of making the journey in about four hours during certain rare conditions. While some aspects of the moon he described would be proven accurate, his ideas concerning the vegetation, seas, and inhabitants would not. His nonexistent creatures were nothing more than part of the dream, but they were probably the first "aliens" ever envisioned in literature.

Following Kepler's lead, several other authors conceived trips into space. But the real beginnings of modern science fiction came later. In the wake of the American Civil War, French author Jules Verne wrote *From the Earth to the Moon*. This satirical look at post-war America confronted the serious problem of putting destructive weapons technology to more constructive uses. The book's answer lay in a noble project to put a man on the moon. Citing the most accurate scientific data available at the time, he envisioned the construction of a huge cannon designed to fire a projectile-like vehicle. While successfully launched into space, the craft did not reach the lunar surface and its final fate was questionable at the end of the book. It was last seen circling the moon, possibly locked in a permanent orbit. Verne's later work, *Round the Moon* (1869), finally ended the suspense. Having circled the moon once, the projectile "splashed down" about 250 miles off the coast of California.

The concept of the rocket ship would later be expanded upon by H.G. Wells. *War of the Worlds*, first printed in 1898, describes an alien invasion from Mars. Nothing could stop the Martian war machines. Ironically, the invaders were defeated the moment they opened the doors of their metal vehicles. They died immediately, not from weapons or technology, but from everyday germs in Earth's atmosphere. Another novel by Wells is *The First Men in the Moon*, published in 1901. In this case, the means of transportation was a metal sphere, constructed from "Cavorite", a substance unaffected by gravitational energy.

Georges Melies, a French film maker noted for short spoofs on scientists and technology, is credited with producing the first space adventure film. *Un Voyage Dans la Lune (A Trip to the Moon)* was a whimsical short, dealing with the construction and launching of the first rocket ship. Verne and Wells were both influential sources from which Melies drew ideas.

Early science fiction appeared primarily in "pulp" magazines. These publications and similar anthology magazines they inspired were a launching pad for budding authors. The first space adventure stories were primarily concerned with "rockets, ray-guns and bug-eyed monsters". In other words, they depended upon the strange allure of fantastic technologies rather than characters. Up until this point there had been no heroes like Flash Gordon or Luke Skywalker, and no villains other than hostile aliens. This was soon to change.

Between February and July of 1912, *All-Story Magazine* published a six-chapter serial entitled "Under the Moon of Mars" (later reprinted as *A Princess of Mars*). It was the first novel written by a new author who had no previous experience in the field. The name credited in the magazine was Norman Bean. This was later revealed as a pseudonym for Edgar Rice Burroughs.

"Under the Moon of Mars" introduced John Carter, who may have been the first "space hero". While no known merchandise was created at the time, the character continued in popularity. Numerous stories based on John Carter were written, and have been continuously reprinted in novelized books, comics, Big Little Books, and other print forms.

Terence X. O'Leary appeared in pulp magazines during the '20s, three of which were exclusive full-length novels. O'Leary used a rocket-style airship to shoot down enemy biplanes. The character disappeared abruptly, possibly due to the appearance of the spectacular space adventurer of the day — Buck Rogers. However, Terence had his moment in space fandom, and his books are still sought after by collectors. The pulp magazines are valued at 50-125 dollars each.

Two novel-length stories by Philip Francis Nowlan,

The three Terence X. O'Leary pulp magazines

"Armageddon 2419 A.D." (*Amazing Stories*, 1928) and its sequel, "The Airlords of Han" (1929), formed the basis for the first space adventure sensation.

Anthony "Buck" Rogers was frozen in time for five hundred years, awakening to find the technologically advanced society of future America. Buck became the hero of the 25th century, foiling the evil schemes of Killer Kane, Ardala, and the dreaded Red Mongols.

One of the major contributions of Buck Rogers, however, was the character's effect on the nation. Space adventure was taken beyond the realm of pulp magazines, spreading out to much larger audiences by means of newspaper and radio syndication. In addition, the avenues for space character merchandise were opened for the first time. Rocket guns, space ships, and even complete uniforms were just a few of the items produced. The hero of the 25th century

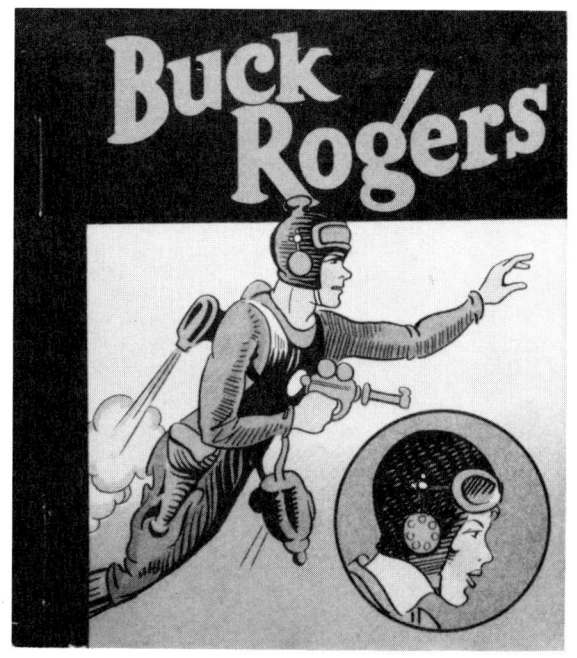

Buck Rogers, the first space adventure hero to be extensively merchandised

dominated toy markets for three years, and interest continued for decades to come.

In response to this success, King Features Syndicate commissioned artist Alex Raymond to create a comic strip to compete with Buck Rogers. "Flash Gordon" was released in 1934. Similar in many respects to Buck, Flash had a beautiful female companion (Dale Arden) and a disheveled scientific genius (Doctor Zarkov) for sidekicks. Ming the Merciless was his nemesis, a regal manifestation of pure evil. Flash had several advantages: the examples of his predeces-

Alex Raymond art from the Flash Gordon *comic strip*

sor, the superb drawings of Alex Raymond, high production budgets for films, and (according to one fan) better-looking women.

Pulp magazines continued to thrive, giving rise to new names and characters. Many of these were inspired by Buck Rogers and earlier sources. Another generation of literature began, introducing new authors who would join Wells and Verne among the masters of science fiction.

Isaac Asimov began writing science fiction professionally in 1938. Since that time he has written countless works, both fiction and non-fiction. The short story "Strange Playfellow" (later retitled "Robbie") was first published in *Super Science Stories* in 1940. This was the first of Asimov's robot stories, which differed surprisingly from the prevalent trends of the period. "Robbie," an early robot, was a young girl's playmate, friend and companion; not a hulking, destructive machine. Asimov's robots are portrayed as very sensitive machines, bound by three "laws of Robotics". First, they must never harm human beings (or allow harm through inaction). Second, robots must obey human commands, unless the First Law would be violated. Finally, robots must protect their own existence as long as this does not conflict with the First or Second Law.

In 1942, *Astounding* magazine published another Asimov story, simply titled "Foundation". This was the first in a series destined to continue much longer than the author intended. The Galactic Empire had ruled over a million planets for 12,000 years. Using a mathematical science called psychohistory, Hari Seldon predicted the fall of the Empire and the long centuries of turmoil to follow. While the fate of the Empire could not be changed, Seldon foresaw a way to shorten the interregnum that would follow. In this endeavor, he set up the Encyclopedia Foundation to preserve the knowledge of the universe. "Foundation" begins the tale of the interregnum, fifty years after the establishment of the Encyclopedia on the planet Terminus. The first eight stories were collected into three volumes — *Foundation, Foundation and Empire, Second Foundation* — and published in 1951, '52 and '53 respectively. A new section was written for the first book as an introduction to the premise behind the series. The trilogy won the only Hugo ever awarded for best all-time series (defeating such prominent competitors as J.R.R. Tolkien's *Lord of the Rings*). Three additional novels have been added to the series: *Foundation's Edge* (1982), *Foundation and Earth* (1986), and *Prelude to Foundation* (1988). None of Asimov's stories have been merchandised, but their influence is undeniable.

Following an unsuccessful political campaign, Robert A. Heinlein turned to writing. His first short story, "Life-Line," appeared in 1939. Although the story is not space adventure, it was the first offering from Heinlein's "future History". This timeline provides a background against which many of his stories appear, creating a continuing link with reoccurring characters and historical references. It extends from the time of "Life-Line" (presumably 1939 or shortly thereafter), through space exploration, to the development of the "first mature culture". A diagram of the timeline appears in several of his published works. Heinlein would be a regular contributor to the realm of space adventure until his death in May of 1988. One of his novels, *Space Cadet* (1948), would later serve as the inspiration for the television series "Tom Corbett — Space Cadet". Also notable among his work is *Stranger in a Strange Land* (1961), the story of a human raised by aliens. Initial hardcover sales were low, but the novel held great appeal for the values of the late '60s. It became a best-seller when released in paperback in 1968.

Yet another prominent name in science fiction is Ray Bradbury, whose work was published as early as 1939. His primary contribution to space adventure is *The Martian Chronicles*, a collection of short stories. Beginning in January of 1999, a female Martian experiences a vision of a visitor from Earth. Shortly thereafter, Earthmen arrive, bringing with them all the flaws of their society. Eventually, both races are almost totally destroyed. The *Chronicles* were published in one volume in 1950, but many of the stories appeared as early as 1946. At least three of these were also collected in other anthologies, *The Vintage Bradbury* (1965) and *S is for Space* (1966). When published in the *Chronicles*, twelve new sections were written for the book to tie the others together. Some of these (such as "Rocket Summer") bear the same titles as earlier Bradbury stories, but are in no way related.

The early '50s marked the second major era of space fascination. The catalyst was television. The excitement and wonders of space first introduced by Buck Rogers in the '30s were now directly broadcast into American homes. The Golden Age of radio was nearing its completion. Television rapidly became the primary media for entertainment.

"Captain Video" first aired in June 1949, bringing a

Cadets Astro, Tom Corbett, and Roger Manning from the TV show "Tom Corbett — Space Cadet," inspired by Robert Heinlein

Captain Video, the Master of Space, was the first space hero to appear on television

8

hoard of scientific gadgets. Despite a definite lack of quality (due to the low budget allotted), it was the first science fiction TV show. The program attracted a huge following, especially when the title role was assumed by Al Hodge in 1951. The character might have lasted beyond 1956 were it not for the demise of the DuMont network, which refused to sell the rights.

"Space Patrol" originated as a local show in Los Angeles, beginning March 1950. Its popularity quickly advanced it to network television six months later. The Patrol was charged with maintaining law, order, and morality throughout the solar system in the twenty-first century. It operated from a base on Terra, a man-made world containing soil from all nine planets at its core. The commander-in-chief was Buzz Correy, a daring young man who made the first trip to Pluto to obtain a soil sample for Terra. The series was simulcast on the ABC radio network until its cancellation in 1955. Much of the merchandise produced

The cast of "Space Patrol"

in conjunction with the show was advertised on both radio and television.

"Tom Corbett — Space Cadet" premiered in October of 1950. While Space Patrol related the exploits of top military officers, Tom Corbett took the opposite end of the scale. Inspired by Robert Heinlein's *Space Cadet* (1948), it was the story of young men growing up in Space Academy, undergoing a rigorous training program. Their goal is to graduate, and be accepted into the ranks of the Solar Guards. Corbett had a tangled history on television — the rights for the show changed hands no less than four times — appearing on two networks (ABC and NBC) simultaneously during 1951. It was heard on ABC radio as well, from January to September of 1952. Tom Corbett seems to have had a better merchandising plan than its contemporaries, producing higher-quality items in greater numbers. In addition, a scientist named Willie Ley was hired as an advisor to lend credibility and accuracy to the program, and, indirectly, to the merchandise which resulted.

Forbidden Planet (MGM) came to the silver screen in 1956. The film passed a major milestone in the advancement of special effects. In addition, it introduced the first "user-friendly" robot in the movies (named "Robby", possibly influenced by Asimov). Elements of this film would greatly influence later projects.

Frank Herbert's novel *Dune* was first serialized in 1963-65 issues of *Analog* magazine. Among its numerous themes, it explores the process of ecological transformation, and the consequences of a charismatic leader who is followed without question. Like *Stranger in a Strange Land*, it became a cult classic during the '60s, spawning five subsequent novels, a reference work, and a major motion picture.

Television made a successful return to space adventure in 1966 with "Star Trek". This new series was created by Gene Roddenberry. In addition to exploring space frontiers "where no man has gone before", the crew of the starship *Enterprise* confronted modern-day issues within the guise of science fiction. Star

Star Trek's famous trio — Dr. Spock, Dr. McCoy, and Captain James T. Kirk

Trek was a "space boom" of itself. While the series ran for a mere three seasons, it attracted a large following of fans who would keep it alive for many years to come. Syndicated reruns were continuously broadcast for over 20 years, and every episode was made available for home video. Licensed character merchandise did not accelerate until after the cancellation of the original TV program.

Planet of the Apes (20th Century-Fox, 1968), adapted Pierre Boulle's 1963 novel of the same name. As a dark warning of the future, it examined the traits that make a race civilized. Many other *Apes* projects would follow, continuing through 1973.

2001: A Space Odyssey (MGM) also appeared in

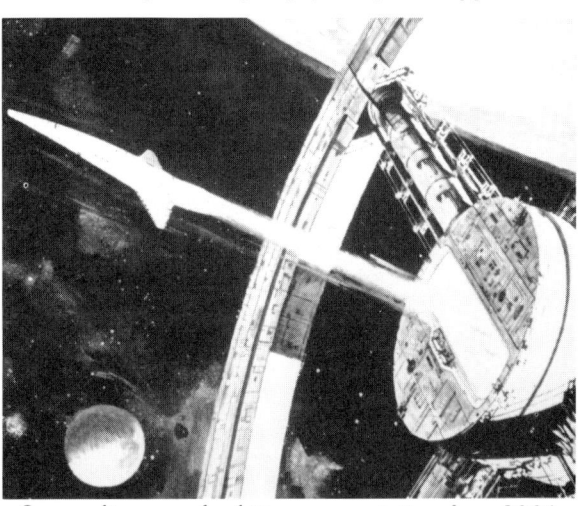

Space clipper and orbiting space station from 2001

9

The original film poster for Star Wars

U.S.S. Cygnus, the mysterious ship from *The Black Hole*

Elliott's bike flies through the air with a little help from E.T.

The creature from Alien frightened its own merchandise off the shelves.

Ming the Merciless and his crafty daughter Aura from the 1980 remake of Flash Gordon.

10

1968, co-created by Stanley Kubrick and Arthur C. Clarke. In spite of debate over the meaning of the film and the scientific accuracy of some segments, the visual effects were of a quality never before seen. The film was based on an earlier story by Arthur C. Clarke, entitled "The Sentinel". Clarke also produced a novelized adaptation, published in the same year. *2010: The Year We Make Contact* was released by MGM in 1982, answering many of the questions raised by the first film. The book edition was once again written by Clarke. A third novel, *2061: Odyssey Three*, was published in 1987.

Since the close of World War II, the space program of the real world had been gradually developing. The successful Russian *Sputnik* mission placed the first artificial satellite in orbit in 1957. Yuri A. Gagarin, a Russian Cosmonaut, was the first man in space in 1961. Aboard *Vostok 1*, he made a single orbit of the Earth with a flight time of one hour, forty-eight minutes. Now the year was 1969, and American astronauts landed on the moon. Fantasy had become real.

George Lucas was responsible for the next major era in space fandom. *Star Wars* (20th Century-Fox, 1977) surprised the world, and quickly become the top-grossing film of the period. New quality standards were set for science fiction, and the character stereotypes of movie serial fame were revived. The style was continued in two subsequent films: *The Empire Strikes Back* (1979) and *Return of the Jedi* (1981). The impact of *Star Wars* was widespread, creating a new public interest in space adventure.

Steven Spielberg took a different approach in *Close Encounters of the Third Kind* (Columbia/EMI, 1978). This sensitive film explores the reactions of Earthbound humans to first contact with alien beings. This time, the visitors turn out to be friendly. The quality of visual effects was comparable to *Star Wars*. Spielberg, however, made little use of these until the final sequence. The result was a gradually escalating feeling of suspense, building toward a spectacular conclusion.

"Battlestar Galactica" (Universal) first appeared on the ABC television network in 1978. Dogfights in space and the constant threat of the evil Cylon Alliance provided the excitement and feeling of *Star Wars* and other "space opera" settings. The main characters were more human, with greater depth. Although a television budget may have put some limits on visual effects, it was a vast improvement over previous TV ventures.

Walt Disney Productions, which turned down the opportunity to produce *Star Wars*, released *The Black Hole* in 1979. A crew in search of other life forms in space finds nothing more than one of their own ships which has been missing for twenty years. This was one of the few films ever released under the Disney label to carry a rating other than "G".

One of the more successful films in the wake of *Star Wars* was *Alien* (20th Century-Fox, 1979). Although it easily fits the qualifications for space adventure, the film also incorporates elements of suspense and horror, defying classification in any one category. A sequel, *Aliens*, was produced in 1986.

With space adventure once again escalating in popularity, earlier material was brought back for post-*Star Wars* fans. Universal revived Buck Rogers in 1979, and Flash Gordon the following year. Ivanhoe Productions filmed a new adaptation of Space Patrol for film and television. The results were considered unsatisfactory, and the project saw only limited release.

The principle rebirth, however, was *Star Trek*. The original cast was reunited at the movies in 1979 (Paramount), picking up the action two and a half years after the end of the "five-year mission" of the original TV series. The familiar ship was completely redone. Paramount went on to produce a new *Trek* film roughly every other year, including *Star Trek II: The Wrath of Khan* (1982), *Star Trek III: The Search for Spock* (1984), *Star Trek IV: The Voyage Home* (1986), and *Star Trek V: The Final Frontier* (1989).

Star Trek returned in 1979 with a new version of the U.S.S. Enterprise

Steven Spielberg returned to space adventure in 1982 with *E.T.* (Universal), the story of a lovable alien who misses the ship going home. Much to the surprise of the merchandising industry, it proved to be far more successful than anticipated. No pictures of the extraterrestrial were released prior to the film. By the time it appeared on the cover of *People* magazine, the merchandisers couldn't get enough E.T. dolls on the shelves.

A movie adaptation of Frank Herbert's *Dune* had been planned for many years, but with little result. Dino De Laurentis eventually brought the plan to fruition, obtaining the rights from the French consortium in 1976. The project was completed in 1984, and released by Universal. While the film was hampered by negative hype in the United States, it was still the sixth largest grossing film of the year. *Dune* enjoyed more success overseas, setting box-office records in France, Germany and Japan.

The Last Starfighter (Universal/Lorimar) was released that same year, noted for its extensive use of computer-generated graphics. Instead of the more common model and blue-screen setup, an animation computer was used to create such effects as a flying car and a high-speed tunnel chase.

Another product of 1984 was "V", the story of a

Paul Atreides, the tragic hero of the Dune *series*

hostile alien invasion. "V" premiered on NBC as a two-night miniseries which ended inconclusively, setting up the plotline for a second, three-night series. Reactions to the miniseries were favorable, but popularity did not carry over when NBC attempted to make it a weekly show.

Steven Spielberg's *Cocoon* (20th Century-Fox, 1985) revealed yet another version of the secret of Atlantis when a group of aliens returns to Earth. In the guise of humans, they attempt to recover other members of their race; friends who stayed behind while their outpost sank beneath the ocean. *Cocoon* maintained the suspense and fantasy inherent to unknown aliens, while confronting the very real issues of aging and death. *Cocoon: The Return* (20th Century-Fox, 1988) was a sequel of little note.

"Star Trek: The Next Generation" (Paramount) introduced the future of the future, halfway into the twenty-fourth century. A weekly series, it introduced a completely new *Galaxy*-class *Enterprise* with more advanced equipment and a fresh crew. A two-hour pilot episode, "Encounter at Farpoint", premiered on the Fox television network in 1987, and was simultaneously published as a novel.

The future of space adventure seems assured with the resumption of regular NASA space shuttle flights and the progression of work on a permanent US space station. George Lucas has announced work in progress on a new trilogy of *Star Wars* films. *Aliens*, *Buck Rogers*, and *Star Trek* have all experienced recent revivals. Interest in space fiction has reached an all-time high, with new merchandise appearing almost every day. The toys of today are the collectibles of tomorrow.

GUIDE TO SPACE ADVENTURE COLLECTING

The following sections contain guidelines for space adventure collectors, both old and new.

Who Is Buying?

The people who buy space adventure memorabilia fall into five categories:

1. Consumers who purchase items as a toy or other plaything to be used and discarded as the child grows older.
2. People who are interested in space travel, UFO's, or contact with alien beings. They may be consumers and/or collectors, purchasing items to complement their interest in space.
3. People who may have owned or wanted to own a particular item as a child, or remember a show or film from that time.
4. Collectors who purchase memorabilia to add it to a collection. These people may confine their interest to one or more specialties or collect everything from a particular time period. Collectors buy memorabilia for their personal enjoyment and investment purposes.
5. Dealers and investors who buy space adventure memorabilia with the intent of realizing a profit from their knowledge and interest.

The last three groups often interact with each other, and are interdependent for the purposes of buying, selling, and trading.

Why Collect?

Collecting anything — stamps, old bottles, primitive tools or baseball cards — has many self-satisfying rewards. Finding a rare or perfect condition piece in some junk shop is like discovering gold. Every antique shop or flea market provides the thrill of the hunt and the chance to meet others who share a collecting interest.

Each item in a collection becomes a trophy that the collector has found, bought, won in an auction, or otherwise traded to obtain. To collect is to succeed at your own pace under whatever terms and goals you set for yourself. Collecting provides a comfortable niche in a highly competitive world — one that the collector controls — as opposed, for example, to job or other pressures they cannot. And every collector "knows" that if they lose interest, they "can get more" than they paid when the collection is sold.

Everything is collected by somebody. The number of what many might consider to be the "odd-ball" collector's items can be confirmed in any collecting journal.

How To Use This Book

Space Adventure Collectibles was designed to be an authoritative and easy to use collector's guide. It utilizes an identification and classification system specially tailored to space adventure collecting.

Items are listed by character or genre, and are arranged chronologically whenever possible. *Star Trek* and *Star Wars* are exceptions. These two categories produced vast quantities of merchandise, and have been broken down into classifications by category.

Each item is assigned a reference code number, usually consisting of one letter and four numbers. Code numbers for Star Trek and Star Wars contain two letters instead of one, due to the large size of these categories. Use of these numbers in dealer and distributor ads and collector's correspondence is encouraged. Permission for such use to conduct buying, selling, and the trade of space adventure memorabilia in letters or advertisements is hereby granted.

The identity code numbers also serve to match the correct listing to a nearby photo. Usually, there is a listing for every photo, but unfortunately, not all items can be depicted. Some items in this volume have been previously listed in the *Tomart's Disneyana*, *Character & Promotional Glasses*, and *Radio Premium* guides. This book utilizes a different system, and the code numbers are NOT consistent with previous publications. In some classifications, a cross section of available material is used for illustration, but no specific items are listed.

The Values in this Price Guide

This book is a collector's and dealer's guide to average prices in a range of conditions. The real value of any particular item is what a buyer is willing to pay. No more. No less. Prices constantly change — up and down.

Many factors influence any given transaction. Not the least of these are perceived value, emotional appeal, or competitive drive for ownership. Everything people buy is motivated by a need or a want. There are few who actually need space adventure collectibles, but a lot of people buy them out of interest or desire. Dealers usually want the highest returns possible and continually test collectors with higher prices.

Supply and demand have always been important factors in determining value, and are a bit more predictable for those knowledgeable in a given area. These people have a feel for how often an item appears for sale. Since everyone has different experience, however, there are many different ideas on which items are rarer or more valuable.

The availability of the items listed in this book is definitely limited. No one can say precisely how limited, but it is certain that no more originals will be manufactured. A few of the more recently produced items may still be found in toy and department stores. For example, Star Wars figures and related playsets turn up once in a while, but in modified packages. The figures remain unchanged, with a few exceptions.

The original quantities of vintage items run anywhere from hundreds up into millions. Generally, the items that generated the greatest interest originally were the items produced in the largest quantities. For example, Buck Rogers pistols were sold in enormous numbers. Since there were so many of them produced back then, they still turn up on a regular basis in attics, old chests of drawers, and even warehouses.

Space Adventure more or less began in the 20th century. All items of character merchandise are collectibles, including many produced within the last ten years. As such, they aren't old enough to consider the known quantities a valid basis for establishing values. There are rare and even some common items in high demand. The value of these items outperforms the space adventure market as a whole — at least until supply catches up with demand.

The idea that the value of collectibles rises automatically with inflation or to the highest price one person was willing to pay in an auction has slightly less credibility than the Moon made of green cheese. Values rise and fall at the whim of ready buyers.

There is no retail market for an entire space adventure collection. There have been numerous examples in recent years where collections of nostalgia collectibles were sold at auctions and estate sales at a fraction of the estimated value. Except for a very limited number of high demand items, the process of turning a good sized collection back into cash can be a long and expensive one.

What is all boils down to is the two ways space adventure collectibles are sold: pre-priced or by auction to the highest bidder.

This book reports market prices based on items sold or traded by dealers and collectors nationwide. It reflects sales on the whole, with the understanding an auction price is the one all other bidders refused to pay.

Collectors who buy at yard sales and flea markets generally purchase for less. Often they have first choice of items offered for sale; sometimes at exceptional bargain prices. But they also incur substantial time and travel expenses.

Mail and gallery auctions are preferred by collectors who don't have the time or the ability to visit major shows. Money spent and current resale value also tend to be of less concern to the auction buyer. The winning bidder must outlast the others who have an emotional fix on ownership or perhaps need the specific piece to "complete" a collection.

It's difficult to say who actually spends more money in pursuit of their collecting interest — the aggressive hunter at low cost outlets or the auction buyer. This much is sure, there are substantial costs involved beyond the money spent on collectibles by the original buyer not normally considered in the "price", and higher overhead costs are included in auction sales where the "price" includes everything.

Collecting should be pursued for the interest and satisfaction involved. There are much better investments at most financial institutions. *Fortune*, *Business Week*, and other business publications have done extensive articles on the pitfalls of speculating in what these magazines categorize as "exotic" investments.

Every attempt has been made to have this price guide reflect the market in its broadest sense. The research effort covers extensive travel each year to attend leading toy, antique, and advertising shows form New York to Glendale, California. Mail auctions are monitored and many leading sales lists are received. The up-to-date values in this edition are a compilation of information received through March, 1990.

There are two more factors affecting value that we can measure more precisely: rarity and condition.

Rarity

Some items are available for years after they were first offered. Examples of this type of continuous distribution include the Buck Rogers rocket pistol, Space Patrol Space-O-Phones, Star Wars action figures, and other similar items. On the other hand, some items are available once or for a brief time. Paper items had less kid tolerance than sturdy metal ones — and thus are rarer — especially punch or cut-out items that would self-destruct when used. Some were designed to be consumed or disposed of — items such as gum and bread wrappers, candy, paper cups, plates, or napkins. A major part of the charm of collecting this type of item is that the items have survived the intended use.

Rarity doesn't always equate to value. In collecting, the strongest demand is often generated by people wishing to obtain items of special interest. Thus rarity is only a part of value. Character popularity, crossovers to other collecting fields (such as pocket knives, robots, wind-up toys, etc.) and the type of item (ring, button, badge, paper punch-out) may become stronger factors, as other collectors often specialize in areas that cross the space adventure line.

Price also has some regional influences. In Los Angeles and New York, prices are substantially higher. Selling prices are lowest in the Midwest — especially around Chicago and in Indiana, Ohio, Minnesota and Pennsylvania. Items still become available on a regular basis in these areas, and thereby fulfill demand. Realizing that these regional price situations exist, and that isolated individuals will always let emotions rule in auction bidding, the values represented in this guide are average estimates taking into account what a given item has sold for over the last two years.

The very existence of a price guide will affect the market — increasing prices, introducing the hobby to many new collectors, as well as opening new areas of interest to established collectors. This is to be expected. However, the advantages of a published record of accepted values outweigh the disadvantages. Among these advantages are the protection of financial investment, easier insurability (and collection) in the event of loss, a better basis for collector trading, item identification, a forum for new discoveries, preservation of more items (yes, people have pitched such items in the past because they didn't think they had any value) and photos helpful in spotting unmarked or unfamiliar items. It will also inspire more dealer interest.

Another factor that enhances value is the completeness of the original box or package. In come cases, the boxes are more attractive than the item itself. Some include instructions, catalogs, and extra parts that made having the toy more fun. The actual box sometimes increases value and demand by perhaps 20 to 50 percent.

Be wary of International merchandise billed as "rare". More often than not, such items are rare in the United States, but are easily found in their country of origin. Some of these are very similar to common items. For example, *Star Trek: The Motion Picture* action figures were released in several other countries, but with different serial numbers and languages. The figures themselves were identical. As such, they are considered to be equivalent for the purpose of identification and worth. The values in this price guide are based on research and travel within the United States.

Fan-produced or homemade items are another complication. These are often found at conventions, but are not available to the general public in most cases. They are produced in small quantities without the permission of the copyright holder, and little or no documentation of their production exists. Since anyone can make their own "limited edition" items, it is impossible to provide an accurate listing. While these items may have great sentimental value to some fans, they have little or no appeal to most collectors. As such, fan-produced items and magazines are not covered in detail.

Condition

Condition, like beauty, is in the eye of the beholder. When money becomes involved, the eye seems to take on an added dimension of x-ray vision or rose-colored glasses — depending on whether you are buying or selling.

However, let there be no mistake about the price spreads set down on the following pages. The top price refers to items in "Mint", like-new condition — no scratches, never repaired, free of any defects whatsoever selling in a top market. If paper, a mint item must be free of marks, creases (other than the original folds), ragged edges or corners, and any other defect or blemish. Mint items probably were never in circulation — original stock, or not used.

The low end price describes items in "Good" condition. That means first and foremost that the item is complete with absolutely no parts or pages missing. Creases, dirt, marks, chips, tears, bends, scratches, minor rust or corrosion damage, repairs without original materials, and similar short comings are factors that depreciate value and regulate such items to the complete, but "Good" classification. Of course, some complete items with excessive wear, major rust, deep cuts, or other mistreatment are less than good; either poor or only a source for repair parts. The value of poor condition items would obviously be less than the lowest price shown.

The range in between Good and Mint is the condition in which most items will be found. Very good, fine, or very fine are the most common grades used. In general, a "Fine" condition item would be one with only minor wear, scratches, blemishes, etc. The item has been in circulation; used, but given some care. The value would be somewhat less than the average in the price range as true "Mint" items command a premium.

Rarity, condition, and the amount of material available in the marketplace all have a direct effect on value. The overriding factor, however, is the number of individuals that wish to acquire any given item and have the money to satisfy their desire.

All prices shown in this book are U.S. dollar values with the dollar signs removed to avoid repetition. The amount shown is for an unboxed item, except in such cases as board games where the box is an integral part of a complete item.

ALIEN/ALIENS

The *Alien* movies brought back the "hostile monster from outer space", combining suspense and horror with space adventure. The creature from the film was considered so frightening that most of the original merchandise was taken off the shelves. The Kenner version of the alien is one of the most highly-sought pieces. Even when found, the figure is usually missing the plastic dome which covered its head, or is otherwise incomplete.

Merchandising was revived in the late '80s with the release of the second film. A few items were available at the Disney/MGM studio tour.

A5100	Film program	5 - 12
A5110	18" Alien (Kenner, 1979)	80 - 200
A5111	Poster, black and white (came w/A5110)	5 - 15
A5115	Jumbo Alien (Tsukuda Hobbys)	80 - 120
A5120	Giant jigsaw puzzle (H. G. Toys, 1979)	15 - 25
A5130	Jigsaw puzzles, Nostromo, Kane looking into egg, or others, ea	5 - 12
A5140	Egg puzzle	8 - 15
A5150	Giant Blaster target set (H.G. Toys, 1979)	40 - 90
A5155	Target game	20 - 40
A5160	Trading cards, set of 84 (Topps, 1979)	8 - 12
A5161	Individual trading cards, ea	.10 - .20
A5162	Stickers for A5160, set of 22	2 - 5
A5163	Individual stickers, ea	.20 - .30
A5164	Box for A5160	5 - 8
A5165	Wrappers for A5160	.25 - 2
A5166	Unopened waxpacks for A5160	.50 - 3
A5170	Board game	15 - 60
A5180	Movie viewer (Kenner, 1979)	15 - 75
A5190	Glow Putty (Larami, 1979)	5 - 10
A5200	Alien mask (25 cast from original mold)	175 - 300

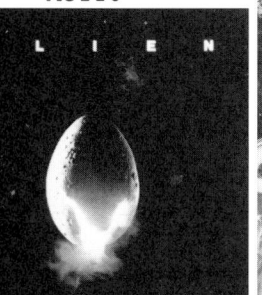

A5110

A5100

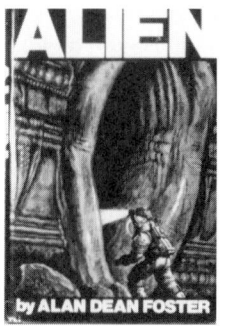

A5150
Alien Blaster Target Game— stop the monster before it attacks

A5120

A5300
by ALAN DEAN FOSTER

A5170

15

A5170

A5220-21

A5180

A5222-23

A5227   A5228

A5510

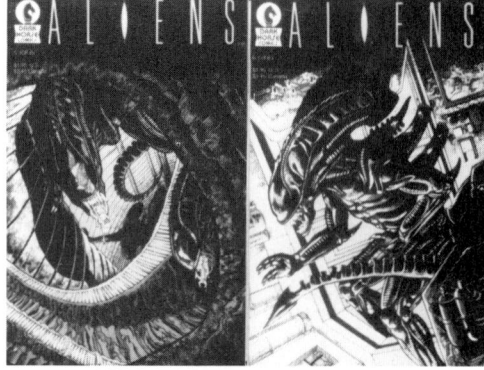

A5224-25

A5500

A5490    A5490

A5495

A5450-53    A5165   A5301   A5401

16

Model kits A5210-15

A5210	Alien w/teeth	35 - 50
A5211	Recasting of A5210, w/o teeth	10 - 25
A5212	Queen & Eggs	4 - 35
A5215	Armored Transport	15 - 40

Comic series A5220-25 (Dark Horse, 1988-89)

A5220	#1	2 - 5
A5221-25	#2-6	1 - 3
A5226	Mini-comic	2 - 6

Second comic series A5227-30 (Dark Horse, 1989)

A5227	#1	2 - 5
A5228-30	#2-4	1 - 3
A5300	*Alien* novel, hardcover	1 - 8
A5301	*Alien* novel, paperback	.50 - 2
A5310	*Alien* illustrated story	5 - 15
A5315	*Alien* photonovel	3 - 8
A5320	*Alien* soundtrack	5 - 10
A5330	Film, Super-8	12 - 40
A5335	Costume (Ben Cooper)	12 - 35
A5400	*Aliens* novel, hardcover	1 - 6
A5401	*Aliens* novel, paperback	.50 - 2
A5415	*Aliens* Official Movie Book	2 - 6
A5420	*Aliens* soundtrack	5 - 10

Cloisonne pins A5450-53

A5450	#1 Warrior #1	5 - 8
A5451	#2 Warrior #2	5 - 8
A5452	#3 Chestburster	5 - 8
A5453	#4 Queen	5 - 8
A5470	*Aliens* promotional T-shirt	6 - 10
A5471	Warrior T-shirt	6 - 10
A5480	Aliens logo mug (plastic)	.50 - 5
A5490	Doorknob signs, ea	1 - 3
A5495	Car signs, ea	1 - 3
A5500	Door signs, ea	2 - 4
A5510	Note pads: "Trust Me I'm the Boss" or "A Note from the Better Half", ea	1 - 2
A5520	Warrior poster	3 - 5
A5521	Warrior 6' poster	3 - 6
A5522	Ripley and Newt poster	3 - 5
A5523	Comic Warrior poster	5 - 15
A5540	Giger's *Alien* book, original	50 - 150
A5541	Same as A5540, reissue	20 - 40
A5550	Mini models (A.E.F., 1988), ea	8 - 15

Video games B5700-01 (Leading Edge, 1990)

| A5700 | Aliens: This Time It's War | 15 - 22 |
| A5701 | Aliens Expansion | 8 - 11 |

BATTLESTAR GALACTICA

For a thousand years, the twelve known colonies of man have been besieged by the Cylon Alliance. This emotionless race of cyborgs, lead by the Imperious Leader, has dedicated itself to the eradication of the human race. At last it seems as though the fighting will be over. The Cylons have sued for peace and the twelve races of mankind are united at last under President Adar. The tone is one of relief, but Adama, commander of the *Battlestar Galactica*, remains suspicious.

Adama's two sons, Apollo and Zac, are the first to discover the treachery. On a routine patrol the brothers discover a Cylon tanker, filled not with fuel but enemy fighters. In the ensuing chase, Apollo barely reaches the *Galactica* in time, but Zac's ship is destroyed. The warning comes too late to save the

B1100-10

B1100

B1331

B1131

B1130

B1200

B1302-03

B1388

B1220

B1270-82

B1241

B1231

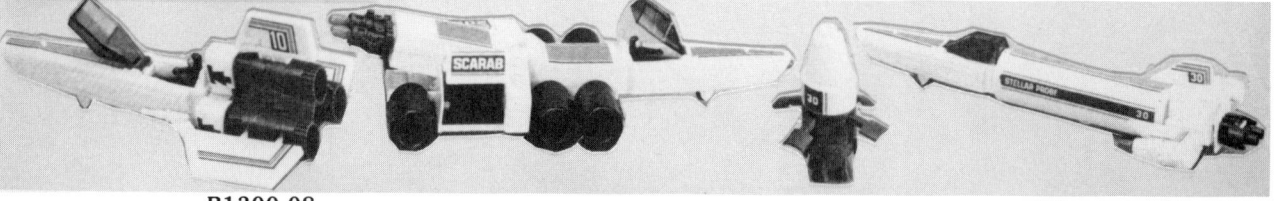

B1300-08

18

B1209-12

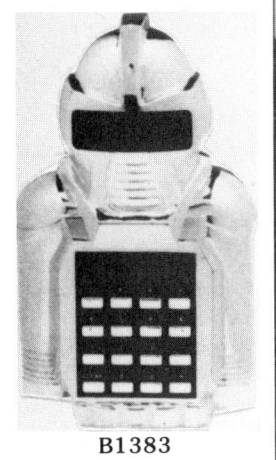

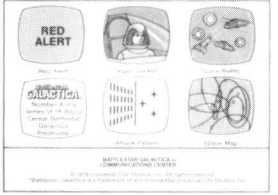

B1383

B1140

B1150

B1334   B1365

B1345

fleet. Adama, not trusting the Alliance, declares a battle stations "drill" and has time to launch fighters. Realizing they have been led to slaughter while their homeworlds remain unprotected, Adama orders the *Galactica* to pull away from the battle, leaving fighters and fleet behind. It is too late. The homeworlds have been destroyed, leaving behind few survivors. President Adar is dead and *Galactica* is the last of the Battlestars.

Following this crushing blow Adama orders the remaining survivors to assemble together any ship that will carry them. In the ancient writings a thirteenth colony was indicated, far out in the universe. Thus a ragtag fleet of 220 ships begins its quest for the last remaining settlement of humankind – a planet called Earth.

"Battlestar Galactica" premiered in 1978. The series was created for television, but the original pilot was also released as a feature film. Produced at Universal City Studios in Hollywood, the series ran for several years on ABC.

Merchandise from the show is fairly common, and most items can be found for less than $35. The most highly sought pieces are probably the radio-controlled Cylon Raider, and model kits of the *Galactica* and *Base Star*. The missle-firing spaceships are also of note, as they were discontinued and replaced with non-firing versions.

Action Figures B1100-21 (Mattel, 1978)
B1100	Adama	6 - 12
B1101	Apollo	6 - 12
B1102	Starbuck	6 - 12
B1103	Daggit (tan or brown)	6 - 12
B1104	Cylon	6 - 12
B1105	Gold Cylon	10 - 20
B1106	Imperious Leader	6 - 12
B1107	Ovion	6 - 12
B1108	Baltaar	8 - 15
B1109	Boray	10 - 20
B1110	Lucifer	10 - 30
B1120	Boxed set of 6: Ovion, Imperious Leader, Cylon, Daggit (brown), Adama, Starbuck	40 - 120
B1121	Boxed set of 4: Imperious Leader, Silver Cylon, Daggit (brown), Ovion	40 - 90

12" Figures B1130-31 (Mattel, 1978)
B1130	Cylon	10 - 30
B1131	Colonial Warrior	10 - 30

Comic adaptations B1140-41
B1140	Marvel Super Special	2 - 4
B1141	Paperback (Marvel, 1978)	1 - 3

Comic Books B1150-73 (Marvel, 1978+)
B1150	#1	.50 - 2
B1151-73	#2-23, ea	.25 - .75

Novels B1200-12
B1200	*Battlestar Galactica*, hardcover	2 - 5
B1201	*Battlestar Galactica*, paperback	.50 - 2
B1202	#2 *The Cylon Death Machine*	.50 - 2
B1203	#3 *The Tombs of Kobol*	.50 - 2
B1204	#4 *The Young Warriors*	.50 - 2
B1205	#5 *Galactica Discovers Earth*	.50 - 2
B1206	#6 *The Living Legend*	.50 - 2

B1395

B1375

B1333

B1337

B1332

B1380

B1360

B1355

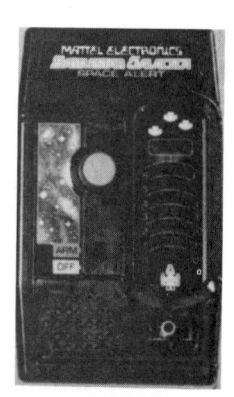

B1390

20

B1207	#7 *War of the Gods*	.50 - 2
B1208	#8 *Greetings from Earth*	.50 - 2
B1209	#9 *Experiment in Terra*	.50 - 2
B1210	#10 *The Long Patrol*	.50 - 2
B1211	#11 *The Nightmare Machine*	.50 - 2
B1212	#12 *"Die, Chameleon!"*	.50 - 2
B1220	Soundtrack record	2 - 6
B1230	Trading cards, set of 132 (Topps, 1978)	8 - 12
B1231	Individual trading cards, ea	.05 - .10
B1232	Stickers for B1230, set of 22	3 - 8
B1233	Individual stickers, ea	.10 - .20
B1234	Box for B1230	3 - 8
B1235	Wrappers for B1230, 3 different	.50 - 1
B1236	Unopened waxpacks for B1230	1 - 2
B1240	Trading cards, set of 36 (Wonder Bread, 1978)	4 - 8
B1241	Individual trading cards, ea	.10 - .70

Model Kits B1260-63 (Monogram, 1978)

B1260	Colonial Viper	15 - 25
B1261	Cylon Raider	10 - 35
B1262	*Galactica*	25 - 40
B1263	*Base Star*	25 - 40

Painted Metal Necklaces B1270-73 (Howard Elton Ltd., 1978)

B1270	Imperious Leader	4 - 8
B1271	Daggit	4 - 8
B1272	Ovion	4 - 8
B1273	Cylon	4 - 8

Rings B1280-82

B1280	Daggit	2 - 5
B1281	Ovion	2 - 5
B1282	Cylon	2 - 5

Glasses B1290-93 (1979)

B1290	Adama	5 - 8
B1291	Apollo	5 - 8
B1292	Starbuck	5 - 8
B1293	Cylon	5 - 8
B1300	Colonial Viper, original version (missile-firing)	15 - 40
B1301	Same as B1300, second or third issue (missiles glued in)	10 - 30
B1302	Cylon Raider, original version (missile-firing)	20 - 45
B1303	Same as B1302, second or third issue (missiles glued in)	10 - 20
B1305	Colonial Scarab, firing	25 - 45
B1306	Colonial Scarab, non-firing	15 - 33
B1307	Colonial Stellar Probe, firing	20 - 40
B1308	Colonial Stellar Probe, non-firing	15 - 30
B1309	Radio-controlled Cylon Raider	75 - 125
B1310	Viper Launch Station (Mattel, 1978)	35 - 60
B1315	Lasermatic Pistol (Mattel, 1978)	10 - 40
B1316	Lasermatic Rifle (Mattel, 1978)	15 - 50
B1320	Board game (Parker Brothers, 1978)	9 - 18
B1325	Colorforms set	8 - 20
B1330	Stuffed Daggit	10 - 20
B1331	Party masks	2 - 5
B1332	Candy cake decoration	2 - 4
B1333	Paper table cloth (Betty Crocker, 1978)	2 - 4
B1334	Napkins	1 - 2

B1320

B1290-93

B1340

B5360

B5340

B5111

B5131-37

B1330

B1325

B5150-54

22

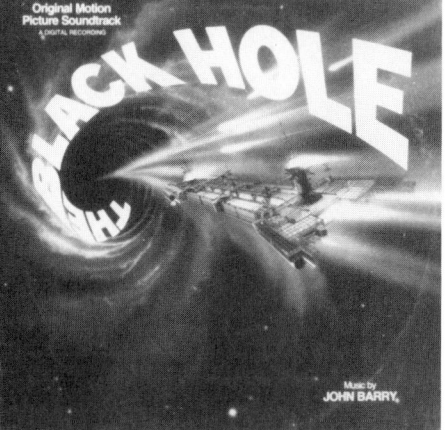

Puzzles B1335-37 (Parker Brothers, 1978)
B1335	Interstellar Battle	4 - 10
B1336	Starbuck	4 - 10
B1337	The Rag-Tag Fleet	4 - 10
B1340	LEM Lander	3 - 8
B1343	Explorer set	3 - 8
B1344	Watch set	3 - 8
B1345	Galactic Cruisers: yellow, blue, green, red or orange	1 - 3
B1348	Wallet w/ID card	4 - 10
B1350	Lunch box (Aladdin, 1979)	10 - 25
B1351	Bottle for B1350	5 - 15
B1355	Folders, ea	2 - 4
B1360	Space Station Kit (General Mills)	10 - 30
B1365	Big G cereal premiums (General Mills), 56 different, ea	1 - 3
B1366	Cereal boxes w/*Battlestar Galactica* ads	5 - 15
B1370	Film program	5 - 10
B1375	Cylon costume	12 - 30
B1380	Cylon bubble machine	10 - 20
B1381	Poster for Cylon bubble machine	5 - 8
B1383	Teaching calculator	10 - 20
B1385	Cylon helmet radio	15 - 30
B1388	Cylon inflatable chair	12 - 20
B1390	Space Alert electronic game	15 - 30
B1393	Vertibird set	15 - 35
B1395	Starfighter combat game (FASA)	5 - 17
B1398	Magazines w/*Battlestar Galactica* covers, ea	1 - 5

Rockets B1450-53 (Estes, 1979)
B1450	Viper Rocket Starter Outfit	20 - 25
B1451	Viper	15 - 20
B1452	Cylon Raider	25 - 30
B1453	Laser Torpedo	10 - 15
B1454	Estes catalog	1 - 2

THE BLACK HOLE

The *U.S.S. Palomino*, a deep-exploration vessel, is returning home. All is proceeding routinely when V.I.N.Cent. (the ship's robot) detects the largest black hole it has ever encountered. Poised on the edge of this deadly destructive force is the starship *U.S.S. Cygnus*, which has been missing for 20 years. The *Cygnus* floats in space — silent and dead — oblivious to the intense gravitational pull of the black hole. While attempting to investigate, the *Palomino* is damaged and forced to land on the *Cygnus's* docking elevator. The crew finds a ship run entirely by robots, with the exception of Dr. Hans Reinhardt — an eccentric scientist who refused to return to Earth when the *Cygnus* mission was declared a failure. Resisting the black hole is the greatest of his achievements. Reinhardt plans to take the *Cygnus* into the hole itself, exploring whatever may exist beyond. But darker forces are at work aboard the ship, as the crew quickly discovers.

The Black Hole was the contribution of Walt Disney Productions to the space science fiction boom created in the wake of *Star Wars*. It was one of the few films produced under the Disney name to carry a "PG" rating. Despite a great deal of publicity prior to its release, the film fared poorly at the box office, and

B5170-71

B5172

B5186

B5320-21

B8802

B5110

B5210

B8300

B8802

B5322

merchandise sales were low.

B5100	Pre-release merchandise folder	3 - 5
B5110	Invitation to preview	2 - 5
B5111	Invitation to reception w/Peter Ellenshaw	3 - 6
B5115	Flasher button	2 - 5
B5120	Novel (Ballantine)	.50 - 2

Action figures B5130-37 (Mego)

B5130	Captain Holland	6 - 15
B5131	Kate McCrae	8 - 18
B5132	Dr. Durant	6 - 15
B5133	Pizer	6 - 15
B5134	V.I.N.Cent	10 - 20
B5135	Harry Booth	6 - 15
B5136	Dr. Reinhardt	6 - 15
B5137	Maximillian	10 - 25

Sold in sets w/other figures B5138-40

B5138	Old Bob	40 - 45
B5139	Starr	30 - 35
B5140	Humanoid	30 - 35

Large figures B5150-55

B5150	Captain Holland	15 - 35
B5151	Kate McCrae	15 - 35
B5152	Dr. Durant	15 - 35
B5153	Pizer	15 - 35
B5154	Harry Booth	15 - 35
B5155	Hans Reinhardt	15 - 35
B5160	Space Alert game (Whitman)	6 - 12
B5161	Voyage of Fear game (Whitman)	5 - 10
B5170	V.I.N.Cent model kit (MPC)	10 - 20
B5171	Maximillian model kit (MPC)	10 - 20
B5172	*U.S.S. Cygnus* model kit (MPC)	12 - 25
B5173	Press-out book	10 - 20
B5180	Color and activity book	2 - 5
B5181	Stamp activity book	3 - 8
B5183	Sticker activity book	3 - 8
B5185	Pop-up book	4 - 15
B5186	Poster book	3 - 8
B5190	Lunch box	10 - 25
B5191	Bottle for B5190	5 - 10
B5200	Trading cards, set of 88 (Topps)	4 - 10
B5201	Individual trading cards, each	.05 - .10
B5202	Stickers for B5200, set of 22	2 - 8
B5203	Individual stickers, each	.10 - .20
B5204	Box for B5200	4 - 8
B5205	Wrappers for B5200	.25 - 1
B5206	Unopened waxpacks for B5200	.50 - 2
B5210	Folders (Pak-Well Corp.), ea	1 - 2

Records B5231-32

B5231	The Story of *The Black Hole*	2 - 7
B5232	Soundtrack from *The Black Hole*	2 - 7
B5250	Storybook	2 - 5

Comic books B5300-02 (Western Publishing)

B5300	#1	1 - 2
B5301	#2	.50 - 1
B5302	#3	.50 - 1

Puzzles B5320-22 (Western Publishing Co., Inc.)

B5320	V.I.N.Cent	4 - 8
B5321	Maximillian and Dr Reinhardt	4 - 8
B5322	Tray puzzles	3 - 7
B5340	Super-8 film clip	10 - 20
B5350	Wrist watch	15 - 30
B5360	View-Master reels	2 - 5
B5400	Pinball machine	300 - 400

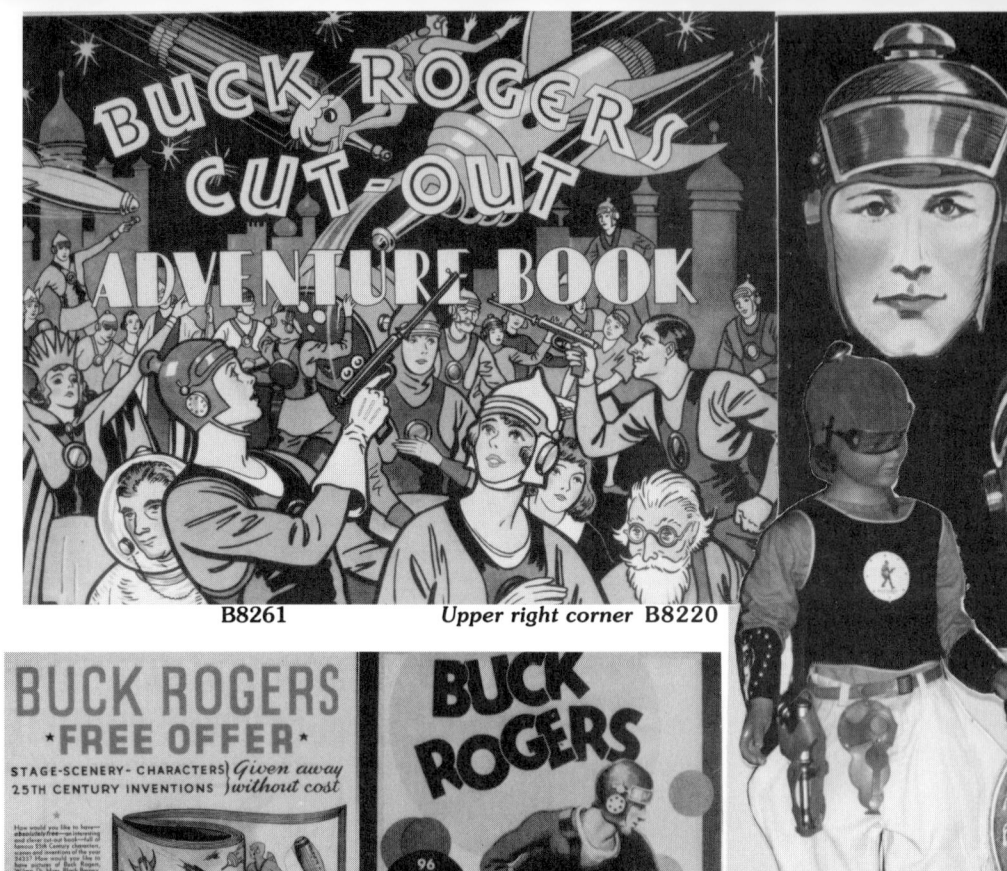

B8261 *Upper right corner* B8220

B8260  B8475

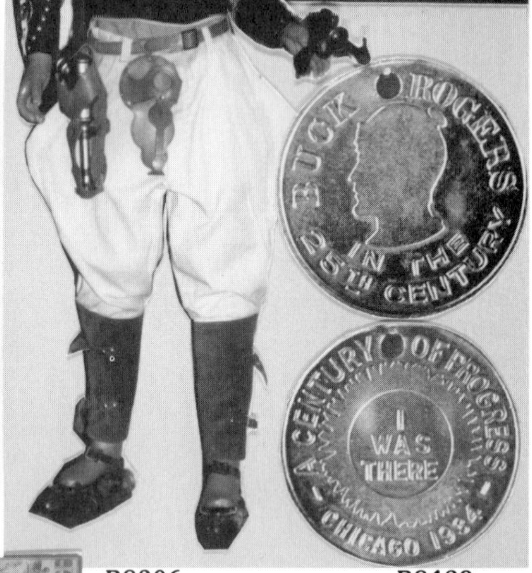

B8306 B8429

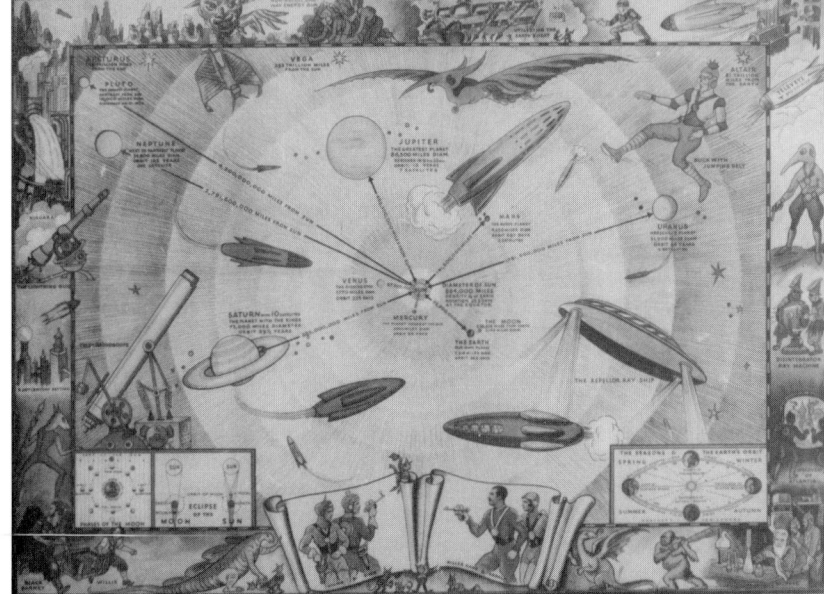

B8190  B8421

BUCK ROGERS in the 25th CENTURY

The first Buck Rogers story, "Armageddon 2419 A.D.", was published in the August 1928 issue of *Amazing Stories*. This pulp novel by Philip Francis Nowlan tells the strange tale of a man "frozen" in time. Anthony "Buck" Rogers, trapped by a cave-in, is preserved in suspended animation by radioactive gases. He reawakens in the 25th century, where he meets beautiful Wilma Deering, the brilliant scientist Doctor Huer, and a reformed, though sometimes not-too-bright Martian air pirate named Black Barney. Reader response was so great a second story, "The Airlords of Han", appeared in the March 1929 issue of *Amazing Stories*. The villains were Killer Kane, his wily girlfriend, Ardella Valmar, and Mongoloid aliens.

The same year, the characters appeared in a comic strip entitled *Buck Rogers 2429 A.D.* Each year the date was increased to remain five hundred years ahead of the present. Eventually, it became known as *Buck Rogers in the 25th Century*. The strip continued to run until 1967, and was briefly resumed from 1979 – 1983.

The radio version of Buck began November 7, 1932, and was heard on CBS. The show had a number of sponsors, including Kellogg's (1932-33), Cocomalt (1933-35), Cream of Wheat (1935-36), and later Popsicle (1939-41) on the Mutual network. World War II interrupted the show, which resumed September 30, 1946, again on Mutual with a variety of sponsors. The final episode was broadcast March 28, 1947. A live-action series ran on ABC television from April 15, 1950 – January 30, 1951, and again in 1953 on the "Adventure Patrol" series weekdays on NBC.

Buck has been seen at the movies on two occasions. The first was a twelve chapter serial produced by Universal in 1939. Later feature versions were called *Planet Outlaws* and *Destination Saturn*. A color feature was done by Universal in 1979. This version attempted to update the characters and add several elements which helped Star Wars succeed. The result was very different from what made Buck Rogers a success in the past. Still an extensive new line of merchandise followed – including books, games, figures and many other toys. A television series spun off from the 1979 film and ran from September 27, 1979 – August 20, 1981 on NBC.

Beginning in 1988 TSR Inc. introduced new Buck Rogers games and novels in conjunction with Flint Dille, grandson of the original copyright holder.

One of the most difficult items to find intact is probably the *Cut-Out Adventure Book*. Young fans were required to drink Cocomalt every day for a month, and have a certificate signed by their mothers as proof. The few copies which remain have the further distinction of surviving the colorful book's intended use.

Some controversy exists regarding the birthstone initial ring, which appeared in a 1940 Popsicle catalog with a Buck Rogers advertisement, but was never explicitly linked with the character. It is included here for those who wish to consider it authentic.

The original Cream of Wheat–sponsored "Solar Scouts" offered 26 premiums. The "Solar Scouts" soon evolved into the "Rocket Rangers" (known as "The Satellite Pioneers" in 1958) with "military" ranks available to boys and girls. It remained active until 1978.

Special thanks to Gene Seger for his help in compiling this section. Some photos used also appeared in *A Celebration of Comic Art and Memorabilia* by Robert Lesser; used by permission of the copyright owner.

1928
B8100	"Armageddon 2419 A.D." (*Amazing Stories*, Aug)	50 - 150

1929
B8101	"The Airlords of Han" (*Amazing Stories*, Mar)	50 - 120
B8110	Newspaper daily strips (1929-67), ea	1 - 5
B8111	Newspaper daily strips (1979-83), ea	.10 - .30
B8112	Newspaper Sunday color comic pages (1930-65), ea	10 - 30
B8113	Newspaper Sunday color comic pages (1979-83), ea	2 - 4
B8120	Original art for B8110-13	500 - 2000

1931
B8123	Planet Venus coloring map	60 - 120

1932
B8125	Newspaper drawings, 8-1/2" x 11" of Buck or Wilma, each has black starry panel behind head	75 - 150
B8128	Iron-on transfer (standing outline of Buck figure) (2 styles), ea	10 - 30

1933
B8175	Buck Rogers Origin storybook (Kellogg's)	50 - 175
B8176	Letter on Kellogg's stationery	10 - 30
B8180	Big Little Book—*Buck Rogers in the 25th Century A.D.* (hard cover)	25 - 50
B8181	Cocomalt Big Little Book—*Buck Rogers 25th Century A.D.* (soft cover)	35 - 70
B8190	Solar System map (Cocomalt)	200 - 600

"Bucktoys" cardboard figures B8200-05 (newspaper premium) (12 issued)
B8200	#1 Buck Rogers	25 - 75
B8201	#2 Wilma Deering	25 - 75
B8202	#3 Killer Kane	25 - 75
B8203	#4 Ardella	25 - 75
B8204	#5 Gyrex-Bullet Space Racer	25 - 75
B8205	#6 Doctor Huer	25 - 75
B8215	Woofian Dictionary (newspaper premium) (buff-color folder)	25 - 50
B8220	Colored face masks of Buck and Wilma (Einson-Freeman Co.) set	150 - 225
B8230	Movie-Jektor film	10 - 40
B8240	Kite folder, #376 (PEP)	15 - 30
B8241	Bird folder, #331 (Corn Flakes)	15 - 30
B8250	Paper gun and helmet, comes in Buck and Wilma versions (Einson-Freeman Co.)	125 - 200
B8251	Boxed store version of B8250	175 - 250
B8260	*Cut-Out Adventure Book* offer sheet, 4-color (was sent w/Solar System map and also w/BLB B8181)	300 - 400
B8261	*Cut-Out Adventure Book*, uncut (Cocomalt)	750 - 2500

27

B8175

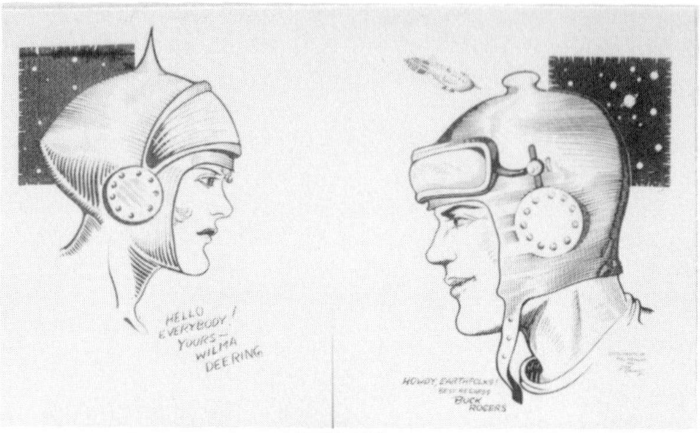

B8125

B8180

B8181

B8251

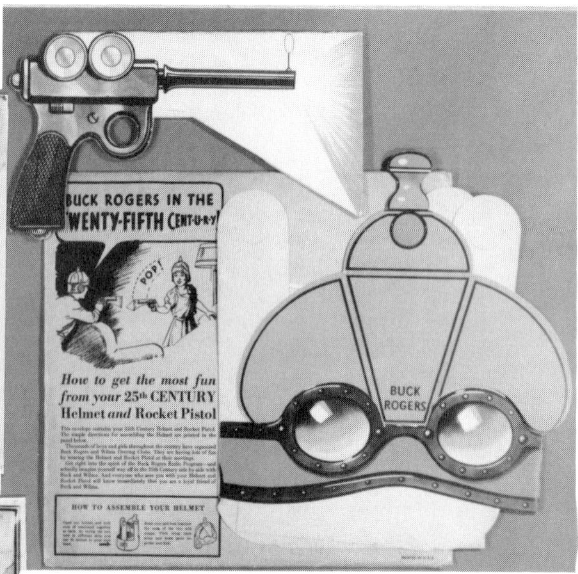

B8250

B8400

B8306

B8350-55

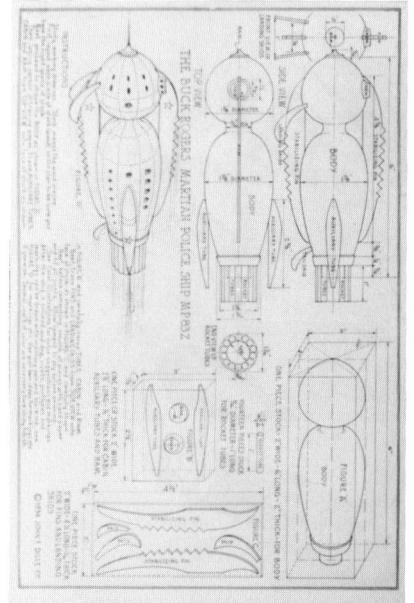

B8310

B8356

B8330

B8351

28

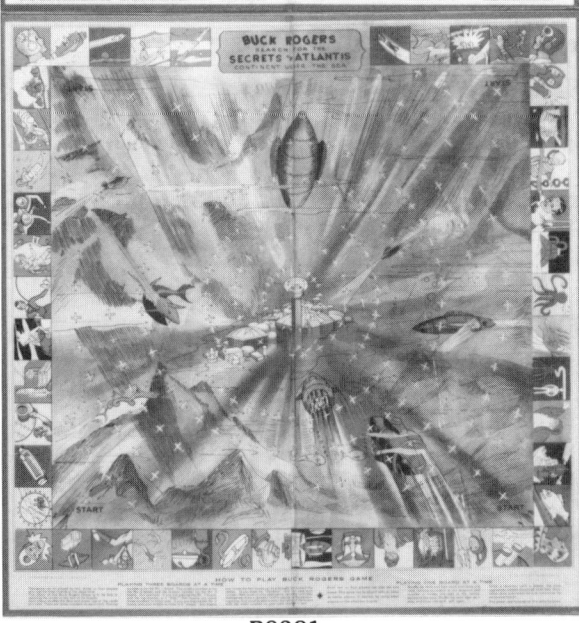

B8262	Mystery Color-By-Number "Puzzle", Buddy w/giant bird	20 - 40

1934

B8300	Rocket pistol, XZ-31 (Daisy)	75 - 125
B8301	Gun and holster combat set, XZ-32 (Daisy)	100 - 450
B8302	Holster only, cloth, XZ-33 (Daisy)	35 - 100
B8305	Helmet, cloth, XZ-42 (Daisy)	100 - 300
B8306	Uniform (Sackman Bros.)	1000 - 3000
B8310	Rocket Ship, wind-up (Louis Marx) (see B8775)	200 - 400
B8315	Rocket Ship motor kit	30 - 80
B8330	Pocketknife, came in red, blue and green (also used as a Solar Scout premium) (Adolph Kastor & Bros. Co.)	200 - 500
B8340	Casting sets w/midget, junior, and electric caster styles, manual, and extra 3 figure mold	75 - 400
B8341	Eight extra molds (2 molds are rare) (Rapaport Bros.), ea	50 - 125

Construction kits for Spaceships B8350-55 (Buck Rogers Co.), also found as built up models

B8350	#1 Battle Cruiser	75 - 200
B8351	#2 Martian Police Ship	75 - 200
B8352	#3 Flash Blast Attack Ship	75 - 200
B8353	#4 Superdreadnought	75 - 200
B8354	#5 Venus Fighting Destroyer	75 - 200
B8355	#6 Pursuit Ship	75 - 200
	#7 War Transport, appeared as blueprint only, but was never released	
B8356	Fighting fleet poster appears on backside of each kit constuction plan (17" x 11")	35 - 75
B8370	Photograph of Buck and Wilma in Grand Canyon (Cocomalt)	50 - 100
B8375	Letters on Buck Rogers stationery (Cocomalt), ea	20 - 45
B8380	Game of the 25th Century	150 - 300
B8381	Interplanetary Games, set of 3 boards in illustrated box	250 - 550
B8382	Cocomalt version of B8381 came in plain red box	250 - 550
B8385	*In a Dangerous Mission* small pop-up book (Blue Ribbon Press)	75 - 200
B8390	Painted lead figures — Buck, Wilma and Killer Kane, set of 3, each in cello bag w/blue folder of radio stations (Cocomalt)	75 - 150
B8395	"Buck Rogers on the Air!" radio station listings	10 - 25

Big Little Books B8400-01

B8400	*Buck Rogers in the City Below the Sea* (2 editions)	25 - 50
B8401	*Buck Rogers on the Moons of Saturn* (2 editions)	25 - 50
B8405	Big Big Book — *On the Planetoid Eros*, #4057 (Whitman)	100 - 300

Big Thrill Chewing Gum Booklets B8410-15 (Goudey Gum Co.), set of 6 in color

B8410	#1 *Thwarting Ancient Demons*	25 - 50
B8411	#2 *A One-Man Army*	25 - 50
B8412	#3 *An Aerial Derelict*	25 - 50
B8413	#4 *The Fight Beneath the Sea*	25 - 50
B8414	#5 *A Handful of Trouble*	25 - 50

B8381

B8370

B8375

B8420

B8380

B8466

B8340

B8530

B8451

B8470

B8410-15

B8456

30

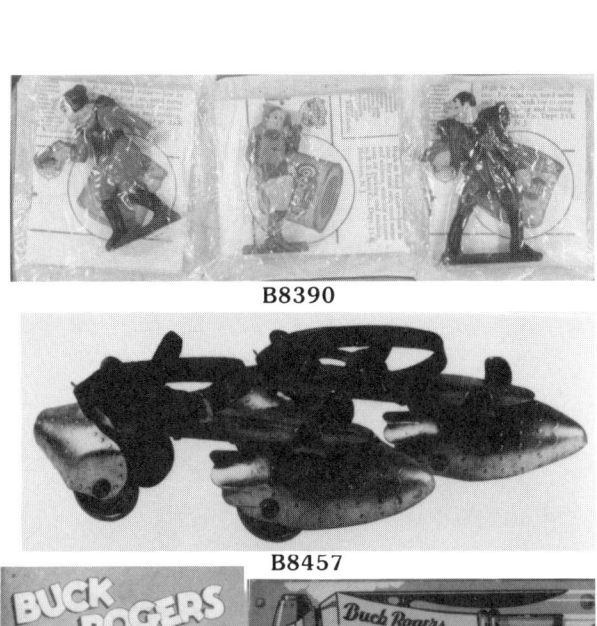

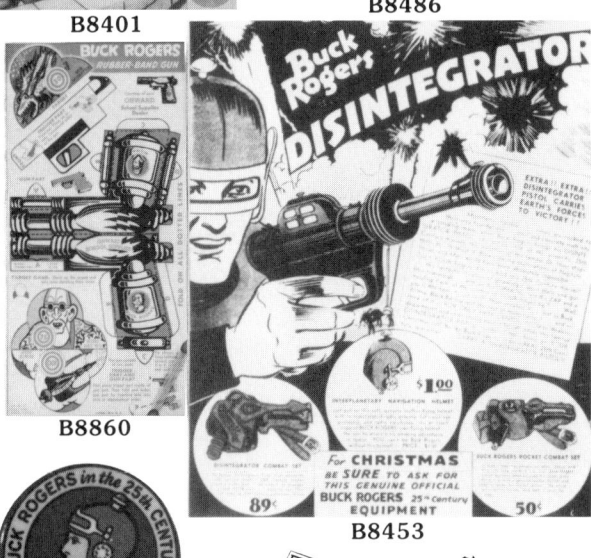

B8415	#6 *Collecting Human Specimens*	25 - 50
B8420	25th Century scientific laboratory, w/3 manuals, large set (Porter Chemical Co.)	800 -2000
B8421	Instruction envelope for B8420	75 - 150
B8429	"I Was There" Century of Progress World's Fair coin	75 - 200
B8430	"I Saw Buck Rogers" pinback, orange and blue (Chicago World's Fair) (Greenduck)	100 - 300
B8431	Buck Rogers pinback (Saturday Chicago American) (Greenduck)	50 - 200
B8432	Pinback, blue on white (*Pittsburgh Post Gazette*) (Bastian Bros.)	75 - 250
B8433	Pinback, blue on white (*Buffalo Evening News*) (Bastian Bros.)	50 - 200

1935

B8440	Printing set, 22 stamps (Superior Type Co.)	150 - 350
B8441	Smaller version of B8440, 7 stamps	60 - 100
B8442	Medium version of B8440, 14 or 15 stamps and alphabet	75 - 135
B8449	Helmet, leather, XZ-34 (Daisy)	300 - 500
B8450	Rocket pistol, XZ-35 (smaller version – 7-3/4") (Daisy)	100 - 165
B8451	Holster for B8450, leather, XZ-36, has round hole (Daisy)	35 - 75
B8452	Gun and holster combat set, XZ-37 (Daisy)	100 - 450
B8453	Disintegrator pistol, XZ-38, copper color (Daisy)	80 - 150
B8454	Holster for B8453, XZ-39 (Daisy)	65 - 135
B8455	Gun and holster, combat set, XZ-40 (Daisy)	150 - 350
B8456	Daisy catalog, yellow and black folder	200 - 300
B8457	Rocket roller skates (Louis Marx) (highest price is for only pair known in original box)	500 - 3000
B8460	Strat-O-Sphere Dispatch balloon w/message (Thornecraft)	25 - 75
B8466	*Strange Adventures in the Spider Ship* pop-up book (Pleasure Books)	125 - 250
B8470	Pocket watch (E. Ingraham Co.)	200 - 700
B8471	Wrist watch (Ingraham)	300 - 900
B8475	Paint Book, #679 (Whitman)	25 - 100
B8480	Toyloons (Lee-Tex Products Co.)	50 - 100
B8481	Rubber balls , various styles (Lee-Tex Products Co.)	20 - 75
B8482	Paddle ball named "Comet Socker" on paddle (Lee-Tex Products Co.)	35 - 75
B8485	Pencil boxes, red, green, and blue styles; over 30 different exist, all made between 1934-38 (American Pencil Co.)	40 - 150
B8486	School crayons ship box, 6 colored pencils (American Pencil Co.)	50 - 125
B8490	Rocket football, silver color (Edward K. Tryon Co.)	100 - 300
B8495	Sweat shirt (sweater)	?
B8500	Ice cream cup lid w/picture of Matthew Crowley (2 different: Dixie and Breyers Ice Cream), ea	25 - 50

32

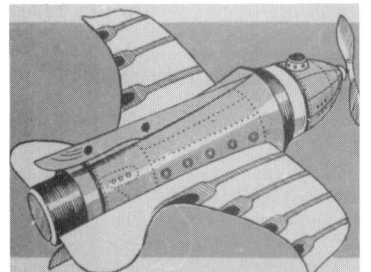

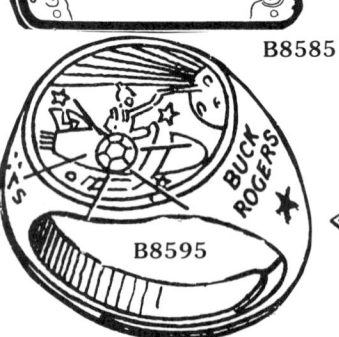

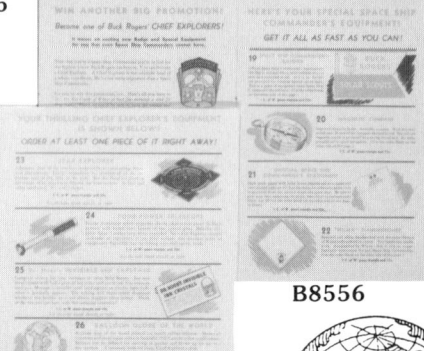

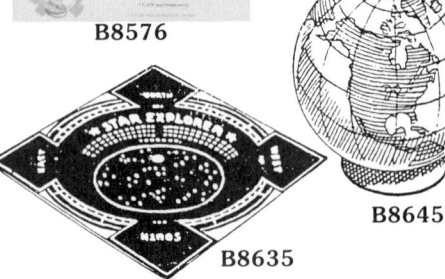

B8505	The 25th Century pinback, 3 colors on blue (Whitehead & Hoag)	35 - 70

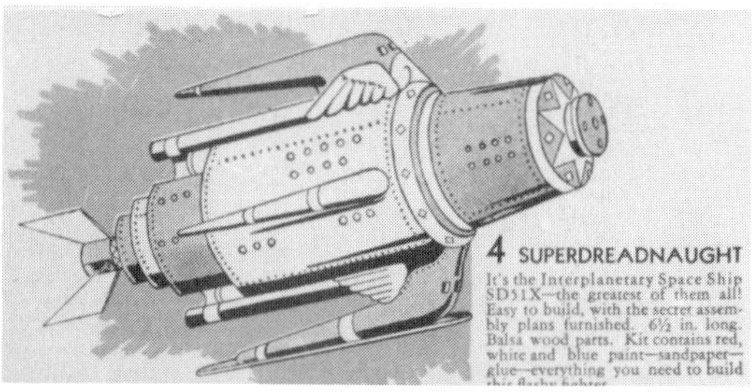

Big Little Books B8530-33 (Whitman)

B8530	*Buck Rogers*, no Whitman number (Tarzan Ice Cream premium)	75 - 175
B8531	*The Depth Men of Jupiter*	25 - 55
B8532	*The Doom Comet*	25 - 55
B8533	*In The City of Floating Globes*, no Whitman number (Cocomalt)	40 - 80
B8540	25th Century catalog, b/w folder, 9" x 12"	75 - 200

1936

B8550	Solar Scouts Radio Club manual	100 - 225
B8551	Solar Scouts member badge, gold color	40 - 55
B8556	Spaceship Commander folder, w/Chief Explorer application	75 - 150
B8557	Spaceship Commander banner	100 - 300
B8558	Spaceship Commander stationery	75 - 150
B8559	Spaceship Commander whistle badge	50 - 125
B8570	Wilma handkerchief	150 - 300
B8575	Chief Explorer badge	100 - 225
B8576	Chief Explorer folder	80 - 200
B8577	Space Ship that flies (Spotswood)	150 - 450
B8578	Superdreadnought model	150 - 300
B8585	School kit bag	75 - 150
B8586	Sweater emblem, 3 colors	200 - 600
B8590	Wilma pendant, brass color w/chain	125 - 225
B8595	Repeller Ray ring (seal ring), brass color w/inset green stone	250 - 750
B8600	Britains lead figures — Buck, Wilma, Kane, Ardella, Doctor Huer, and Robot, set of 6, name on pedestal base	600 - 2200
B8601	Reproductions of B8600, set of 6 (dp miniatures) no name on pedestal base (1989)	55 - 65
B8602	Pencil box, #35228	40 - 80
B8603	Movie projector, unmarked (Irwin), generic	50 - 90
B8604	Films for B8603, set of 6 Buck Rogers (Irwin)	50 - 200
B8605	16mm "Buck Rogers on Jupiter"	5 - 25
B8610	Lite-Blaster flashlight	75 - 300
B8625	Liquid Helium water pistol, XZ-44, red/yellow (Daisy)	75 - 350
B8626	Same as B8625 but copper finish	50 - 150
B8630	Magnetic compass, unmarked, also sold in stores	25 - 45
B8635	Star Explorer chart, unmarked, also sold to schools	20 - 60
B8640	Four-power telescope, unmarked, also sold in stores	20 - 40
B8645	Balloon Globe of the World, unmarked, in mailer (Lou Fox)	80 - 150
B8646	Doctor Huer's Invisible Ink Crystals	50 - 150
B8650	All-Fair card game, 36 cards (E.E. Fairchild)	150 - 375
B8655	"Buck Rogers in the 25th Century" strip cards, #425-448, 24 in color, perforated (John F. Dille Co.), ea	10 - 40

B8726

B8700-02

B8485

B8661

B8650

B8485

B8655

34

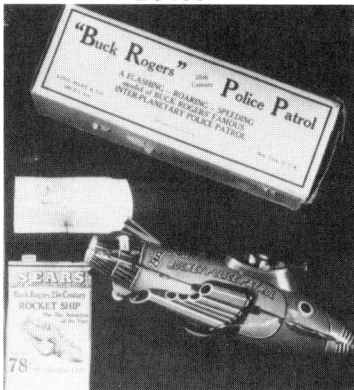

ID	Description	Price
B8660	Big Little Book — *The Planetoid Plot*	20 - 45
B8661	Dandy picture of Buck Rogers, b/w, 8-1/2" x 5-1/2"	50 - 150
B8666	Buck Rogers and Doctor Huer pinback, black on blue	45 - 150

1937

ID	Description	Price
B8670	Rocket Rangers pinback, blue on white	100 - 200
B8680	Chemistry set w/manual, simple set (Gropper Co.)	150 - 600
B8681	Same as B8680, advanced set	200 - 800
B8690	Sneakers (U.S. Rubber Co.)	35 - 125

Tootsietoy Rocket Ships B8700-02 (Dowst Mfg. Co.) (paint colors changed several times for each spaceship)

ID	Description	Price
B8700	Flash Blast Attack Ship	50 - 150
B8701	Venus Duo-Destroyer	50 - 150
B8702	Buck Rogers Battle Cruiser	50 - 150
B8703	Cast figures of Buck (gray) and Wilma (gold), 1-3/4" tall, ea	75 - 125
B8704	Tootsietoy Battle Fleet, boxed set containing B8700-03 and *U.S.N. Los Angeles Dirigible* (which is not marked)	250 - 500
B8710	Hearing Aid "Acousticon" Jr (Dictograph Products Co.)	?
B8711	Large color and white pinback (for B8710), 2-1/4"	150 - 450
B8712	Composition books and tablets w/story chapter on cover, ea	20 - 60
B8715	Rocket Rangers enlistment blank	15 - 40
B8716	Confidential Rocket Ranger bulletins, ea	15 - 40
B8717	Membership cards, ea	30 - 130

Fireworks B8720-26 (National Fireworks Co., Inc.)

ID	Description	Price
B8720	"Chase of Killer Kane"	50 - 100
B8721	"The Sun Gun of Saturn"	50 - 100
B8722	"The Battle of Mars"	50 - 100
B8723	"Battle Fleet of Rocket Ships"	50 - 100
B8724	"Fireless Rocket Ships"	50 - 100
B8725	Set of 5 B8720-24	500 - 2000
B8726	Catalog	50 - 200
B8727	Spencer Fireworks catalog	25 - 100
B8728	Combat game, interlocking panels w/stand-up figures (Warren Paper Products)	150 - 300
B8730	Club member pinback, 3 colors (Shaw, Toronto)	150 - 500
B8731	Gang member pinback, red lettering on white	35 - 175

1938

ID	Description	Price
B8750	Better Little Book—*In The Interplanetary War With Venus*	15 - 50

1939

ID	Description	Price
B8770	Whistling rocket ship (Muffets)	20 - 75
B8775	Police patrol ship, wind-up (Marx) (see B8310)	300 - 500
B8780	Telescope (Popsicle premium)	30 - 90
B8787	Serial prints (16mm film reels in 12 b/w chapters) (Universal)	100 - 300
B8800	Serial lobby cards (85 different) in various one-shade colors, 14" x 11", ea	25 - 115
B8801	Reprints of B8800, ea	5 - 20

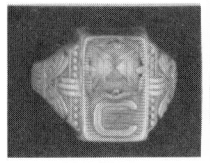

B8871
B9000   B9230 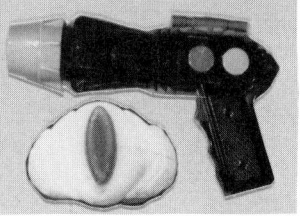
B8870 
B9054 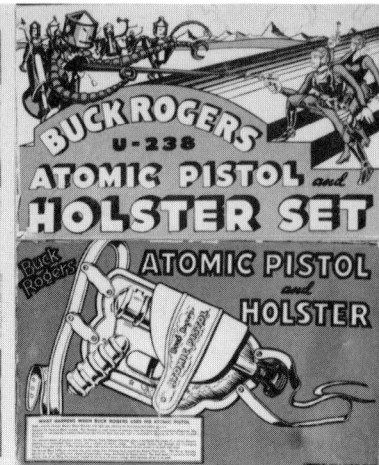
B9257 
B9251 
B8955 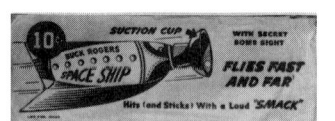
B9254 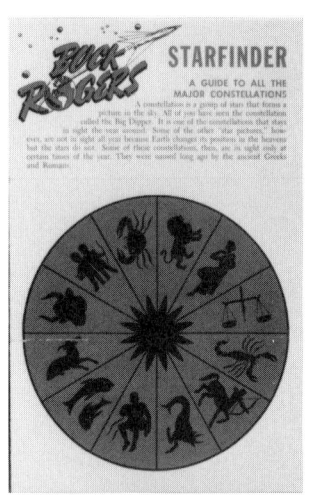
B9030 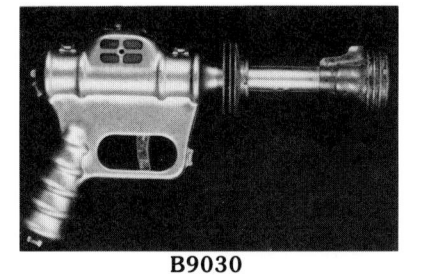
B9100 
B9221 
B9075 

36

B8802	Serial posters, several sizes for each chapter	300 - 1000
B8803	Serial stills (original)	5 - 50
B8804	Serial press book, 3 versions: Universal, Filmcraft, Planet Outlaws, ea	100 - 350
B8805	Strange World Adventures Club pinback, 2 colors (Philadelphia)	200 - 400
B8806	Membership card for B8805	25 - 75

1940

B8830	Better Little Book—*Buck Rogers vs. The Fiend of Space*	15 - 40
B8840	Matchbook ((Diamond), Popsicle and Creamsicle versions, each w/April 6 and May 4 radio ads	10 - 30

***Buck Rogers in the 25th Century* comic books**
B8851-56 (Eastern Color Printing Co.)

B8851	Buck Rogers, #1, issued 1940	20 - 150
B8852	Buck Rogers, #2, issued 1941	20 - 130
B8853	Buck Rogers, #3, issued 1942	20 - 130
B8854	Buck Rogers, #4, issued 1942	20 - 130
B8855	Buck Rogers, #5, issued 1943 (second half is Skyroads)	20 - 130
B8856	Buck Rogers, #6, issued 1943	20 - 130
B8860	Rubber band gun (Onward School Supplies)	15 - 40
B8870	Popsicle Pete's Radio Gift News, 2 issued in color, 15" x 10"	20 - 60
B8871	Birthstone initial ring (generic)	60 - 200
B8872	Amoco series pennycards and board, 3" b/w (Calex Mfg.), ea	5 - 25

1941

B8900	Better Little Book—*The Overturned World*	20 - 45
B8910	Rocket Rangers *Flying Needle* rocket ship plan (red on white)	15 - 45

1942

B8950	Dog tag w/chain (dated 1935)	20 - 130
B8955	Paperboard spaceship w/suction cup (Morton Salt)	25 - 75
B8956	Punch-O-Bag, balloon w/characters in color, 2 dif envelopes (Morton Salt)	35 - 110

1943

B8975	Better Little Book—*The Super Dwarf of Space*	20 - 45

1944

B8990	Rocket Rangers iron-on transfers, set of 3 – Buck Rogers, Wilma Deering, Pursuit Ship, red and blue	15 - 75
B9000	Ring of Saturn w/red stone, glow-in-the-dark white plastic formed on crocodile base (Post Corn Toasties)	100 - 400
B9001	Red and black folder for B9000	30 - 100

1945

B9030	Atomic pistol, U-235 (Daisy), 2 versions, nickel and black	75 - 150
B9031	Black and white adventure book folder for B9030	30 - 100
B9032	Buck Rogers and His Atomic Bomber, boxed set of 3 inlaid jigsaw puzzles (Puzzle Craft)	50 - 200

1946

B9050	Blotter w/color scene (Chicago Herald American)	15 - 35
B9054	Atomic pistol, U-238 (Daisy), gold color, leather holster and colored announcement folded flyer, set	100 - 275
B9075	Strato-kite, came flat or rolled (The Aero-Kite Co.)	20 - 50

1947

B9100	Drawing of Pluton (Yager)	20 - 60

1948

B9120	Two-way Trans-Ceiver (DA-Myco)	75 - 100

1949

B9130	Comic Traders series A-3 Color cards (2):Buck Rogers, Flame D'Amour, ea	5 - 15

1950-59

B9175	Tru-Vue Stereo Film Card T-3 (oblong) and viewer	15 - 30
B9190	Flying saucer, paper plates	25 - 60
B9200	Comic books, #1-3, actual cover #100,101,9, (Toby press, 1951) ea	5 - 12
B9220	Inlaid puzzle, space station scene, 14" x 10" in paperboard sleeve (Milton Bradley, 1952)	20 - 30
B9221	Space Ranger kit (Sylvania, 1952)	25 - 75
B9222	Space Ranger HaloLight ring (Sylvania, 1952)	40 - 80
B9229	Rocket Rangers member oblong tab (L.J. Imber, 1954)	35 - 75
B9230	Sonic ray gun, plastic, w/code folder (Norton-Honer, 1952-55)	25 - 65
B9231	Space glasses (N-H, 1955)	25 - 60
B9232	Super-Scope (N-H, 1955)	20 - 50
B9233	Super-Foto camera (N-H, 1955)	20 - 50
B9235	Walkie Talkies (Remco)	50 - 95
B9240	Drawing of Buck, his friends and enemies (Yager)	20 - 45
B9250	Satellite Pioneers pinback, green or blue (Greenduck, 1958), ea	10 - 30
B9251	Satellite Pioneers round tab (Greenduck, 1958)	30 - 120
B9252	Satellite Pioneers membership card	15 - 55
B9253	Satellite Pioneers Cadet Commission w/autographed postcard (1958)	20 - 60
B9254	Satellite Pioneers Starfinder (1958)	20 - 50
B9255	Satellite Pioneers Secret Order #1	15 - 45
B9256	Satellite Pioneers Map of the Solar System (1958)	15 - 45
B9257	Confidential Satellite Pioneers Bulletins	5 - 18

1960-69

B9260	Magic Erasable Dot Picture set (Transogram)	20 - 75
B9265	Reprint of "Armageddonn 2419 A.D." (*Amazing Stories*, Apr 1961)	5 - 10
B9266	Reprint of "Airlords of Han" (*Amazing Stories*, May 1962)	5 - 10
B9270	Gold Key Comics #1 (1964)	2 - 10
B9271	Paint-By-Number (not Craft Master)	8 - 35
B9278	Captain Action outfit (doll not included) (Ideal, 1967)	75 - 150
B9279	Captain Action card game (4 show Buck Rogers) (Kool-Pops, General Foods) (1967)	10 - 20
B9300	The Buck Rogers Idea poster	

B9331

B9345

B9695

B9430

B9420-28

B9360

B9440-46

38

	(S.D. Warren Co., 1969)	10 - 35
B9301	Paper Disintegrator noisemaker and postcard (came w/B9300) (S.D. Warren Co., 1969)	25 - 65
B9310	Buck profile ring	25 - 50

1970-78

B9325	Pocket watch (Huckleberry Time)	50 - 200
B9326	Pendant watch (Huckleberry Time)	50 - 225
B9327	Wrist watch (Huckleberry Time)	35 - 125
B9328	Clock (Huckleberry Time)	25 - 65

Reproduction recordings of the Buck Rogers radio broadcasts B9330-39 LP and audio cassette version available

B9330	1971 Radiola prelease #6, radio program, Apr 4, 1939	5 - 10
B9331	1973 Mark 56 record #602, 2 undated radio programs	5 - 10
B9335	1979 Golden Age GA5035, first 4 radio programs, Nov 1932	5 - 10
B9336	1979 Wonderland WLP-3005, 4 radio programs, May, 1940	5 - 10
B9337	1979 MCA-3097, original motion picture soundtrack	5 - 10
B9339	1980 GNP Crescendo 2133, has music excerpts from 1979 movie	5 - 10
B9345	1981 MCA 13-002, stereo videodisc, 1979 motion picture	5 - 10
B9350	Sweatshirt (Varsity House, Inc., 1974)	5 - 15
B9352	Frazetta portfolio of 9 *Famous Funnies* covers (Chochran, 1975)	15 - 30
B9353	Drawing of Buck, Wilma, and Black Barney in space (Dworkins)	4 - 8
B9360	Adventures in the 25th Century game (Transogram)	20 - 40
B9362	View-Master J-1 series, 4 reels	8 - 20
B9363	Greeting card (Bantam)	2 - 10
B9390	Toy wrist watch (GLJ Toys, 1978)	8 - 15

1979-87

B9395	*Armageddon 2419 A.D.*, novel (Ace)	2 - 6
B9400	Souvenir film program	5 - 10
B9401	Lobby cards, ea	5 - 10
B9402	Stills, ea	2 - 8
B9403	Press book	10 - 20
B9404	Posters	10 - 20

Small action figures and vehicles B9420-35 (Mego)

B9420	Buck Rogers	10 - 14
B9421	Wilma Deering	15 - 20
B9422	Doctor Huer	12 - 15
B9423	Twiki	14 - 18
B9424	Killer Kane	10 - 12
B9425	Ardella	15 - 20
B9426	Tiger Man	10 - 12
B9427	Draconian Guard	12 - 15
B9428	Draco	12 - 15
B9430	Landrover	20 - 50
B9431	Star Fighter	20 - 50
B9432	Draconian Marauder	20 - 50
B9433	Star Fighter Command Center	25 - 75
B9435	Laserscope Fighter	20 - 50

Large action figures B9440-46 (Mego)

B9440	Buck Rogers	10 - 45
B9441	Walking Twiki	10 - 35
B9442	Doctor Huer	20 - 50

B9460

B9466

B9465

B9485

B9447

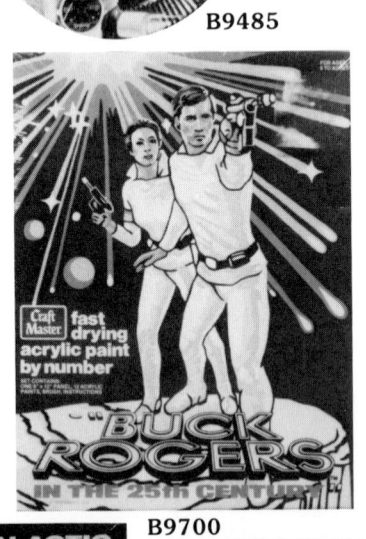

B9700

B9727

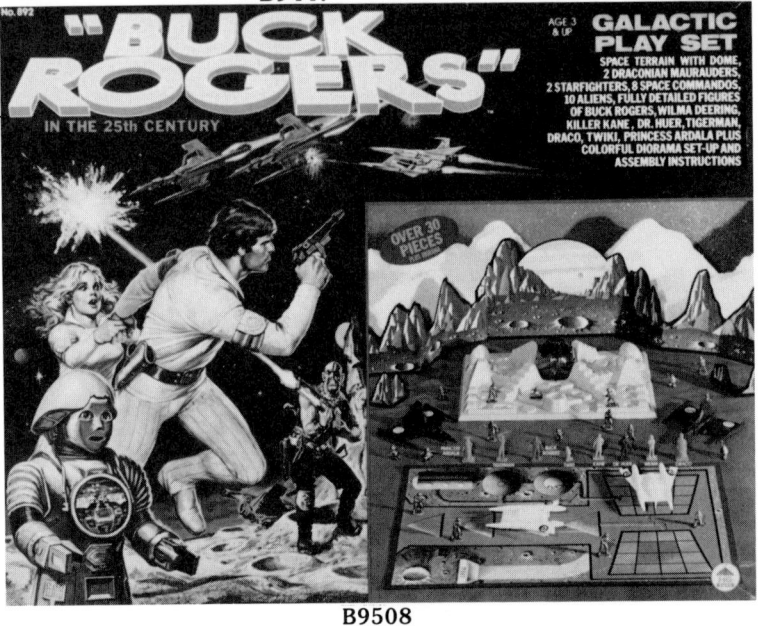

B9508

B9496

40

B9443	Killer Kane	20 - 50
B9444	Draco	15 - 40
B9445	Tiger Man	20 - 50
B9446	Draconian Guard	20 - 50]
B9447	Spaceport playset (Mego)	50 - 150
B9451	Radio-controlled Twiki, inflatable (Daewoo)	50 - 100
B9452	Galaxy gun and holster set (Nichols-Kusan)	18 - 35
B9453	Utility belt, including play watch, decoders, eyeglasses, and disk-shooting gun (Remco)	15 - 25
B9455	Die-cast Starfighter (Corgi), 2 sizes	12 - 25
B9460	Board game (Milton Bradley)	20 - 40
B9465	Lunch box (Aladdin)	8 - 15
B9466	Thermos for B9465	6 - 9
B9470	Comic books (Gold Key/Whitman), #2-16, (issues #8 & 9 are rare; #10 was never released), ea	1 - 6
B9485	Paper plates, 2 sizes (Paper Art, 1979)	2 - 8
B9495	Giant Film Adaptation (Marvel)	2 - 4
B9496	Jigsaw puzzles (Milton Bradley), ea	5 - 15
B9500	Trading cards, set of 88 (Topps)	6 - 12
B9501	Individual trading cards, ea	.05- .10
B9502	Stickers for B9500, set of 22	3 - 7
B9503	Individual stickers, ea	.15 - .35
B9504	Box for B9500	5 - 10
B9505	Wrappers for B9500	.25 - 1
B9506	Unopened waxpacks for B9500	2 - 5
B9508	Galactic play set (H-G Toys Inc.)	15 - 25

Model kits B9510-11 (Monogram)
B9510	Draconian Marauder	10 - 35
B9511	Starfighter	10 - 35

Plastic tumblers B9512-19 (Coca-Cola)
B9512	16 oz, 8 dif, ea	2 - 5
B9513	20 oz, 5 dif, ea	2 - 5
B9514	Video game plastic tumbler, 2 designs (Slurpee, 1982, blue and 7-Eleven (Southland), 1983, red)	2 - 5

Glass tumblers B9520-23 (Coca-Cola)
B9520	Buck Rogers	20 - 40
B9521	Wilma Deering	20 - 40
B9522	Twiki	20 - 40
B9523	Draco	20 - 40
B9540	Target set, 2 styles (Fleetwood)	8 - 20
B9600	Gas-Powered Flying Starfighter (Cox)	35 - 75
B9601	View-Master L-15 series, 3 stereo reels (Showtime)	10 - 20
B9610	Communications set (H-G Toys)	7 - 15
B9615	Sticker set, 240 (Panini)	8 - 18
B9675	Space Communicators (Corgi)	10 - 20
B9676	Large postcard (Quick Fox)	1 - 3

Novels B9680-86
B9680	*Buck Rogers in the 25th Century* (film adaptation) (Dell)	2 - 5
B9681	#2 *That Man on Beta* (Dell)	2 - 5
B9682	*Fotonovel* Vol. 12, 1979 movie	1 - 6
B9683	*Mordred* (Ace)	1 - 6
B9684	*Warrior's Blood* (Ace)	1 - 6
B9685	*Warrior's World* (Ace)	1 - 6
B9686	*Rogers' Rangers* (Ace)	1 - 6
B9695	Colorforms Adventure set	4 - 20
B9690	Planet of Zoom video game (Sega)	5 - 10
B9700	Paint-by-number set (Craft Master)	10 - 25

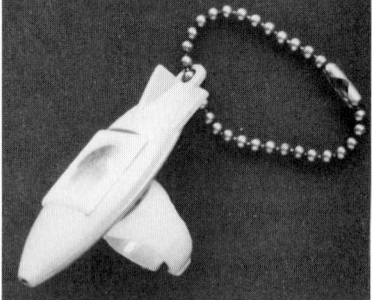

B9720　　　　　Upper right corner C1160

C1140

C1231-33

C1150

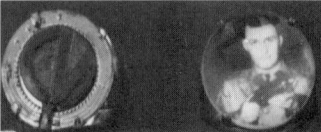

C1130　　　C1120

C1240

C1290

C1175

42

C1112   C1315

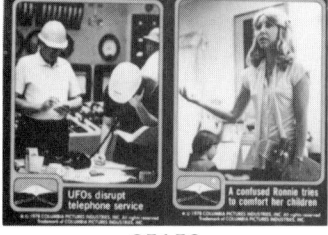

C5153   C5155

B9710	Little Golden Book—*Buck Rogers and the Children of Hopetown*	5 - 10
B9711	Pop-up Buck Rogers (Random House)	5 - 10
B9715	Photo of Twiki, given at Detroit Autorama	1 - 5

1988-90

B9719	1988 mobile, large logo w/flying figure of Buck underneath	10 - 20
B9720	Battle for the 25th Century Game (TSR)	10 - 40
B9721	Martian Wars Game (TSR)	10 - 40

Novels B9725-28 (TSR)

B9725	*Arrival*, Anthology	2 - 4
B9726	*Rebellion 2456*, Murdock	2 - 4
B9727	*Hammer of Mars*, Murdock	2 - 4
B9728	*Armageddon off Vesta*, Murdock	2 - 4
B9729	TSR poster given away rolled, also inserted in *Dragon Magazine*, #146, 31-1/2" x 21" (1989)	4 - 8
B9730	25th Century wings pin	5 - 10
B9740	Cosmic Heroes Comic Book series begins (Malibu Graphics, 1988) ea	1 - 2

1990

Novels B9750-52 (TSR)

B9750	*Rude Awakening* (Graphic Novel)	1 - 3
B9751	*First Power*	1 - 3
B9752	*Prime Squared*	1 - 3

CAPTAIN VIDEO

Captain Video, television's first space hero, premiered in June of 1949. The show was by far one of the most popular of its time, even though an embarrassingly low budget was allotted for the series. The Captain was a master scientist and inventor, and leader of an elite corps of men known as the Video Rangers. The most important of his inventions was a futuristic version of the TV set: the Remote Tele-Carrier. This amazing device allowed our hero to see anyone, anywhere, unhindered by distance, walls, or concealment. In the early days of the series, he would look in on the "Video Rangers of the Wild West". These "agents" took up a 10-minute segment in the middle of each show. Thus, in addition to its technological merits, the Remote Tele-Carrier gave the actors a break, and enabled the DuMont network to pad out the show with old western footage.

Meanwhile, the Captain had his hands full saving the world of the 22nd century. His adventures dealt with high-tech intrigue and espionage. Constantly in search of new weapons and strange devices, the Captain struggled to remain one technological step ahead of his enemies. Chief among these adversaries were the mad genius Dr. Pauli and the death-ray shooting robot, Tobor. Joining the Captain in his exploits was a 15-year-old recruit from the Video Rangers, who became the idol of many young fans.

The original Captain was radio and stage actor Richard Coogan. The man famous for the role, however, was Al Hodge, the radio voice of The Green Hornet. Hodge assumed the role in 1951, and took the successful show to new heights — at the expense of his acting career. Eventually the 30-minute daily broadcast became exclusively Captain Video. "The Secret Files of Captain Video" was added as a

C1181

C1181    C5120

C5110

C5170   C1220   C5180

C5125    C5128    C5190

C5160   C5120-23

Saturday show in 1953. Propelling him into the stars was a standard '50s style rocket ship - the *X-9*. The ship was later called the *Galaxy*, then destroyed and rebuilt as the *Galaxy II*.

The Master of Space was also played by Judd Holdren in a 15-episode serial. The year was 1951. The movie version, produced by Columbia Pictures, could not match the performance of Al Hodge. The film was very forgettable and material from it is difficult to find.

In the end, it was neither Dr. Pauli nor the numerous menaces from outer space that caused the demise of the character. Despite widespread demand and high ratings, budget concerns and a failing network eventually killed the show. The series was cancelled in 1956. The same year, Hodge hosted "Captain Video's Cartoons", an hour-long segment of the six-hour show "Wonder Time". This was to be the last appearance of the Captain, who was finally taken off the air sometime in 1956. NBC attempted unsuccessfully to purchase the rights to the show.

C1100	Membership card	8 - 16
C1110	Photo of Captain Video	5 - 15
C1112	Premium photo of Captain Video and Video Ranger	10 - 30
C1120	Photo ring	25 - 50
C1130	Secret Seal ring	40 - 175
C1140	Rocket ring	50 - 175
C1150	Flying Saucer ring (w/both saucers)	50 - 350
C1160	Rite-O-Lite gun kit	15 - 30
C1170	Plastic Space Men, (Post Raisin Bran), ea	5 - 12
C1175	Interplanetary Space Men (larger than cereal premiums), boxed set	35 - 90
C1180	Space vehicles, hard plastic, boxed set	35 - 90
C1181	Space vehicles, individually boxed	15 - 25
C1200	Purity Bread tab	15 - 25
C1210	Glo-Photo pendent (plastic)	40 - 150
C1220	Mysto-Coder	35 - 115

Comic Books C1231-36 (Fawcett, 1951)

C1231	#1	15 - 150
C1232-36	#2-6	10 - 100
C1240	Space game (Milton Bradley Co.)	30 - 100
C1250	Goggles	30 - 70
C1260	Lobby cards	5 - 15
C1270	Six-In-One record album	20 - 60
C1280	Secret Ray gun	40 - 80
C1290	Galaxy ride-on vehicle	350 - 500
C1300	Inflatable rocket ship	75 - 150
C1304	Space Port (Superior)	400 - 650
C1310	Serial poster, large	400 - 675
C1315	Serial posters, episodes, ea	200 - 500

CLOSE ENCOUNTERS OF THE THIRD KIND

This innovative motion picture deviates from the usual trends in space adventure. The main characters of the film are not dashing heroes, protecting the universe from cunning villains as they rocket through the galaxies. It is a story of ordinary people with unremarkable lives, struggling to comprehend the mysteries of alien contact. The effects of this encounter are explored primarily in the reactions of three very different people: a scientist, an ordinary man, and a young child. The aliens are frightening, not because they are evil or sinister, but because they are unknown. The film has a constant mood of tension, coalescing into a message of hope. We are not alone.

C5110	Official Collector's Edition	1 - 3
C5120	Novel, hardback	2 - 5
C5121	Novel, first edition, paperback	1 - 2
C5122	Novel, later editions, paperback	.50 - 2
C5123	Novel, revised ending	.50 - 1
C5124	Fotonovel	1 - 2

Soundtrack recordings C5125-27

C5125	Record	3 - 8
C5126	Cassette	1 - 4
C5127	Compact disc	5 - 10
C5128	Music from *Close Encounters*	2 - 6
C5130	Alien figure (Imperial, 1977)	8 - 25
C5140	Trading cards, set of 24 (Wonder Bread, 1977)	4 - 12
C5141	Individual trading cards, ea	.18 - .50
C5150	Trading cards, set of 66 (Topps, 1978)	5 - 12
C5151	Individual trading cards, ea	.02 - .08
C5152	Stickers for C5150, set of 11	2 - 8
C5153	Individual stickers, ea	.10 - .20
C5154	Box for C5150	4 - 9
C5155	Wrappers for C5150	1 - 2
C5156	Unopened waxpacks for C5150	2 - 3
C5160	Lunch box (King Seeley Thermos, 1978)	10 - 25
C5161	Thermos for C5160	5 - 12
C5170	Board game (Parker Brothers)	10 - 20
C5180	Marvel Special Edition graphic novel	1 - 2
C5190	*Science Fantasy* magazine	1 - 4
C5200	Postcard book (1980)	5 - 15

Buttons C5210-15

C5210	Close Encounters	1 - 2
C5211	I've Seen One	1 - 2
C5212	Contact	1 - 2
C5213	A Close Encounter	1 - 2
C5214	Watch the skies	1 - 2
C5215	We are not alone	1 - 2
C5220	Pinball machine	400 - 550

Skywatchers Club premiums C5230-31

C5230	UFO Sighting map	2 - 5
C5231	Skywatcher newsletter	2 - 5

DUNE

The *Dune* series was the masterwork of science-fiction writer Frank Herbert. It is a vast, sweeping epic, spanning six novels. Although set far in the distant future, *Dune* contains many allegorical elements designed to mirror aspects of the modern world.

In the year 10191 the most important planet in the universe is Arrakis, more commonly known as Dune. It is an inhospitable desert world, thrashed by destructive windstorms and home to monstrous sandworms. Yet beneath the sands lies the spice melange — the most precious substance in the universe. Though addictive, the spice extends the life span of the body

C5200

C5130

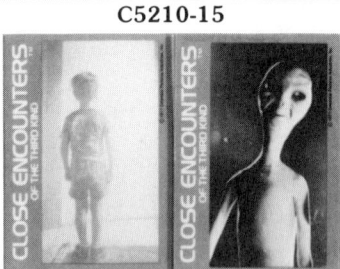

D8155

D8110

C5210-15

D8184

C5153

D8132

C5151

D8117

D8310

D8116

D8300-03

46

and expands the awareness of the mind. Every major power group in the known universe depends on it. Whoever controls the spice controls the universe.

The series explores the events surrounding Paul Atreides, heir to one of the feudal families who rule the known universe. His father, Duke Leto, is ordered by the Padishah Emperor to assume control of Arrakis. Though presumably a token of good faith, the move conceals treachery destined to destroy House Atreides. The Duke is killed, but Paul and his mother escape into the deep desert. Here they ally themselves with the Fremen, a warrior people accustomed to the harsh life of the planet. In fulfillment of an ancient prophecy, Paul is accepted among them as their promised messiah, and becomes the religious leader Muad'Dib. With his guidance, spice production is brought to a standstill until the Emperor himself is forced into a confrontation. The Fremen overpower the Emperor's military forces, and Paul reveals that he can destroy the spice if his demands are not met. Treachery fails to defeat him. At last the Emperor is forced to comply. Assuming the throne, Paul becomes Emperor and religious leader of the known universe.

Later books detail the consequences of Paul's actions: the holy war of the Fremen, the ecological transformation (and eventual destruction) of the planet Arrakis, and the power struggles through the reign of Paul's children and subsequent generations. The series emphasizes the destructive effects of heros. Despite his noble intentions, Paul sets off a chain of events from which the universe must struggle to recover for thousands of years after his death.

The original story, entitled "Dune World", was serialized in *Analog* magazine from Dec 1963 - Feb 1964. "The Prophet of Dune" followed in 1965 from Jan - May. These two stories were combined and published as the novel *Dune* by the Chilton Book Company. The book won the Nebula award in 1965 and the Hugo in 1966.

After several false starts, a motion picture adaptation of the first book was released by Universal in 1984. Assorted character merchandise was offered for a few months. The first and only issue of the *Dune Newsletter* made an attempt to get a fan club going, but the idea never caught on. A re-edited version of the film was shown on television in 1988.

D8100	*Analog* magazines: Dec 1963 - Feb 1964 ("Dune World"), ea	3 - 6
D8101	*Analog* magazines: Jan 1965 - May 1965 ("The Prophet of Dune"), ea	2 - 4
D8102	*Galaxy* magazines: July 1969 - Oct 1969 ("Dune Messiah"), ea	2 - 6
D8104	*Playboy* magazine: Jan 1981 issue (preview of *God Emperor of Dune*)	1 - 4
D8110	*Dune*, hardcover novel, first edition	3 - 10
D8111	*Dune Messiah*, hardcover novel	2 - 5
D8112	*Children of Dune*, hardcover novel	2 - 5
D8113	*God Emperor of Dune*, hardcover novel	2 - 5
D8114	*Heretics of Dune*, hardcover novel	2 - 5
D8115	*Chapterhouse: Dune*, hardcover novel	2 - 5
D8116	*Dune*, film edition paperback	1 - 2
D8117	Other paperback novels, ea	.50 - 5

D8185

D8181

D8183

D8225-27

D8114-15

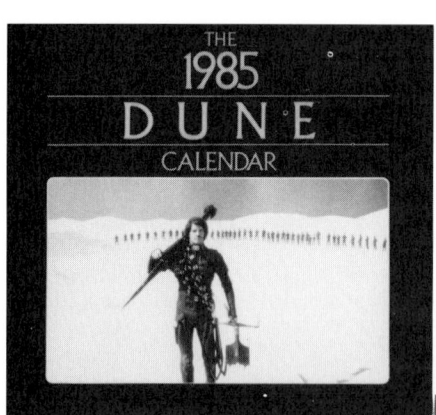

D8200

D8235

D8330

D8220

48

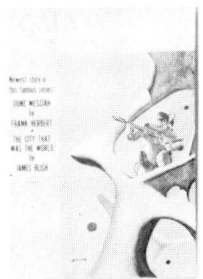

ID	Item	Price
D8130	*The Dune Encyclopedia*	5 - 10
D8131	*The Making of Dune*	2 - 5
D8132	*The Maker of Dune*	2 - 5
D8135	Official Collector's Edition magazine	1 - 3
D8150	Film pre-release button (Two Moons)	1 - 2
D8151	Logo button	1 - 2
D8152	Two Moons button	1 - 2
D8153	Paul and Feyd button	1 - 2
D8154	Sandworm button	1 - 2
D8155	Game (Avalon Hill)	8 - 15
D8156	Spice Harvest (Module for D8155)	10 - 15
D8157	The Duel (Module for D8155)	10 - 15
D8159	Film pre-release poster (A World Beyond Your Dreams)	2 - 4
D8160	Film poster	4 - 8
D8161	A World Beyond Your Dreams poster	2 - 4
D8162	Two Moons poster	2 - 4
D8163	Paul and Feyd poster	2 - 4
D8164	Sandworm poster	2 - 4
D8165	Terminology sheet	.50 - 1
D8167	Flyer (novel promotion)	.50 - 1
D8170	Storybook	2 - 5
D8180	Trading cards, set of 132	8 - 14
D8181	Individual trading cards, ea	.10 - .20
D8182	Stickers for D8180, set of 44 (Large sticker set was difficult to complete)	6 - 15
D8183	Individual stickers, ea	.10 - .40
D8184	Box for D8180	4 - 8
D8185	Wrappers for D8180	2 - 4
D8186	Unopened waxpacks for D8180	1 - 3
D8187	Paper plates, 2 sizes, ea	1 - 3
D8200	Calender, 1985	5 - 10
D8210	Fan club newsletter	2 - 5
D8220	Book cover	1 - 2
D8225-27	Comic miniseries (Marvel) #1-3, ea	1 - 2
D8230	Graphic novel	1 - 3
D8235	Board game (Parker Brothers)	8 - 15
D8240	Taped interview: David Lynch/Frank Herbert (Waldenbooks, 1984)	1 - 4

Film soundtrack album D8241-43

ID	Item	Price
D8241	Record	2 - 6
D8242	Cassette	1 - 4
D8243	Compact disc	5 - 10
D8250	*The Notebooks of Frank Herbert's Dune* (Perigee, 1988)	5 - 10

LJN (1984) D8300-41

Action figures D8300-05

ID	Item	Price
D8300	Paul Atreides	10 - 15
D8301	Stilgar the Fremen	10 - 15
D8302	Baron Harkonnen	10 - 15
D8303	Feyd	15 - 20
D8304	Rabban	10 - 15
D8305	Sardaukar Warrior	15 - 25
D8310	Spice Scout	12 - 25

Battery-operated vehicles D8320-22

ID	Item	Price
D8320	Sand Roller	8 - 15
D8321	Sand Tracker	8 - 15
D8322	Sand Crawler	8 - 15
D8330	Sandworm	10 - 25
D8340	Fremen Tarpel gun	20 - 30
D8341	Sardaukar pistol	25 - 40

Grosset & Dunlap (1984) D8400-10

ID	Item	Price
D8400	Activity book	2 - 5
D8401	Coloring and activity book	2 - 5

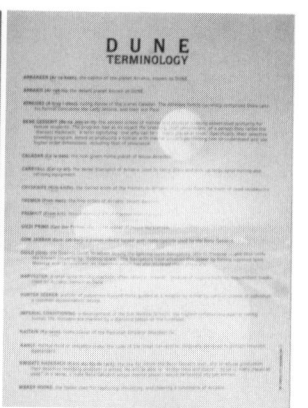

D8502

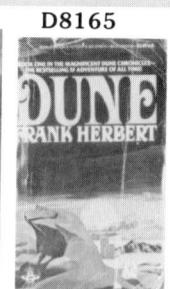

D8167

D8165

D8322

D8117

D8340

E2030

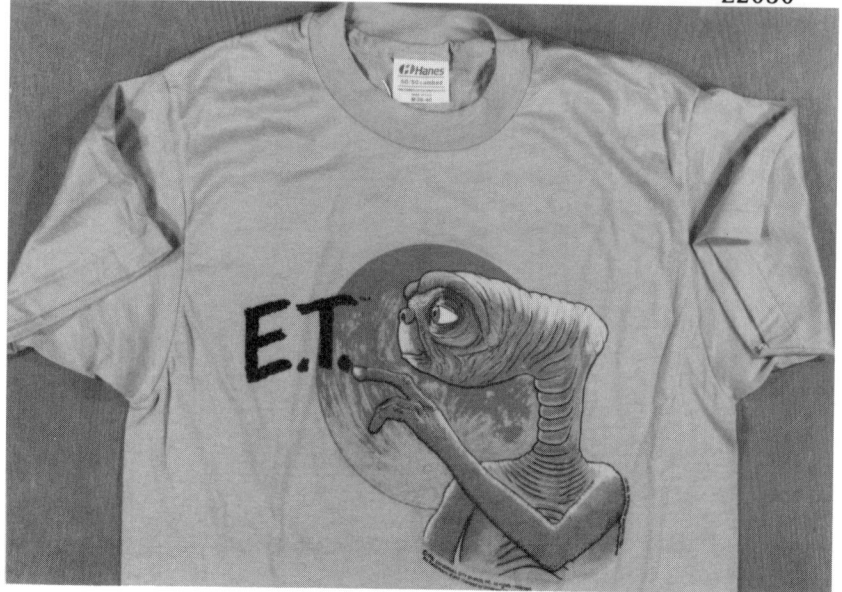

E2063

E2010

E1075

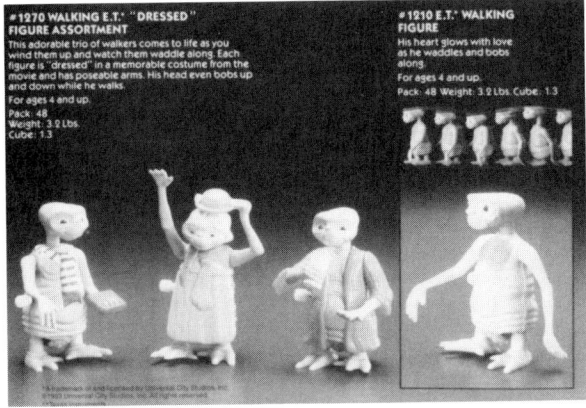

D8402	Coloring book	2 - 5
D8403	Cut-out activity book	8 - 12
D8404	Puzzles, Games, Mazes and Activities book	2 - 4
D8410	Pop-Up panorama book	8 - 20

Model kits D8500-02 Revell (1985)

D8500	Ornithopter	10 - 20
D8501	Sand Crawler	10 - 20
D8502	Sandworm	15 - 25

E.T.

E.T. (short for extraterrestrial) is Steven Spielberg's classic tale of a loveable alien who missed the ship. Alone on a strange world and hunted by the government, the visitor befriends a human boy and his family. With their help, it is able to contact its people and return home.

Following the film's release in 1982, the initial rush for E.T. merchandise was phenomenal. Manufacturers were unable to keep up with all the requests. Numerous bootleg E.T.'s, mostly plush toys, sprang up to fill in the gap. By the time the market recouped, the movie-inspired demand had already died down. The major manufacturer was LJN. The character also had numerous tie-ins with Reese's Pieces. Home video editions of the film were not released until 1988, generating a brief promotional effort.

E1000	Novel, hardcover	2 - 6
E1001	Novel, paperback	.50 - 2
E1002	*The Book of the Green Planet*	.50 - 2

Soundtrack recordings E1005-7

E1005	Record	2 - 6
E1006	Cassette	1 - 4
E1007	Compact disc	5 - 10
E1010	Talking figure	8 - 20
E1011	Talking figure - dressed	8 - 20
E1012	Walking figure - glowing heart	5 - 12
E1013	Walking figure - scarf	5 - 12
E1014	Walking figure - dress and hat	5 - 12
E1015	Walking figure - robe	5 - 12
E1016	Action figure - glowing heart	2 - 8
E1017	Action figure - scarf	2 - 8
E1018	Action figure - dress and hat	2 - 8
E1019	Action figure - robe	2 - 8

2" E.T. figures E1020-25

E1020	w/blanket and Speak 'n Spell	2 - 5
E1021	Holding plant	2 - 5
E1022	In costume	2 - 5
E1023	Holding beer can	2 - 5
E1024	Reading book	2 - 5
E1025	w/phone	2 - 5
E1026	Hugging doll	3 - 6
E1027	In robe w/telephone	3 - 6
E1028	w/sheet over head	3 - 6
E1029	Lifting potted flower in left hand	3 - 6
E1030	Right hand pointing, no phone	3 - 6
E1031	w/umbrella and suitcase	3 - 6
E1032	Family gift set (includes Elliott, Gertie, Michael, Mom, the intruder and E1029)	15 - 45
E1035	Pop-up spaceship	4 - 8
E1037	Powered bicycle figure	8 - 15
E1040	Stunt spaceship	4 - 8

51

E1011

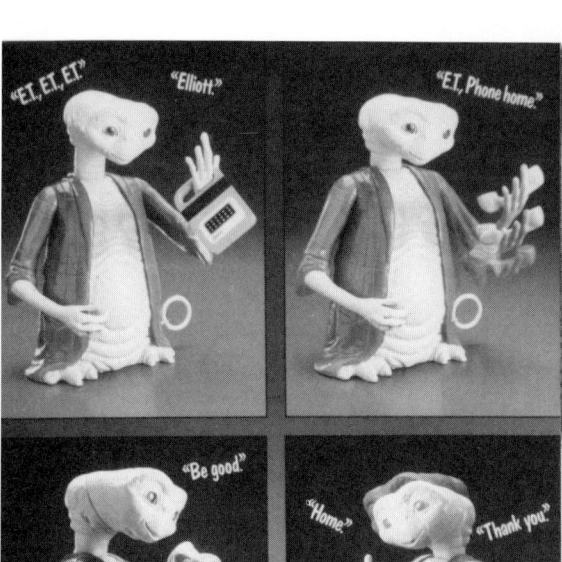

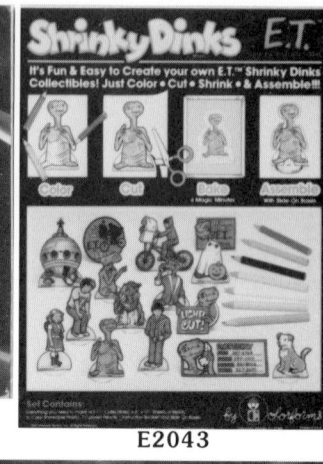

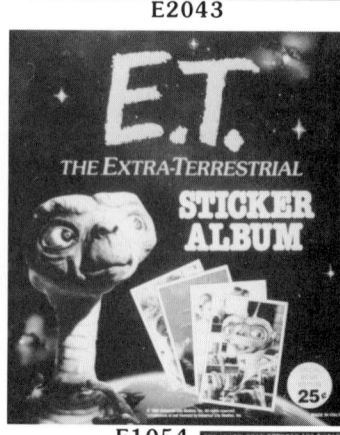

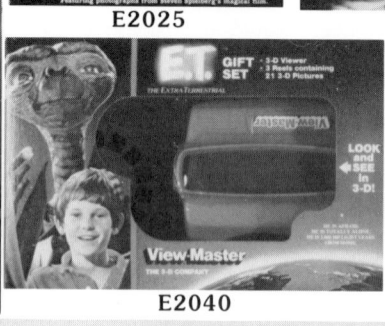

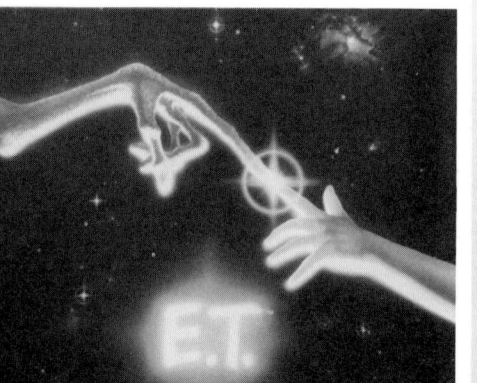

E1010

E2043

E2025

E1054

E1043

E1037

E2040

E2002

E3155

E2091

E2050

52

E1060

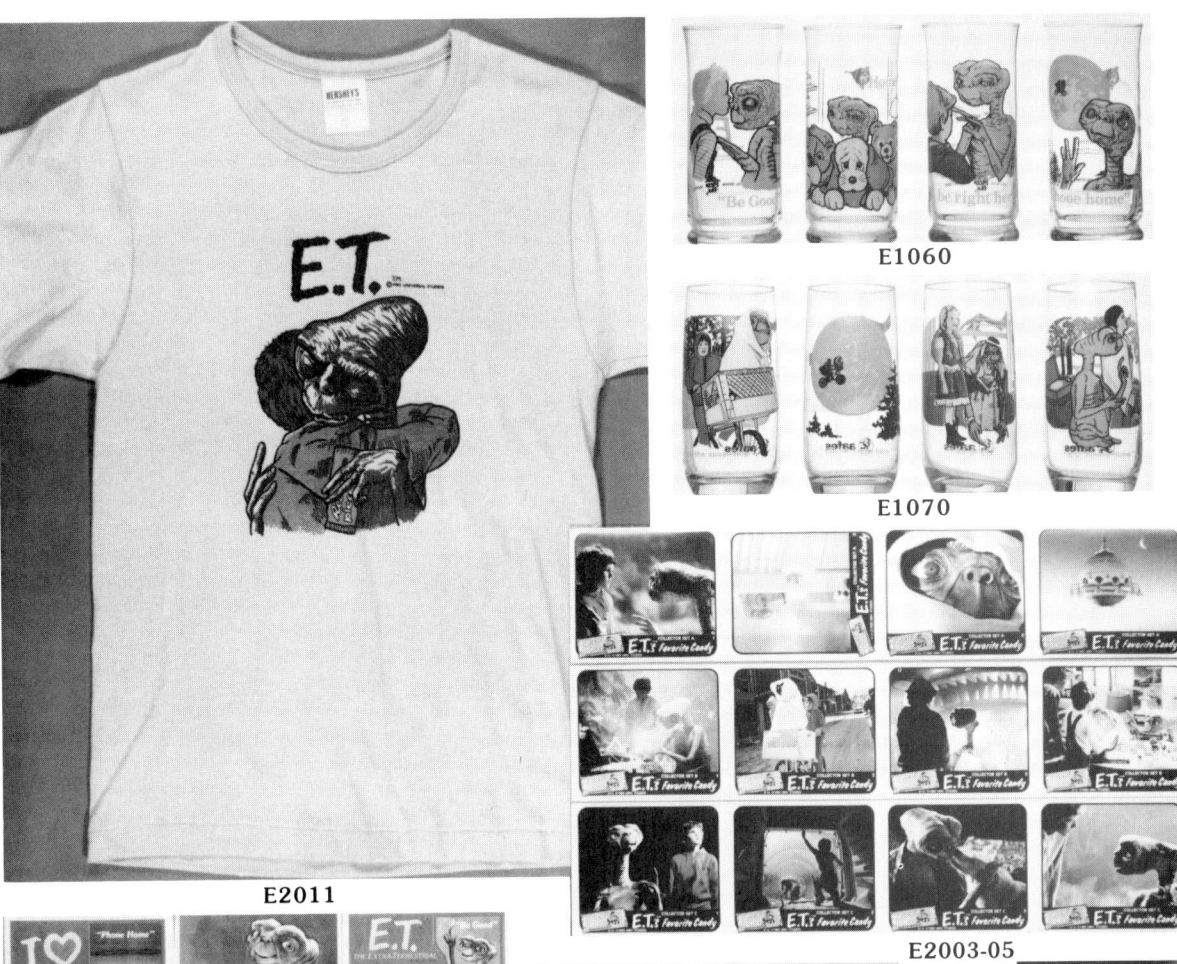

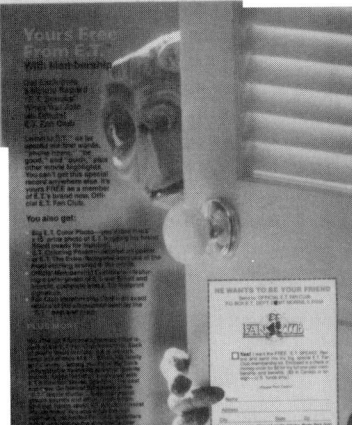

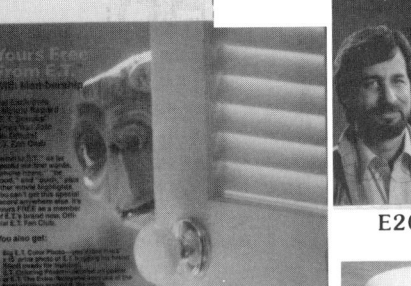

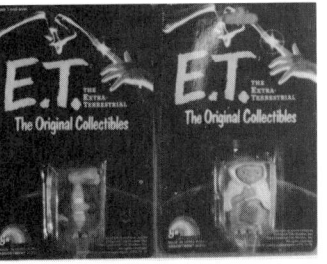

E1070

E2011

E2003-05

E2065

E2090

E2130

E1076

E2110

E1020-25

E2055

53

E2095

E2001

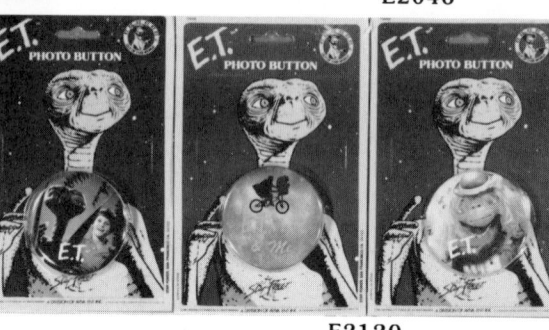

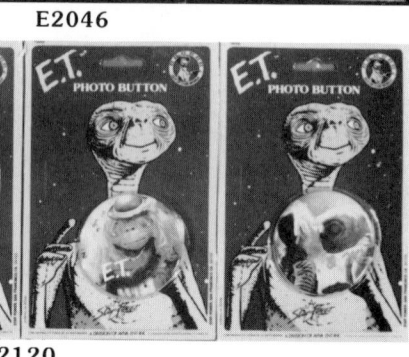

E2020

E3150

E2060

E2046

E2080   E2075   E2026

E2120

E2100-01

E2102   E2068   E1080

54

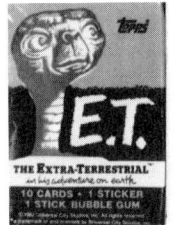

ID	Description	Price
E1043	E.T. and spaceship launcher	5 - 10
E1045	Trading cards, set of 88 (Topps)	5 - 10
E1046	Individual trading cards, ea	.05 - .10
E1047	Stickers for B1045, set of 9	2 - 4
E1048	Individual stickers, ea	.10 - .40
E1049	Box for B1045	3 - 8
E1050	Wrappers for B1045	.25 - 1
E1051	Unopened waxpacks for B1045	.50 - 2
E1052	Sticker set, 120 (Topps)	8 - 20
E1053	Individual stickers, ea	.10 - .25
E1054	Sticker album (Topps)	1 - 4
E1060	Glasses (Pizza Hut), "Home", "Phone Home", "I'll Be Right Here", or "Be Good", ea	2 - 3
E1070	Glasses (AAFES/Paramount), "E.T. Phone Home", To The Space Ship, "I'll Be Right Here", or "Be Good", ea	4 - 6
E1075	Lunch box (Aladdin)	8 - 16
E1076	Bottle for E1075	4 - 8
E1080	E.T. cereal box	5 - 25
E1081	E.T./Michael Jackson poster	1 - 3
E1082	E.T./Michael Jackson tape	1 - 4
E1083	E.T. premium book	2 - 6
E2000	Reese's Pieces wrappers w/E.T.	2 - 7
E2001	Poster offer sticker (Reese's Pieces)	1 - 2
E2002	Reese's Pieces box w/E.T. walking figure	10 - 25
E2003-05	Reese's Collector's stickers, set A, B, and C, ea	2 - 5
E2010	T-shirt	7 - 12
E2011	T-shirt (Hershey's)	8 - 15
E2020	Tray	6 - 10
E2025	Storybook	2 - 5
E2026	Book and record set	2 - 6
E2030	Board game (Parker Brothers)	9 - 18
E2035	Card game (Parker Brothers)	5 - 12
E2040	View-Master set	5 - 10
E2043	Shrinky Dinks	4 - 8
E2046	Suncatchers, 4 different, ea	1 - 2
E2050	Fun Art coloring set	3 - 8
E2055	Paper cups	1 - 2
E2060	Message pad	.50 - 1
E2063	Finger light	2 - 10
E2065	Sticker sets, 3 different, ea	.50 - 1
E2068	Puffy stickers	.75 - 1.50
E2075	Address book	.50 - 2
E2080	Keychain	1 - 2
E2090	Spielberg/E.T. postcard	.50 - 2
E2091	Calendar, 1983	5 - 10
E2095	Balloons	1 - 3
E2100	Watch, numeral dial	20 - 40
E2101	Watch, digital	20 - 40
E2102	Melody Glow Alarm Watch	8 - 15
E2110	Jewelry, pin, necklace, 6 different	1 - 4
E2120	Photo buttons, ea	2 - 4

Fan club premiums E2130-35

ID	Description	Price
E2130	Application	1 - 2
E2131	Membership certificate	2 - 4
E3132	Membership card	1 - 2
E3133	"E.T. Speaks" record	3 - 6
E3134	8" x 10" photo of E.T. and Elliott	1 - 3
E3135	Coloring poster	2 - 4
E3150	Pepsi box w/videocassette offer	2 - 5
E3151	Pepsi premium poster	2 - 4

F5165

F5301

F5303

F5304

F5661

F5376

F5660

F5326-28

56

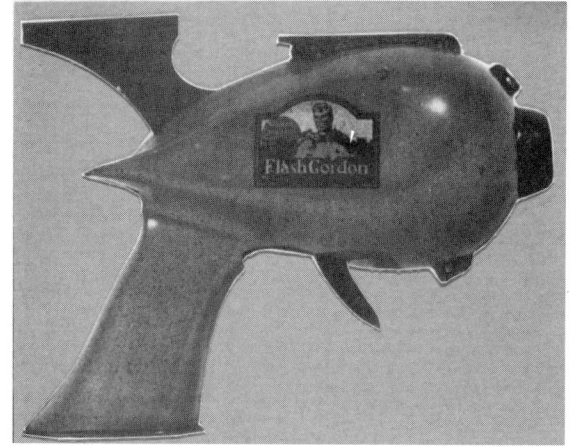

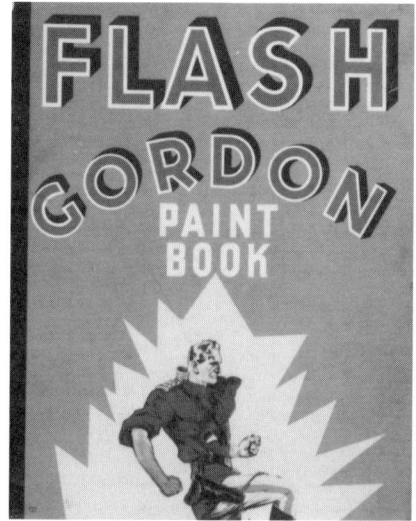

E3155	Videocassette	5 - 30
E3156	Video disc	10 - 35
E3160	Magazines w/E.T. covers	1 - 4

FLASH GORDON

In response to *Buck Rogers*, King Features Syndicate commissioned Alex Raymond to create a new space adventure. The focal point of this series was typical of the period: Flash Gordon, a dashing male hero; Dale Arden, a beautiful girl to shriek, scream, faint, and make a good hostage; and Dr. Hans Zarkov, a master scientist.

In contrast to other science fiction heroes of the time, Flash and his companions lived in modern times rather than the distant future. Departing from Earth in a rocket ship built by Dr. Zarkov, the three travel to ongo, a recently discovered planet. Here they ncounter strange new races and cultures in various ages of technological advancement. Ming the Merciless, self-proclaimed emperor of the Universe, presides over the planet and rules with an iron fist. Moved by the plight of Ming's subjects, Flash becomes the bane of the emperor, a champion of justice, and a hero to the people of both Earth and Mongo.

The series began on June 7, 1934, and quickly expanded to other levels. Although the artistic talent of Alex Raymond was a major factor in the success of the strip, there is evidence to suggest that Don Moore was the author until the early forties.

The first of three Flash Gordon serials was released by Universal in 1936, with a plot line based on the comic strip. Simply titled *Flash Gordon*, it was the first space adventure serial ever produced, and one of the most expensive. The second serial was originally titled *Flash Gordon and the Witch Queen of Mongo*. On Halloween night, 1938, Orson Wells and the Mercury Theater shocked the nation with the infamous "War of the Worlds" broadcast. Suddenly "Mars" was the buzzword. To capitalize on the situation, the film was renamed *Flash Gordon's Trip to Mars* (1938). Many of the usual denizens of Mongo (including Ming) suddenly found reasons to come to Mars. This film is considered the worst of the three.

Flash Gordon Conquers the Universe (1940) Brought back many of the successful elements of the first film. Ming, having been burned alive and disintegrated (respectively) in previous adventures, miraculously returned to threaten the universe yet again. This time the evil dictator is destroyed once and for all in a huge explosion. Maybe.

Larry "Buster" Crabbe played the title role in all three films. Re-edited versions of the serials were released as motion picture features entitled: *Rocket Ship*, *Mars Attacks the World*, and *Flash Gordon Conquers the Universe*.

Television ventures were considerably less successful. A low-budget series ran for one season in 1953. Though the actors were well-chosen physically, they spoke with accents that betrayed the program's West Berlin origin. (The show was produced in Germany to cut costs.) Ming never appeared in the series. An animated version was also produced in later years.

Universal reintroduced the characters in the 1980

F5112

F5800-04

F5511   F5514

F5792

F5645

F5640   F5831

F5635

F5647

F5370

F5840-48

F5625

58

film, *Flash Gordon*. This film went back to the beginning. Once again, it was based on the early comic strips, but designed to appeal to modern audiences. The Universe is saved when Ming is impaled on the spire of a '30s style rocket ship. But an evil chuckle closed the film, reassuring us he will back.

F5110	Newspaper color comic pages, ea	5 - 35
F5111	Original art for F5110	100+
F5112	*Into the Water World of Mongo* reprint	5 - 20
F5115	Lead casting set (Home Foundry, 1934)	350 - 1200
F5120	Wind-up Rocket Fighter	300 - 1500
F5130	Pencil box	40 - 100
F5131	Crayon box	30 - 90
F5132	Paint book	30 - 125
F5140	Signal Pistol	50 - 450
F5150	City of the Sea Caves picture disk	25 - 85
F5160	*Tournament of Death* pop-up book	100 - 350
F5165	Strip cards, each	5 - 25

Big Little Books F5200-04 (Whitman)

F5200	*The Monsters of Mongo* (1935)	25 - 125
F5201	*The Tournaments of Mongo* (1935)	25 - 125
F5202	*The Witch Queen of Mongo* (1936)	25 - 125
F5203	*Vs. the Emperor of Mongo* (1936)	40 - 150
F5204	*The Water World of Mongo* (1937)	25 - 125
F5210	Photo of Flash and Dale	2 - 4
F5220	Serial posters, ea	500 - 1000
F5250	Film posters, ea	450 - 900

Dell Fast-Action books F5276-77

F5276	Same as F5203, paperback	30 - 125
F5277	*The Ape Men of Mor*	35 - 110

Better Little Books F5300-04 (Whitman)

F5300	*The Perils of Mongo* (1940)	20 - 75
F5301	*The Ice World of Mongo* (1942)	20 - 75
F5302	*The Red Sword Invaders* (1945)	20 - 75
F5303	*The Jungles of Mongo*	20 - 75
F5304	*The Fiery Desert of Mongo* (1948)	20 - 75

Dell Four-Color Comics F5320-27

F5320	#10	40 - 350
F5321	#84	25 - 190
F5322	#173	10 - 75
F5323	#190	9 - 70
F5324	#204	8 - 55
F5325	#247	8 - 55
F5326	#424	5 - 40
F5327	#512	3 - 20
F5328	#2 (not a Four-Color Comic)	4 - 20
F5329	Macy's giveaway comic (1943)	35 - 150
F5330	Gordon Bread giveaway comics, #1 and 2, ea	5 - 50
F5340	Space Target	30 - 50
F5350	World Battle Fronts WWII map (1943)	25 - 50
F5360	Wood composition figure of Flash (1944)	100 - 300
F5365-68	Comic books #1-4 (1950-51) ea	10 - 100
F5370	*Flash Gordon* (Treasure Book)	2 - 4
F5375	Pencil box (1951)	25 - 55

F5750-51

F5797-98

F5795

F5602

F5530

F5680-84

F5421

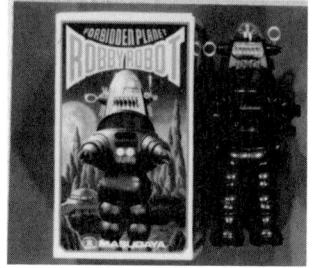

F7201

F5130

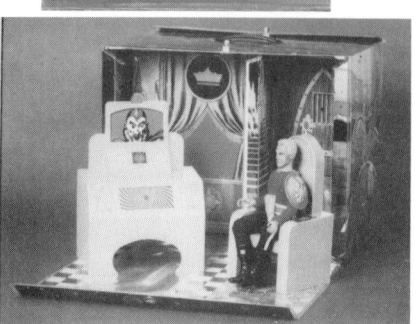

F5610

F5600-03

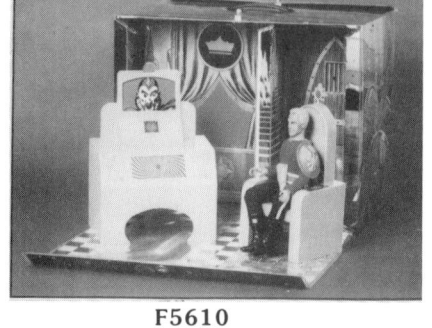

F7135

F7200

F7100

F7140

60

F5376	3 Puzzle boxed set (Milton Bradley, 1951)	45 - 100
F5390	Tray puzzle (Milton Bradley, 1951)	12 - 45
F5420	Space outfit including belt, goggles, and wrist compass (Esquire Novelty Co., 1951)	50 - 125
F5421	Space compass	15 - 35
F5422	Kite	30 - 60
F5425	Gordon Bread wrappers	60 - 200
F5450	Gold Key Comic (1965)	2 - 10
F5451	Board game (Transogram, 1965)	35 - 50
F5459	Army giveaway comic (1968)	1 - 7
F5460-96	Comic Books #1-37 (1968+), ea	1 - 10
F5499	Giant comic album (1972)	1 - 3
F5500	Original radio broadcasts record (1973)	5 - 12
F5505	Flash Gordon Starship (Tootsietoy)	5 - 15
F5506	Ming Starship (Tootsietoy)	5 - 15
F5507	Flash Gordon Large Box, set w/3 figures, 2 ships (Tootsietoy)	15 - 40

Paperback novels F5510-14 (Avon, 1974)

F5510	*The Lion Men of Mongo*	1 - 3
F5511	*The Plague of Sound*	1 - 3
F5512	*The Space Circus*	1 - 3
F5513	*The Time Trap of Ming*	1 - 3
F5514	*The Witch Queen of Mongo*	1 - 3
F5530	Button, Flash and Ming	4 - 8

Action Figures F5600-03 (Mego, 1976)

F5600	Flash	15 - 25
F5601	Dale	20 - 30
F5602	Dr. Zarkov	15 - 25
F5603	Ming	15 - 25
F5610	Action figure playset	50 - 135
F5620	3-color Raygun (Nasta, 1976)	10 - 20
F5623	Sparkling Ray Gun (Nasta, 1976)	10 - 20
F5625	Space Water Pistol (Nasta, 1976)	10 - 20
F5630	World of Mongo playset (Mego, 1977)	35 - 75
F5635	Adventure on the Moons of Mongo game (House of Games, 1977)	10 - 20
F5638	View-Master packet w/three reels (1977)	5 - 10
F5640	Medals and insignia (Larami Corp., 1978)	2 - 4
F5645	Paper plates (Unique Industries, 1978)	2 - 4
F5646	Paper cups (Unique Industries, 1978)	2 - 4
F5647	Table cover (Unique Industries, 1978)	2 - 6
F5649	Loot bags	1 - 2
F5660	Candy box display	20 - 30
F5661	Candy boxes, 8 different, ea	4 - 10

Movie buttons F5680-84

F5680	Flash	2 - 4
F5681	Ming	2 - 4
F5682	Vultan	2 - 4
F5683	Aura	2 - 4
F5684	Barin	2 - 4
F5750	Flash action figure from "Defenders of the Earth"	10 - 20
F5751	Ming action figure from "Defenders of the Earth"	10 - 20

Action figures F5755-60 (1979)

F5755	Flash	8 - 10
F5756	Dr. Zarkov	8 - 12
F5757	Thun the Lion Man	8 - 12
F5758	Ming the Merciles	8 - 12
F5759	Beastman	8 - 12
F5760	Lizard Lady	10 - 20
F5770	Stun gun (Mattel, 1979)	10 - 20
F5780	Ming Space Shuttle (Mattel, 1979)	5 - 15
F5785	Inflatable Rocket Ship (Mattel, 1979)	25 - 35
F5790	Film program (1979)	2 - 8
F5791	Film soundtrack record	3 - 7
F5792	Film paperback	.50 - 3
F5793	Film comic adaptation	1 - 3
F5794	Same as F5693, hardcover	4 - 7
F5795	Lobby cards, ea	1 - 2
F5796	Ming punch-out (from *Playboy* magazine, Jan 1981)	1 - 2
F5797	*The Flash Gordon Book*	4 - 7
F5798	*Flash Gordon The Movie* (Golden Book)	5 - 10

Paperback novels F5800-04 (Grosset and Dunlap, 1980)

F5800	*Massacre in the 23rd Century*	.50 - 1
F5801	*War of the Citadels*	.50 - 1
F5802	*Crisis on Citadel II*	.50 - 1
F5803	*Forces from the Federation*	.50 - 1
F5804	*Citadels Under Attack*	.50 - 1
F5830	MIP Soft Target set (King Features, 1981)	5 - 30
F5831	Sunglasses (JA-RU, 1981)	2 - 4
F5840-48	Comic series (DC, 1988-89), 9 issues, ea	1 - 2

FORBIDDEN PLANET

This is considered to be one of the better science fiction films of the 1950s and is by far the most commonly known. Roughly based on Shakespeare's *The Tempest*, it is the story of a space patrol crew sent to investigate a missing expedition. In addition to improving special effects of the day, it introduced the first "loveable" robot, Robby. From this character comes the only known merchandise based on the film. Robby later appeared in *The Invisible Boy* and elsewhere, becoming a symbol of high-technology for the '60s and early '70s. Robby toy robots were produced in authorized and unauthorized versions, and have been reproduced in several forms and materials over the years. The robots most associated with the character are listed even if they were called by another name. Robots named Robby but having little or no resemblance to film design, on the other hand, are not included.

Robots pictured are from the Robert Lesser Collection.

F7100	Film poster	375 - 750
F7110	Lobby cards, 8 different, ea	30 - 75

Soundtrack recordings F7121-23

F7121	Record	10 - 60
F7122	Cassette	5 - 15
F7123	Compact disc	10 - 20
F7125	7" record w/illustrated sleeve	5 - 20
F7126	Videocassette	10 - 20
F7130	Mechanized robot	1000 - 3500
F7133	Battery operated robot	1000 - 3000
F7135	Piston action robot	250 - 400
F7136	Robby space patrol car	10000 - 25000

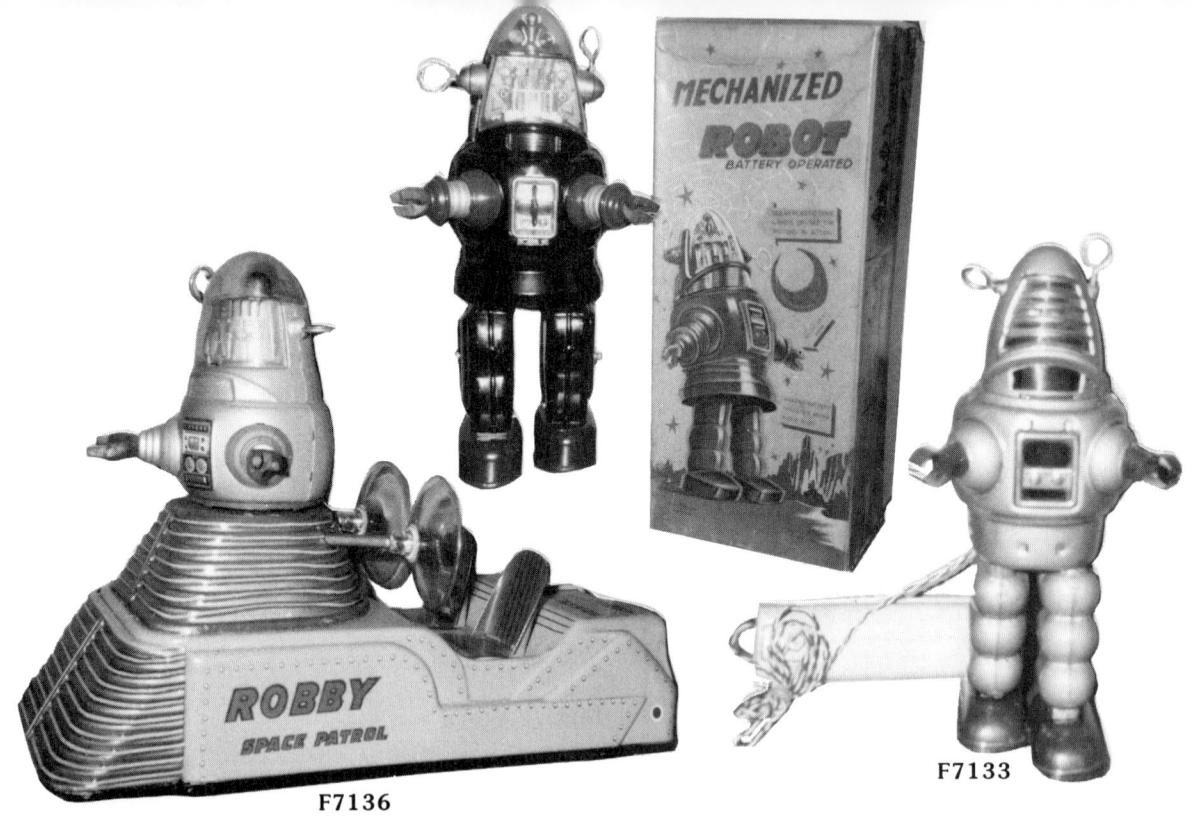

F7136

F7133

F7126

F7140

J7150　　J7326　　J7325　　J7400　　J7420

F7140	*Invisible Boy* poster	50 - 150
F7141	*Invisible Boy* lobby cards	20 - 65
F7160	Starlog poster	5 - 10
F7200	16" Talking Robby (Masudaya)	80 - 100
F7201	5" Robby, wind-up (Masudaya)	8 - 15

JOHN CARTER OF MARS

John Carter was the first published character created by the now-famous Edgar Rice Burroughs. Rocket ships had not yet begun to dominate space fiction as the principle method of travel. Instead, John Carter "projected" himself between planets by sheer force of will. "The Martian Tales," as they came to be called, originally appeared as serials and short stories in pulp magazines. The only *Amazing Stories Annual* ever published contained a complete John Carter novel. The stories were later published as novels, big little books, and comic books.

J7100	*All-Story Magazines*: Feb 1912 - July 1912 ("Under the Moon of Mars"), ea	50 - 75
J7110	*All-Story Magazines*: Jan 1913 - May 1913 ("The Gods of Mars"), ea	40 - 75
J7120	*All-Story Magazines*: Dec 1913 - March 1914 ("The Warlord of Mars"), ea	40 - 75
J7130	*All-Story Weekly* magazines, April 1916 ("Thuvia, Maid of Mars"), ea	40 - 75
J7140	*Argosy All-Story Weekly* magazines, Feb 1922 - Apr 1922 ("The Chessmen of Mars"), ea	35 - 70
J7150	*Amazing Stories Annual*, 1927 ("The Master Mind of Mars")	100 - 200
J7160	*Blue Book Magazines*, Apr 1930 - Sept 1930 ("A Fighting Man of Mars"), ea	20 - 35
J7170	*Blue Book Magazines*, Nov 1934 - Apr 1935 ("Swords of Mars"), ea	20 - 35
J7180	*Argosy* magazines, Jan 7, 1939 - Febr 11, 1939 ("Synthetic Men of Mars"), ea	15 - 30
J7190	*Amazing Stories*, Jan 1941 ("John Carter and the Giant of Mars")	15 - 30
J7200	*Amazing Stories*, Mar 1941 ("The City of Mummies")	12 - 25
J7201	*Amazing Stories*, June 1941 ("Black Pirates of Barsoom")	12 - 25
J7202	*Amazing Stories*, Aug 1941 ("Yellow Men of Mars")	12 - 25
J7203	*Amazing Stories*, Oct 1941 ("Invisible Men of Mars")	12 - 25
J7210	*Amazing Stories*, Feb 1943 ("Skeleton Men of Jupiter")	12 - 25

Original hardcover novels J7300-10 (w/dustcover)

J7300	*A Princess of Mars*	50 - 150
J7301	*The Gods of Mars*	50 - 100
J7302	*The Warlord of Mars*	50 - 100
J7303	*Thuvia, Maid of Mars*	25 - 75
J7304	*The Chessmen of Mars*	25 - 75
J7305	*The Master Mind of Mars*	25 - 75
J7306	*A Fighting Man of Mars*	25 - 75
J7307	*Swords of Mars*	25 - 75
J7308	*Synthetic Men of Mars*	25 - 75
J7309	*Llana of Gathol* (includes stories from J7200-03)	20 - 50
J7310	*John Carter of Mars* (includes stories from J7190 and J7210)	20 - 50
J7325	Better Little Book (1940)	15 - 30
J7326	Dell Fast-Action book (1940)	15 - 30

Four-color comics J7330-32

J7330	#375	15 - 75
J7331	#437	8 - 60
J7332	#488	5 - 50
J7340-42	Gold Key Comics (Reprints of J7330-32) #1-3, ea	5 - 25
J7350	Comic, reprints of '40s comic strips (House of Greystroke, 1970)	2 - 14

***John Carter, Warlord of Mars* comics J7370-92** (Marvel)

J7370	#1	1 - 3
J7371-87	#2-18, ea	1 - 2
J7390-92	Annuals, #1-3, ea	1 - 3
J7400	Paperback reprints of John Carter stories (Ace), ea	1 - 2
J7420	Paperback reprints of John Carter stories (Del Rey), ea	1 - 2

Heratage Games J7450-51

J7450	Role playing game	10 - 20
J7451	Sets of 25mm lead figures, ea	5 - 10

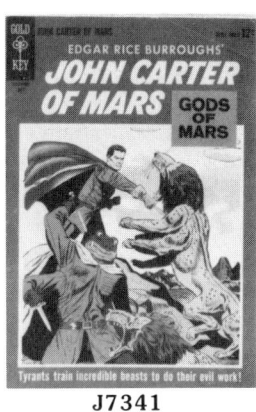

J7331 J7341

J7379 J7380

PLANET OF THE APES

Twentieth Century Fox turned the tables on the human race in this 1968 film. Astronauts traveling at speeds greater than light leave their time and planet behind. Something goes wrong on the ship, however, and the expedition crash-lands on a strange planet in the distant future. Thus, for the first time, man encounters the Planet of the Apes, a world ruled by Simians where men are little more than animals. Humans are kept in submission, for ancient writings say that man is a violent race who destroys his own lands. Taylor, the last surviving astronaut, eventually escapes the apes and rides into an area of the planet which has been marked forbidden. There he discovers the shocking truth when he finds the Statue of Liberty buried in sand. The Planet of the Apes is not a far-off world, it is post-apocalypse Earth.

The film went on to produce four sequels: *Beneath the Planet of the Apes* (1970), *Escape from the Planet of the Apes* (1971), *Conquest of the Planet of the Apes* (1972), and *Battle for the Planet of the Apes* (1973). In addition, a television show and an animated cartoon series resulted. A new series of *Apes* comic books began in April 1990.

The *Planet of the Apes* is based on a novel by Pierre Boulle. Most items carry a 1967 copyright date, but were produced in the '70s.

Film novels P6000-25
P6000	*Planet of the Apes*, hardcover	2 - 7
P6001	*Planet of the Apes*, paperback, first edition	1 - 2
P6002	*Planet of the Apes*, paperback, later editions	.50 - 1.50
P6010	*Beneath the Planet of the Apes*	.50 - 1
P6015	*Escape from the Planet of the Apes*	.50 - 1
P6020	*Conquest of the Planet of the Apes*	.50 - 1
P6025	*Battle for the Planet of the Apes*	.50 - 1

TV novels P6030-31
P6030	*#1 Man the Fugitive*	.25 - 1
P6031	*#2 Escape to Tomorrow*	.25 - 1

Action figures P6040-49 (Mego)
P6040	Cornelius	8 - 35
P6041	Dr. Zaius	8 - 35
P6042	Zira	8 - 35
P6043	Soldier Ape	8 - 35
P6044	Astronaut	8 - 35
P6045	Galen	8 - 35
P6046	General Ursus	8 - 35
P6047	General Urko	8 - 35
P6048	Astronaut Burke	15 - 45
P6049	Astronaut Verdon	15 - 45
P6050	Action Stallion, brown	10 - 40
P6051	Same as P6050, but yellow palomino	10 - 40
P6053	Catapult and wagon	8 - 20
P6054	Fortress	20 - 50
P6055	Treehouse	20 - 50
P6056	Village playset	20 - 50
P6057	Battering ram	4 - 15
P6058	Jail	4 - 15
P6059	Dr. Zaius' Throne	4 - 10
P6060	Forbidden Zone Trap	20 - 50
P6063	Knickerbocker water rifle (1966)	10 - 20
P6066	15" plaster statues: Zira, Dr. Zaius,	

64

2001 a space odyssey
A NOVEL BY ARTHUR C. CLARKE
STANLEY KUBRICK and ARTHUR C. CLARKE
MARVEL COMICS GROUP
30¢
BEGIN A NEW JOURNEY TO THE STARS-AND BEYOND!!
2001: A SPACE ODYSSEY
PREMIERE ISSUE!
S1E-13 ST X
STEREO
Music from the Motion Picture Sound Track
2001 a space odyssey
CINERAMA
MGM
THE MOON BUS
From the Movie of the Century
2001 A SPACE ODYSSEY
Nº 37
MARVEL SUPER SPECIAL
$2.00
2010
2001 a space odyssey
A NOVEL BY ARTHUR C. CLARKE
BASED ON THE SCREENPLAY OF THE MGM FILM BY
STANLEY KUBRICK and ARTHUR C. CLARKE
2001 a space odyssey
2001 a space odyssey

BUCK ROGERS SIEGE OF GIGANTICA
BUCK ROGERS COLORFORMS ADVENTURE SET
SPACE GLOW PUTTY
FLASH GORDON
DR. ZARKOV
Flash Gordon 3 PUZZLES
FLASH GORDON PAINT BOOK
fast drying acrylic paint by number
"BUCK ROGERS" IN THE 25th CENTURY
TABLECOVER
54 IN. X 88 IN.
THE MOVIE FLASH GORDON
BUCK ROGERS IN THE 25th CENTURY
LASERSCOPE FIGHTER WITH SIMULATED LASERS AND EXPLOSION
DRACONIAN MARAUDER
WALKING TWIKI
FLASH GORDON MEDALS and INSIGNIA
"BUCK ROGERS" IN THE 25th CENTURY
GALACTIC PLAY SET
BUCK ROGERS
FLASH GORDON
Buck Rogers Official Utility Belt
BUCK ROGERS SOLAR SCOUTS
The Pop-Up BUCK ROGERS
STRANGE ADVENTURES IN THE SPIDER-SHIP
DOOM COMET
SCHOOL CRAYONS
SPACE SHIP

CAPTAIN VIDEO
TOM CORBETT SPACE CADET
PUSH-OUTS
Kellogg's CORN FLAKES
CUT-OUTS of Space Cadet VISOR
SPACE CADET
ATOMIC CADET PISTOL
FLASHLITE
CAPTAIN VIDEO
SPARKLING SPACE GUN
Official TOM CORBETT SPACE CADET
PLASTIC
SPACE GUN
ROCKY JONES, Space Ranger
COLORING BOOK
SPACE CADET NEWS
SPACE CADET SQUADRONS FORM ALL OVER USA!
Tom Corbett SPACE CADET COLORING BOOK
TOM CORBETT SPACE CADET
BUCK ROGERS
MARVEL COMICS GROUP
EDGAR RICE BURROUGHS'
JOHN CARTER WARLORD OF MARS
SPACE CADET
Captain VIDEO
BREAD END LABEL ALBUM
SPACE DROME
SUPERIOR SPACE PORT
TOM CORBETT SPACE ACADEMY
SPACE ACADEMY
THE SPACE PIONEERS
THE ROBOT ROCKET
DANGER IN DEEP SPACE
TREACHERY IN OUTER SPACE
CAREY ROCKWELL
Rite-O-Lite
TOP SECRET!

SPACE: 1999
ADVENTURE PLAYSET
WALT DISNEY STUDIOS'
THE BLACK HOLE
V.I.N.CENT.
Original Motion Picture Soundtrack
THE BLACK HOLE
VOYAGE OF FEAR
GAME
RACE TO THE EDGE OF THE UNKNOWN!
SPACE: 1999
A GAME ADAPTED FROM THE TELEVISION SERIES
SPACE:1999
MOON BASE ALPHA
Control room & launch monitor center!
SPACE: 1999 UTILITY BELT
DISC SHOOTING STUN GUN WITH 8 DISCS
Dinky

E.T.
Finger Light
25¢
NEW! HIT MOVIE!
E.T.
THE EXTRA-TERRESTRIAL
MOVIE PHOTO CARDS BUBBLE GUM
General Mills
NEW
E.T.
CEREAL
Peanut butter & chocolate-flavored crispy, sweetened 2-grain cereal
E.T. Storybook Album Offer!
15¢ COUPON INSIDE!
THE EXTRA-TERRESTRIAL
in his adventure on earth
E.T.
BALLOONS
E.T. GIFT SET
View-Master
E.T.
THE EXTRA-TERRESTRIAL
Storybook
E.T.
THE EXTRA-TERRESTRIAL
CALENDAR
1983
E.T.
E.T.
THE EXTRA-TERRESTRIAL
E.T.
ACTION FIGURE
E.T.
E.T.
THE EXTRA-TERRESTRIAL
CARD GAME
E.T.
THE EXTRA-TERRESTRIAL
E.T.
THE EXTRA-TERRESTRIAL
STICKER ALBUM
25¢
E.T.
The Original Collectibles
E.T.
The Original Collectibles
E.T.
PHOTO BUTTON
E.T.
PHOTO BUTTON
E.T.
PHOTO BUTTON
E.T.
PHOTO BUTTON
E.T.
PHOTO BUTTON
Yours Free From E.T.
E.T. phone home!
Message Pad
E.T.
ADDRESSES
I ♥ E.T.
"Phone Home"
E.T.
"Be Good"
E.T.
THE EXTRA-TERRESTRIAL
"I'll Be Right Here"
E.T.

BUCK ROGERS in the 25th CENTURY
FLASH
GORDON
FLASH GORDON
STAR WARS TM
NATIONAL PUBLIC RADIO
KBPS-1450
TM © LFL 1981
ROCKY JONES
SPACE RANGER
SILVERCUP BREAD
PURITY BREAD
CAPT. VIDEO
SPACE RANGER
BUCK ROGERS
SATELLITE PIONEERS
ROCKET RANGERS
CHIEF EXPLORER
BUCK ROGERS
SOLAR SCOUTS
STAR WARS
THE EMPIRE STRIKES BACK
STAR WARS
RETURN OF THE JEDI
THE FIRST TEN YEARS
1977 1987
DUNE
COMING CHRISTMAS WORLD WIDE
OFFICIAL STAR WARS FAN CLUB
REBEL RECRUITER
SPACE CADET
STAR WARS
REVENGE OF THE JEDI
DARTH VADAR LIVES
2001
a space odyssey
"A MIND-STRETCHING EXPERIENCE"
soundtrack album on
MGM RECORDS
FLASH GORDON
Ming the Merciless
STAR WARS
FACTORS ETC. INC. D. IMAGE FACTORY INC., CA. • © 1977 TWENTIETH CENTURY FOX FILM CORP.
DARTH VADER

Space Patrol
SPACE SHIP COMMANDER
COMMANDER
Space Patrol
Space Patrol
INLAID PUZZLE
WITH FRAME AND TRAY
DECCA
OFFICIAL
Space Patrol
STAMPS &
OFFICIAL
Space Patrol
ROCKET LITE
OFFICIAL
Space Patrol
ATOMIC
PISTOL
Sensational
SUPER
300 FT BEAM
Space Patrol
OFFICIAL WALKIE-TALKIE
SPACE-A-PHONES
A REAL TWO-WAY SPACE-A-PHONE SYSTEM
TOYS OF TOMORROW
Space Patrol
ROCKET
GUN
Space Patrol
Space Patrol

DUNE
FREMEN
TARPEL GUN
ELECTRONIC SOUNDS
FLASHING LIGHTS
THE DUNE STORYBOOK
By Joan D. Vinge
Adapted from a screenplay by David Lynch
Based on the novel by Frank Herbert
FRANK HERBERT'S DUNE
A WORLD BEYOND YOUR EXPERIENCE, BEYOND YOUR IMAGINATION.
DUNE
COMING SOON TO SELECT THEATRES
ALIEN
THE ILLUSTRATED STORY
by Archie Goodwin and Walter Simonson
ALIEN
MOVIE NOVEL
OVER 1,000 FULL-COLOR PHOTOS
V
The Resistance
45'ER
Sound Pistol & Holster
The Resistance
M-16
Sound Rifle
Try Me!
RAPID FIRE MACHINE GUN SOUND
ENEMY VISITOR
ACTION FIGURE
ALIEN
GAME
AN EXCITING NEW GAME OF ELIMINATION AND ESCAPE! FOR 2 TO 4 PLAYERS
200 Piece
Jigsaw Puzzle, 11" x 17"
Relive The Legend. Fulfill The Prophecy.
DUNE
A PARKER BROTHERS ADVENTURE GAME
ITEM 521
36 CT.
DUNE
TRADING CARDS & STICKERS
ALIEN
DUNE
SANDWORM
DUNE
SPICE SCOUT
DUNE
ACTION FIGURE
GIANT POSTER SIZE 3 FEET TALL
ALIEN
Jigsaw Puzzle
250 Pc.
ALIENS
ALIEN
by ALAN DEAN FOSTER
45'ER
ACTION SET
2 WALKIE TALKIES
DUNE
Battle-Matic Action
ITEM 537
36 CT.
They're Here!
TRADING CARDS AND STICKERS
42 Inch Inflatable
BOP BAG
DUNE
COLORING BOOK
MARVEL COMICS
DUNE
THE OFFICIAL COMIC BOOK
DUNE
FRANK HERBERT
ALIENS
ALIEN
DUNE
TRADING CARDS & STICKERS

P6050

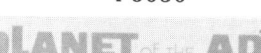

P6060

P6090-94    P6083   P6220

P6078   P6209    P6207   P6045-49

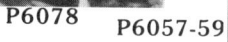

P6077    P6053   P6054

73

P6184

P6235

P6040-44

P6080

P6042

P6190

P6056

74

P6150-51

P6101

P6109

P6126

P6117

P6127

P6128

	Cornelius (Tuscany Statues,1973) ea	25 - 35
P6068	Bike Reflector (1974)	5 - 10
P6070	Furry Galen Doll (Well Made Toys)	3 - 6
P6071	Furry Dr. Zaius (Well Made Toys)	3 - 6
P6075	Galen bank (Play Pal Plastics)	5 - 15
P6076	Dr. Zaius bank (Play Pal Plastics)	5 - 15
P6077	Mix 'n Mold kit, Cornelius	8 - 35
P6078	Mix 'n Mold kit, Dr. Zaius	8 - 35
P6080	Quick Draw Cartoon set (Pressman)	8 - 15
P6083	Pencil coloring set	6 - 12
P6085	Colorforms set	6 - 15

Bend 'n Flex figures P6090-94

P6090	Astronaut	5 - 15
P6091	Dr. Zaius	5 - 15
P6092	Dr. Zira	5 - 15
P6093	Cornelius	5 - 15
P6094	Soldier Ape	5 - 15

Comic magazines P6100-28 (Marvel, 1974-77)

P6100	#1	.50 - 2
P6101-28	#2-29, ea	.25 - 1

Adventures on the Planet of the Apes comics
P6135-45 (Marvel, 1975-76)

P6135	#1	.50 - 2
P6136-45	#2-11, ea	.25 - 1
P6150-51	Parachutists (AHI, 1976), ea	3 - 7
P6155	Board game (Milton Bradley)	8 - 15

Model kits P6160-64 (Addar)

P6160	Cornelius	10 - 35
P6161	Dr. Zaius	10 - 35
P6162	Dr. Zira	10 - 35
P6163	General Aldo	15 - 45
P6164	General Ursus	15 - 45
P6165	Ape on stallion	40 - 50

Bottle scene model kits P6170-72 (Addar)

P6170	Treehouse	15 - 25
P6171	Cornfield Roundup	15 - 25
P6172	Jail wagon	15 - 25

Puzzles P6180-82, cylinder packaged

P6180	Cornelius, Zira and Lucas	5 - 12
P6181	General Aldo	5 - 12
P6182	On Patrol	5 - 12
P6184	Poster puzzle	6 - 15
P6185	Lunch box (Aladdin)	8 - 30
P6186	Bottle for P6185	4 - 15
P6190	Record, "Mountain of the Delphi"	1 - 5
P6200	Trading cards, set of 44 (movie series), ea	10 - 30
P6201	Individual trading cards, ea	.10 - .60
P6202	Box for P6200	6 - 15
P6203	Wrappers for P6200	3 - 5
P6204	Unopened waxpacks for P6200	4 - 10
P6206	TV trading cards, set of 66	10 - 25
P6207	Individual TV trading cards, ea	.10 - .50
P6208	Box for P6206	5 - 25
P6209	Wrappers for P6206	2 - 5
P6210	Unopened waxpacks for P6206	3 - 10
P6215	Chimp scope (Larami)	10 - 30
P6220	Picture activity album	5 - 15
P6225	Talking View-Master packet	8 - 15
P6230	Target game	10 - 30
P6232	Wastebasket	5 - 30
P6235	Punch-out Adv. playset (Amsco)	20 - 40
P6250	Fanner gun	15 - 35
P6251	Rapid fire gun w/ape mask	20 - 40
P6252	Tommy burst gun w/ape mask	20 - 40

75

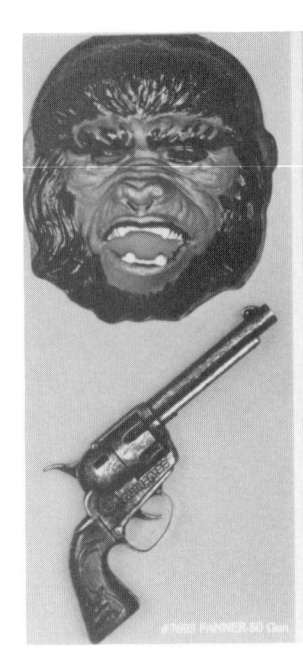

P6150-52

R7122

P6155

P6160-61    P6162

R7121

S1010-13    S1171    S1225

76

P6260	Candy boxes	6 - 10
P6300	Comic series (Adventure Comics, 1990), #1	1 - 2.50

ROCKY JONES, SPACE RANGER

This filmed television series first appeared on Feb. 27, 1954, a few years too late in the Space Boom to catch on. Rocky Jones was the daring leader of the Space Rangers. Whizzing through the solar system in the *Orbit Jet*, Rocky and his companions carried black-and-white justice throughout the galaxy.

The show did not last long enough to produce much merchandise, but a few store-bought items did crop up. The wings were sold individually or on display cards of 30.

R7100	Wings (pinback)	15 - 30
R7111	Membership pinback	15 - 30
R7121-22	Coloring books (2), ea	25 - 40
R7130	Wrist watch	75 - 150
R7135-38	*Space Adventures* comics, #15-18, ea	8 - 24
R7140	2-record (45rpm) set w/booklet (1954)	20 - 60

SPACE: 1999

In the year 1999, the moon is knocked out of orbit when a nuclear waste dump explodes. Moonbase Alpha and its crew is sent hurtling through space, never to return. At the mercy of fate, the colonists hope their path will take them close enough to an Earth-like planet where they can settle and begin anew. *Space: 1999* was produced by the Independent Television Corporation. Although it was rejected by all three television networks, it was later seen in syndication. Merchandise was produced during 1975-76, and reissued as late as 1979.

Large action figures S1010-13 (Mattel)
S1010	Commander Koenig	10 - 25
S1011	Dr. Russell	10 - 25
S1012	Professor Bergman	10 - 25
S1013	Zython	15 - 35
S1015	Moon Base Alpha, vinyl	25 - 50
S1020	Lunch box (King Seely Thermos)	12 - 30
S1030	Wrist watch/roll viewer w/2 rolls (L-Toys)	5 - 10
S1040	Eagle Transport model kit (MPC)	10 - 25
S1041	Alien and Car model kit (MPC)	10 - 20
S1042	Moon Base Alpha model kit (MPC)	25 - 50
S1100	Control Room (Mattel)	10 - 40
S1110	Stun Gun flashlight	10 - 25
S1111	Utility belt	10 - 25
S1120	Colorforms set	8 - 20
S1130	Puzzle (H. G. Toys)	7 - 15
S1140	Notebook	2 - 8
S1150	Board game (Milton Bradley)	12 - 20
S1160	Eagle One Transporter w/3" action figures of Koenig, Dr. Russell, and Professor Bergman	40 - 125

Small action figures S1161-67
S1161	Commander Koenig	5 - 15
S1162	Commander Koenig in space suit	5 - 15

S1150

S1111

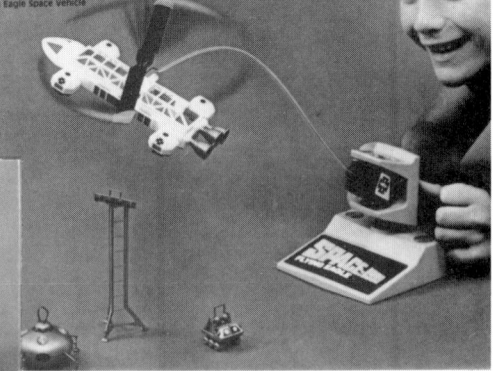

S1195

S1210

S1241

S1270

S1271

S1275

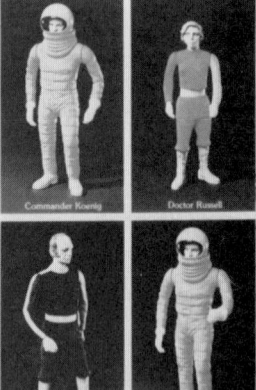

S1015

S1260

S1161-67

S1160

78

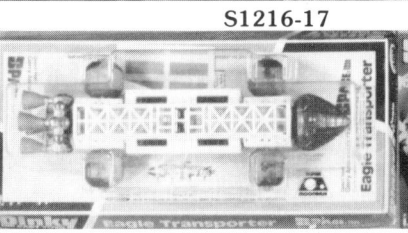

ID	Description	Price
S1163	Dr. Russell	5 - 15
S1164	Dr. Russell in space suit	5 - 15
S1165	Professor Bergman	5 - 15
S1166	Pilot	5 - 15
S1167	Crew set, includes S1162, S1163, S1165	20 - 60
S1170	Trading cards, set of 66 (Donruss)	7 - 15
S1171	Individual trading cards, ea	.10 - .30
S1172	Box for S1170	3 - 8
S1173	Wrappers for S1170	1 - 4
S1174	Unopened waxpacks for S1170	2 - 8
S1180	Eagle One Transporter, die-cast metal and plastic, red and white (Dinky)	20 - 40
S1181	Same as S1180 w/nuclear waste canisters, green and white	
S1190	Parachutist (AHI)	20 - 40
S1195	Flying Eagle	
S1200	Eagle Transporter model kit (Airfix)	8 - 20
S1201	Hawk Spaceship model kit (Airfix)	8 - 20
S1205	Record	3 - 9
S1210	Punch-out Adventure playset (Amsco)	20 - 40
S1215	Cut and Color book	7 - 18
S1216	Coloring book	5 - 10
S1217	Activity book	5 - 10

Comic magazines S1225-32 (Charlton)

S1225	#1	1 - 3
S1226-32	#2-8, ea	.50 - 2

Comic books S1233-39 (Charlton)

S1233	#1	1 - 2
S1234-39	#2-7, ea	.50 - 1

Paperback novels S1240-41

S1240	*Breakaway*	.50 - 1.50
S1241	*Moon Odyssey*	.50 - 1.50
S1250	View-Master packet	8 - 15
S1251	Talking View-Master packet	8 - 15
S1255	Chestpack/AM radio	10 - 30
S1260	Magazines w/*Space: 1999* covers	.50 - 1
S1270	Rocket gun	10 - 20
S1271	Superscope	10 - 20
S1272	Throw dart game	10 - 20
S1273	Astro Popper	10 - 20
S1274	Color TV and stamp set	10 - 20
S1275	Galaxy Time Meter	10 - 20
S1276	Color TV movies	10 - 20
S1277	Stamp set	10 - 20

80

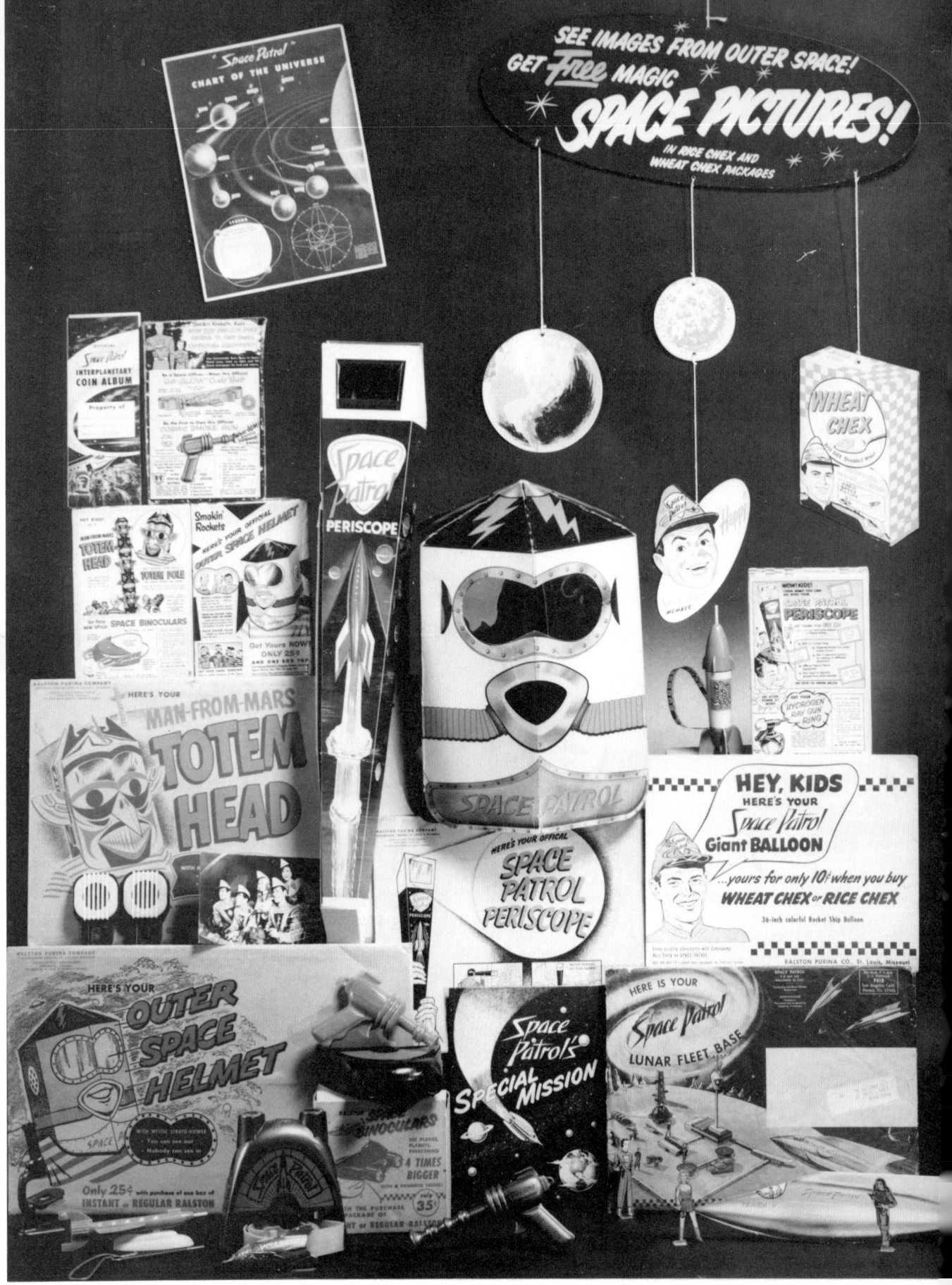

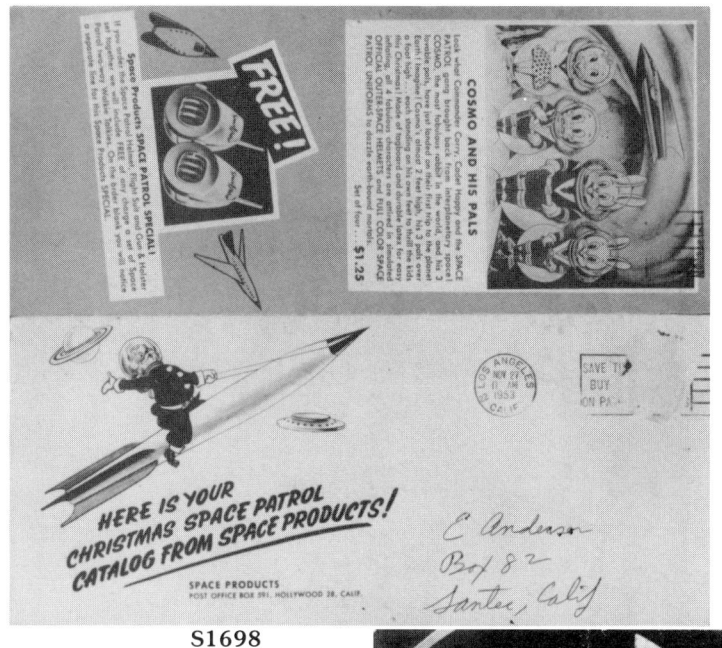

S1698

S1698

S1600

S1599

S1697

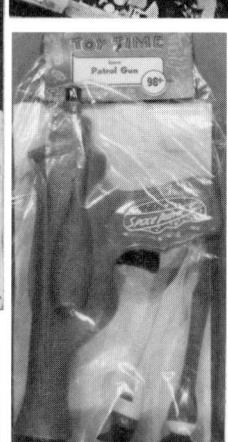

S1653-54

S1679

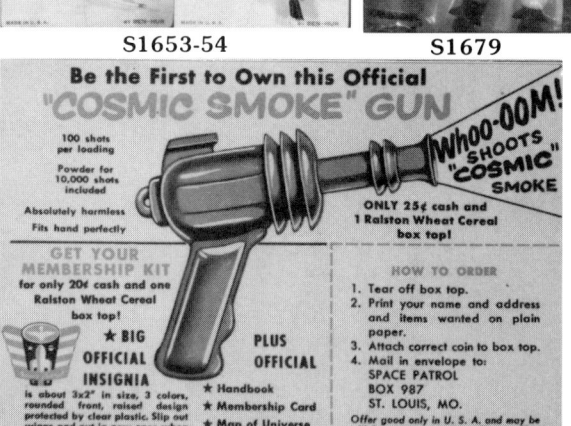

S1602

S1604

81

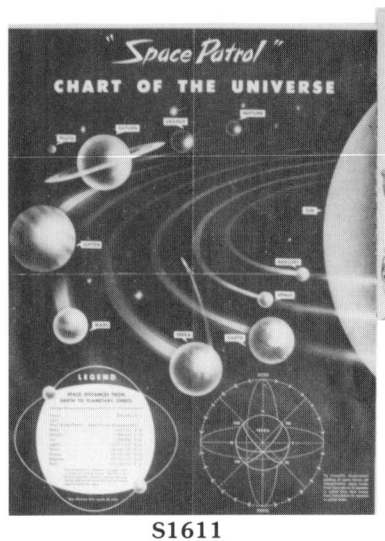

S1611   "Space Patrol" CHART OF THE UNIVERSE

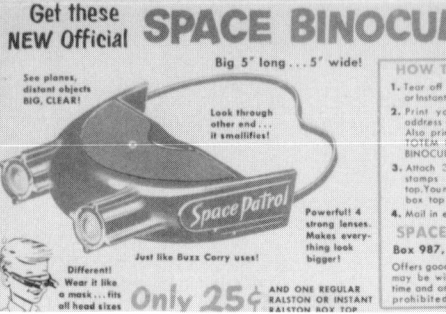

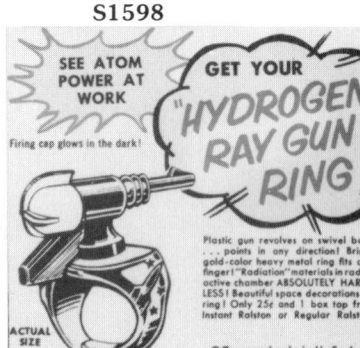

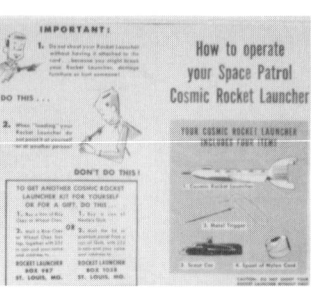

S1605   Get these NEW Official SPACE BINOCULARS

S1616   How to operate your Space Patrol Cosmic Rocket Launcher

S1687   INTERPLANETARY SPACE PATROL CREDITS — TERRA

S1607   RALSTON SPACE BINOCULARS

S1598   "Space Patrol"

S1595   "Space Patrol" certificate

S1617   WOW! KIDS! LOOK WHAT YOU CAN DO WITH YOUR SPACE PATROL PERISCOPE

S1618   GET YOUR "HYDROGEN" RAY GUN RING

S1656   Space Patrol belt

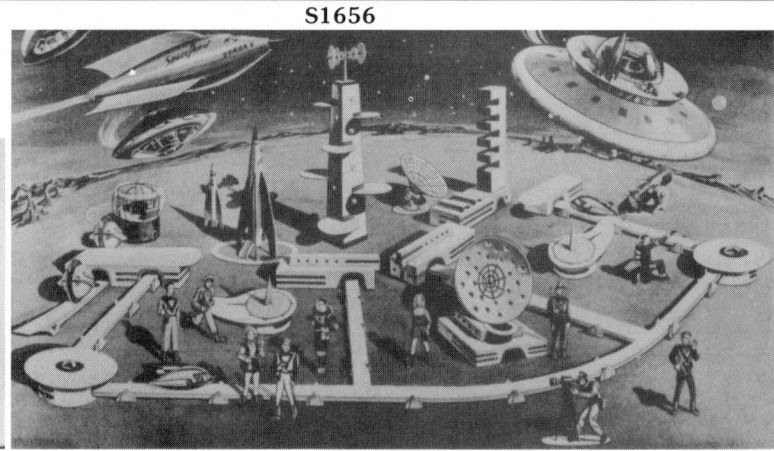

S1625   Space Patrol OFFICIAL WALKIE-TALKIE SPACE-A-PHONES

S1628

82

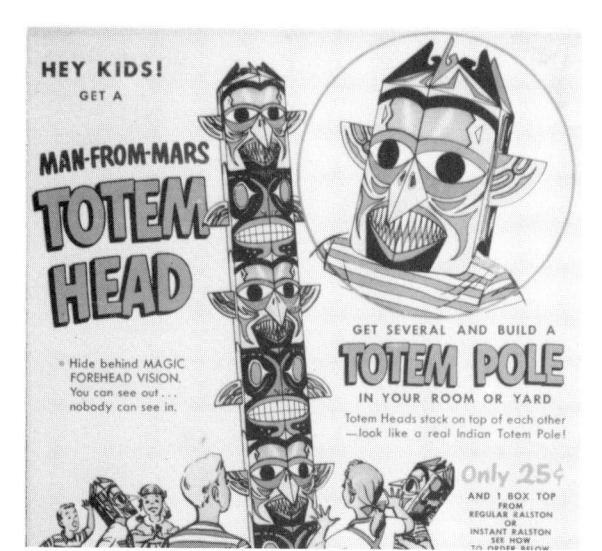

SPACE PATROL

The exploration of the solar system was nearly complete by the thirtieth century, creating a need for a universal government system. The leaders of the various planets met on Earth and established the United Planets of the Universe.

To prevent political conflicts, the United Planets government was located on a man-made planet. This world was known as Terra and contained soil from each of the nine planets in its core. Buzz Corry became the first man ever to reach Pluto when he flew there to obtain a capsule of soil for Terra's core.

The Space Patrol was created as the military force for this new system, with Buzz Corry as commander-in-chief. Companions included the comic Cadet Happy, girlfriend Carol, second in command Major Robertson, and rehabilitated criminal Tonga. Together they lead the Space Patrol in the never-ending battle to preserve "right, goodness and justice" in the solar system. With villains like Dr. Rylard Scarno, Mr. Proteus and Prince Bacharatti bent on ruling the universe, it was no easy task.

"Space Patrol" was launched into popularity on March 13, 1950, when the first broadcast premiered on ABC. It was one of the more enduring space exploration shows on television, and ran until February 26, 1955.

While the most commonly remembered format of the show was a 1/2 hour, it was originally presented in 15-minute daily segments with "cliff-hanger" endings common. The primary sponsor of Space Patrol was the Ralston Purina Co., but the final season of the show was presented by Nestlé Chocolate.

Space Patrol items came two ways: toys and premiums. Premiums were found in cereal boxes, sold in stores (with a purchase of Ralston Products) or mailed in with box tops and a few coins. Many premiums were produced in different colors, or had subtle design variations, depending on where the item was obtained. The most commonly noted example of this is the Cosmic Smoke Gun, originally a box top premium. A slightly different version was later released for sale in stores. The store version was molded in green plastic instead of the original red, and had a longer barrel.

Space-O-Phones and Space-A-Phones can be confusing. The Space-O-Phones were a premium offer, molded in blue and yellow plastic. Two different color combinations were made. Yellow phones with blue grills are more difficult to find. Space-A-Phones were sold in stores. They are shaped differently, larger, and molded in various combinations of red and white or black and white. As with most store-bought Space Patrol items, they are more difficult to come by than the premiums.

Binoculars are either black or green. The green variety, distributed in supermarkets, is less common. The Cosmic Rocket Launcher and Totem Head were jointly offered by Ralston and Nestlé Chocolate. Weather Bird Shoes also co-sponsored the Interplanetary coin giveaway. Jet Black, Sun Gold, and Midnight Blue coins were found, one to a box, in the cereal, while the shoe dealerships handed out Starlight Silver. The first three could be used to enter the "Name the Planet" contest and are thus more difficult to find. The Space Patrol Rocket cockpit is the only official

FLEET COMMANDER	SECRET CODE MASTER	BUZZ CORRY	JET CAR TROOPER	SPACE NURSE	
CLEARING THE SPACE LANES	COSMIC SCIENTIST	CADET HAPPY	INTERPLANETARY GUARD	ROCKET ASTROGATOR	
MONORAIL LINER	SAUCER ATTACK	ROCKET OVER CANALI	STARDRIVE	READY FOR ACTION	
EXPERIMENTAL ROCKET	WAR OF THE PLANETS	SATURN	TERRA CITY	DESERT OF MARS	
JETTING THROUGH SPACE	ROCKET TEST PILOT	SOLAR SPACE RACE	LUNAR GYRO JET	ROCKET CARRIER SHIP	
MULTIPLE SUN SYSTEM	VENUS	NEPTUNE	EXPEDITION TO RHEA	ROCKET OVER THE MOON	

SPACE PATROL EMERGENCY KIT

Going some place? Then you'll need this Space Patrol Emergency Kit. Indispensable for interplanetary travel around any neighborhood — a real First Aid Kit with zip strips, tape, bandage, etc. The handle is a real ROCKET SHIP SIGNAL FLASHLIGHT. It flashes . . . and the inner lid shows the complete Morse Code. A direction Compass Rose is ingraved on the back of the carrying case . . . you'll never get lost when you carry your Space Patrol Emergency Kit. $2.98

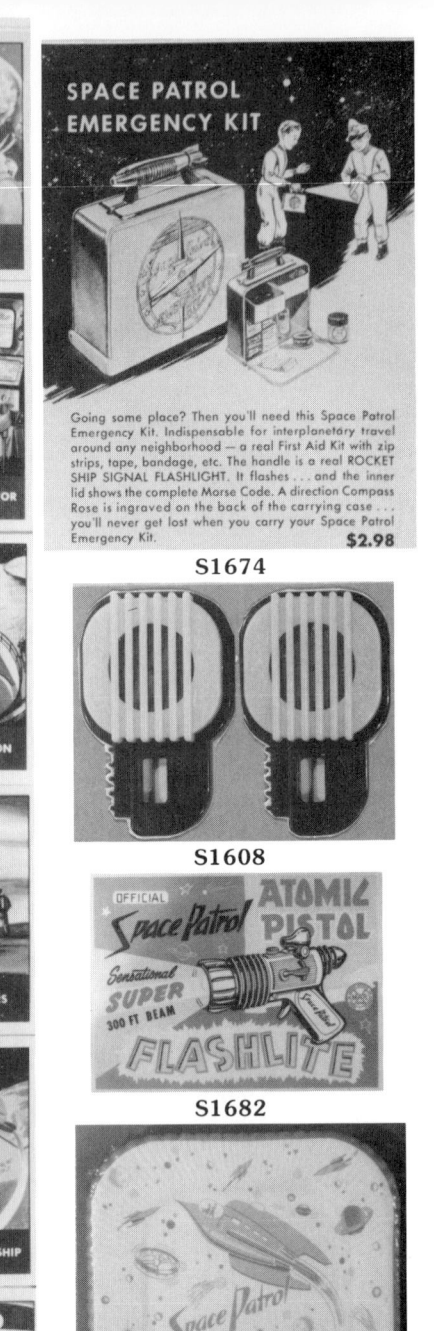

S1674

S1608

S1682

S1641

S1623

S1642    S1641   S1640 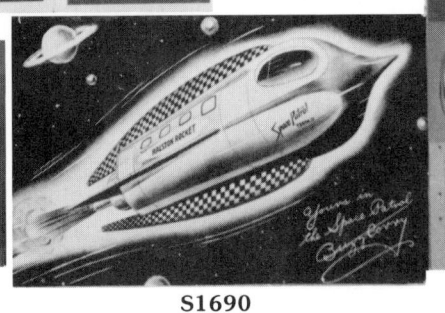   S1690    S1625

premium offered exclusively by Nestlé. The Hydrogen Ray Gun ring appears to have been offered only as a Ralston mail-in premium. Although offered through the program, the Neddy Nestlé Space Jet is not labelled "Space Patrol".

The Lunar Fleet Base was a premium. A similar Terra City punch-out set was a store item which sold for $1.

The Diplomatic Pouch was marketed through the mail as the Space Patrol Stamp, Coin & Ball Point Pen set. The contents included a sheet of 100 stamps (2 each of 50 different), 6 plastic coins, 6 pieces of paper currency, 8 sheets of official Space Patrol stationery, a 16-page stamp album, a 3-fold coin album, and a ball point pen shaped like a rocket ship. Everything but the pen was packaged in a paper case marked "Diplomatic Pouch". The entire set sold for $1. Diplomatic Pouches were also sold in stores, but without the pen.

The major toy manufacturers were Beelman, Plastic Novelties, Inc., Toys of Tomorrow, Ltd., and U. S. Plastics. The first Space Patrol toys began appearing in 1950. The monorail, ball point pen, Space-A-Phones, and Nestlé Rocket Cockpit are the most difficult to find.

S1595	Membership card	10 - 35
S1596	Handbook	30 - 90
S1597	Handbook, reprint	3 - 6
S1598	Badge, plastic	50 - 175
S1599	Photo	6 - 16
S1600	Decoder buckle and belt	75 - 180
S1601	Cosmic Smoke Gun, green, long barrel	80 - 200
S1602	Cosmic Smoke Gun, red, short barrel	80 - 200
S1603	Ring, plastic	200 - 450
S1604	Rocket Ship balloon, in envelope	75 - 225
S1605	Binoculars, black	50 - 120
S1607	Binoculars, store version in box, green	75 - 250
S1608	Space-O-Phones, blue backs, yellow grills	50 - 150
S1609	Space-O-Phones, yellow backs, blue grills	75 - 175
S1610	Premium catalog	30 - 75
S1611	Chart of Universe	35 - 75
S1612	Printing ring w/ink pad	75 - 300
S1613	Project-O-Scope, complete w/film	100 - 300
S1614	Lunar Fleet Base	100 - 700
S1615	Apology card	10 - 30
S1616	Cosmic Rocket Launcher	150 - 600
S1617	Periscope	85 - 200
S1618	Hydrogen Ray Gun ring	75 - 175
S1619	Microscope	80 - 150
S1620	Martian Totem Head	50 - 140
S1621	Space helmet	90 - 200
S1622	Control panel cockpit (Nestlé)	650 - 1000
S1623	Trading cards, 40, ea	10 - 20
S1625	Space-A-Phones, various colors	150 - 300
S1628	City of Terra (similar to S1614, but sold in stores)	300 - 600
S1629	Order form for S1628	40 - 80
S1630	Comic book, #1	75 - 175

S1596

S1689

S1613

S1635

85

S1670

S1681

S1661

S1700

86

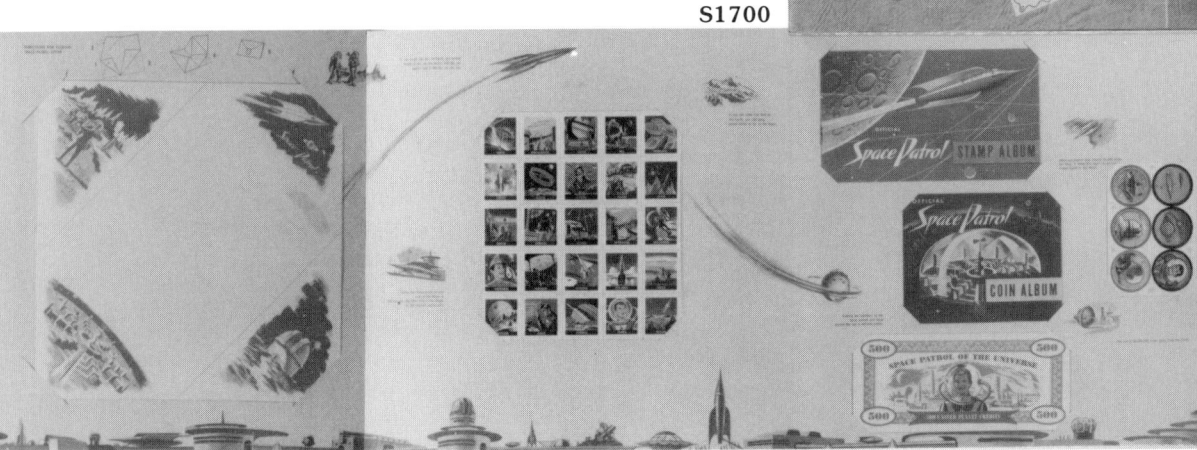

S1696

S1702-03

S1679

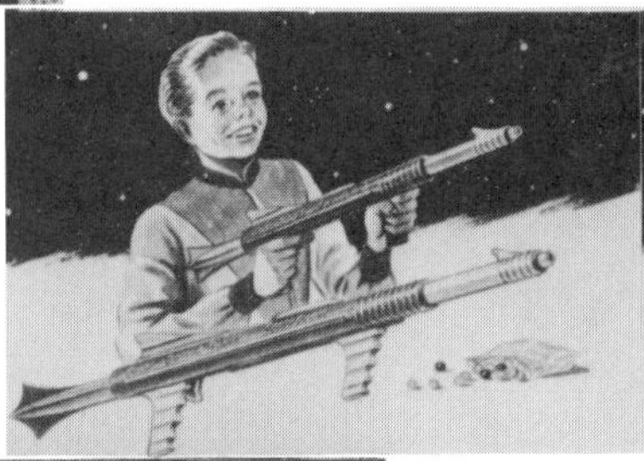

S1671

S1650

BOYS' AND GIRLS' COSMIC CAP

Are you wearing the official Space Patrol headgear? It's now available in four sizes... small-medium-large and extra large, in bright colors with visor, real goggles and Space Patrol insignia. It completes every well dressed Space Patroller's wardrobe. **$1.69**

S1675

S1692

S1630-31

SPACE PATROL STAMP, COIN & BALL POINT PEN SET

Never before have you ever seen such an assortment!

1. 100 full color stamps with 50 different designs, from 50 different planets. Gummed and perforated.
2. 6 full color plastic coins. 3. 6 pieces of paper currency.
4. 8 sheets of official Space Patrol stationery.
5. 16 page stamp album. 6. 3-fold coin album.
7. Space Patrol Ball Point Pen.
8. Complete set packed in Space Patrol case. **$1.00**

S1700   S1701

S1694

87

S1634

S1679-80

SPACE PATROL ROCKET GUN AND HOLSTER SET

Here you have it! That thrilling full size missile space gun complete with two rubber capped rockets! One rocket has exciting noise action the other a secret compartment. Real leather belt and holster with ammunition clip to carry one guided missile. A rocket gun for real Space Patrollers. **$3.79**

S1645

Back of S1690

S1680

S1683

S1693

S1676

S1643

S1621

Code	Item	Price
S1631	Comic book, #2	75 - 175
S1634	Monorail	1500 - 3500
S1635	Inlaid puzzle	30 - 60
S1640	Paper cups	10 - 30
S1641	Paper plates	10 - 30
S1642	Napkins	8 - 15
S1643	Table cover	25 - 50
S1645	Cadet Happy postcard	25 - 50
S1650	Space bank	400 - 800
S1653	Rocket barrette (Ben Hur)	75 - 150
S1654	Pistol barrette (Ben Hur)	75 - 150
S1656	Belt	200 - 300
S1657	Belt w/secret compartment	150 - 350
S1661	Magic Space pictures, 24, ea	4 - 10
S1665	Uniform shirt	250 - 400
S1666	Flight suit	500 - 700
S1670	Rocket ship (inflatable)	100 - 400
S1671	Auto-Sonic rifle	200 - 800
S1674	Emergency kit	250 - 650
S1675	Cosmic cap	75 - 200
S1676	Cosmic Rayn Protector	75 - 150
S1679	Rocket gun w/2 darts	60 - 150
S1680	Holster for S1679	100 - 225
S1681	Rocket Lite	100 - 200
S1682	Atomic Pistol flashlight (Marx Toys)	100 - 250
S1683	Wrist watch w/compass in box	300 - 600
S1684	Watch only	40 - 90
S1685	TV promotion folder	75 - 150
S1686	Ralston promotional folder	75 - 150
S1687	Coins, 4 values of Moon, Saturn, and Terra, gold, blue, or black, ea	7 - 30
S1688	Same as S1687, but silver	5 - 20
S1689	Interplanetary coin album	60 - 160
S1690	Ralston rocket card	25 - 50
S1691	Color book	10 - 50
S1692	Special Mission Blood Booster flyer	35 - 175
S1693	Blood Booster tab	25 - 110
S1694	Nestlé grocery promotional folder	100 - 200
S1695	Store displays	350+
S1696	Window sign	100 - 200
S1697	Supply Depot toy catalog	75 - 175
S1698	Toy catalog	75 - 175
S1700	Diplomatic pouch	50 - 150
S1701	Rocket-shaped ball point pen (came w/Diplomatic pouch)	100 - 200
S1702	Adventure record, #1	75 - 150
S1703	Adventure record, #2	75 - 150
S1704	Magazines w/Space Patrol covers	10 - 60
S1710	Cereal boxes	100 - 600

STAR TREK

In 1963, Gene Roddenberry conceived the *Star Trek* series as a method of confronting modern-day issues against a background of science fiction. The show communicates its messages through its characters — the crew of the deep space-exploration vessel *Enterprise* — whose five-year mission is "to explore strange new worlds, to seek out new life forms and new civilizations, to boldly go where no one has gone before." The members of the crew come from different racial, cultural, gender, and ethnic backgrounds. Working together, they learn and promote values such as justice, racial tolerance, morality and peace among themselves and the beings they encounter.

The original pilot episode of *Star Trek* was called "The Cage." Although pleased with the concept, the NBC network rejected the pilot and asked Roddenberry to do another. The return of the original cast was not possible, however, and the crew of the ship had to be almost totally re-created.

The series premiered in 1966. After two seasons it was slated for cancellation, but letters from fans poured in. NBC decided to continue for another season, but moved the show from 7:30 Monday night to 10:00 PM on Fridays. This poor time slot effectively ended the television days of the original show.

Popularity did not diminish. *Star Trek* was kept alive through syndicated re-runs, and original novels were produced. An animated *Star Trek* premiered on September 15, 1973, producing 22 half-hour episodes. Animation was done by Filmation House, with members of the original cast providing voices. Letters from eager Trek fans even convinced NASA to name the first space shuttle *Enterprise*.

"Star Trek II" was to be one of the major productions for a new television network conceived by Paramount Studios. The plan was announced in 1977. The old cast was to be reunited on a refitted *Enterprise* and would set out on a second five-year mission. Paramount's network plan was later discarded due to lack of affiliates, but not before a great deal of production had been completed for *Star Trek*.

With the success of *Star Wars*, the film industry gained a renewed interest in space adventure. The sets designed for the television show were dismantled and rebuilt on a larger scale.

Star Trek: The Motion Picture was released in December of 1979, incorporating many of the new ideas created for the aborted series. These included the refitted *Enterprise*, new crew members, and new uniforms. The film met with mixed reactions, but was profitable enough to make up for losses amassed in preparation for the cancelled television production and encourage sequels.

Star Trek II: The Wrath of Khan (1982), *Star Trek III: The Search for Spock* (1984) and *Star Trek IV: The Voyage Home* (1986) comprised an inter-related trilogy. *Star Trek V: The Final Frontier* was released in the summer of 1989.

"Star Trek: The Next Generation" premiered on the Fox TV network in 1987. This was the future of *Star Trek*, with a new crew and a more advanced *Enterprise*, designed to carry crew members and their families on extended missions of ten to fifteen years. Computer-generated special effects were used extensively.

The *Star Trek* dream has been shared in a unique way by many fans, sometimes referred to as "Trekkies" or "Trekkers." Trek enthusiasts played an active role in preventing the cancellation the original TV show, and have since swelled in size. The official fan club alone numbers 35,000 people. National and regional conventions are held regularly.

Fans and fan/dealers have also been the source of numerous "fanzine" publications and unlicensed *Star Trek* merchandise, mainly uniforms, tribbles, insignia pins, buttons, reproductions of props, posters, T-

ST1500

ST1501

ST1504-09

ST1520 ST1521

ST1518-19

ST1514 ST1515 ST1516

ST1542

90

ST1543

ST1517

ST1700 ST1701

ST1702 ST1704

ST1705 ST1706

shirts and other artifacts. Most of this material remains available at conventions or by mail. This work, with rare exceptions, deals only with items licensed by Paramount.

Despite its short initial life span as a television series, *Star Trek* has maintained its popularity for more than twenty years. A few items were produced during the early days of the show, but the major surge in licensed merchandise began in 1973. Due to the large amount of merchandise produced, this section has been classified by category, using a system similar to the yellow pages of a phone book. Certain large classifications, such as Advertisements, are so vast that a complete listing is impossible. In these situations, general guidelines for the field are given and a few examples are shown, but no details are provided on specific pieces.

Star Trek code numbers begin with "ST" instead of "S" due to the vast amount of merchandise which has been produced, and to allow room for future items to be included.

For simplification, several common designations have been abbreviated in the following list. These include the original television show (TV), *Star Trek: The Motion Picture* (STTMP), *Star Trek II: The Wrath of Khan* (STII), *Star Trek III: The Search for Spock* (STIII), *Star Trek IV: The Voyage Home* (STIV), *Star Trek V: The Final Frontier* (ST5) and "Star Trek: The Next Generation" (NG).

Action Figures

Star Trek figures of any size tend to follow similar patterns. Figures of major cast members (Kirk, Spock, McCoy, and the like) are fairly common, while aliens and less prominent characters are more difficult to find. In some cases, this is partially due to consumers, but later rarities resulted from lower production runs of certain characters. The first figures appeared in 1974, along with a few accessories. Two series of aliens were made in 1976. Smaller plastic figures were later produced in conjunction with some of the films, beginning in 1979. "Star Trek: The Next Generation" produced its own line of figures as well. In addition to the usual scarcity of aliens, only one Data figure was included in each carton. The figure of Lieutenant Yar often brings higher prices, as the character was killed in the first season.

Although loose figures can still be sold, only figures in their original bubble pack will go for higher prices. Many of them came with easily-lost plastic accessories, which are also important to the value of the item. Star Trek action figures were produced by Mego Corporation and the Lewis Galoob Toy Company. Five limited edition figures were made by the Lewis Galoob Toy Company for *Star Trek V: The Final Frontier*.

Television-style action figures ST1500-13 (Mego, 1974-76)

ST1500 Kirk	15 - 35
ST1501 Spock	15 - 35
ST1502 McCoy	10 - 30
ST1503 Scotty	10 - 30
ST1504 Uhura	10 - 35
ST1505 Klingon	15 - 45

ST1707 ST1708 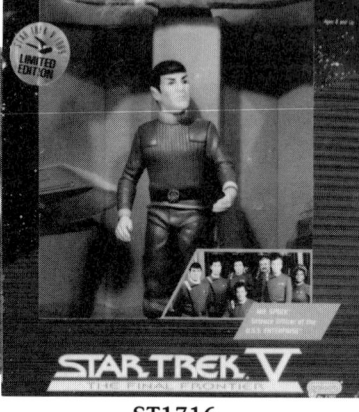 ST1716  ST1715

ST1750

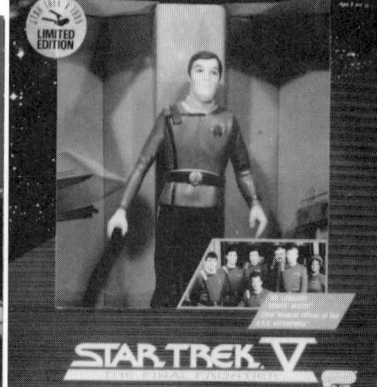

ST1717

ST1802

ST1718-19

92

ST1709

ST1710

ST1760

ST1802   ST1802

ST1506 Gorn	35 - 100
ST1507 Cheron	35 - 100
ST1508 The Keeper	35 - 100
ST1509 Neptunian	35 - 100
ST1510 Andorian	75 - 150
ST1511 Mugato	75 - 150
ST1512 Romulan	75 - 150
ST1513 Talos	75 - 150

***Star Trek: The Motion Picture* 12" figures ST1514-19** (Mego, 1979)

ST1514 Kirk	25 - 35
ST1515 Spock	25 - 35
ST1516 Ilia	25 - 35
ST1517 Decker	70 - 85
ST1518 Klingon	40 - 55
ST1519 Arcturian	40 - 55

Star Trek: The Motion Picture (1979), 3-3/4"

ST1520 Kirk	5 - 15
ST1521 Spock	5 - 15
ST1522 McCoy	5 - 15
ST1523 Scotty	5 - 15
ST1524 Decker	10 - 20
ST1525 Ilia	6 - 15
ST1526 Klingon	10 - 20
ST1527 Arcturian	12 - 30
ST1528 Betelgeusian	12 - 30
ST1529 Megarite	12 - 30
ST1530 Rigellian	12 - 30
ST1531 Zaranite	12 - 30

Star Trek III: The Search for Spock ERTL (1984)

ST1540 Kirk	5 - 10
ST1541 Spock	5 - 10
ST1542 Scotty	5 - 10
ST1543 Kruge and his dog	10 - 18

"Star Trek: The Next Generation" (Lewis Galoob Toy Co., 1988)

ST1700 Picard	2 - 6
ST1701 Riker	2 - 4
ST1702 Data	5 - 10
ST1703 Same as ST1702, but blue skin	20 - 40
ST1704 La Forge	2 - 6
ST1705 Yar	6 - 12
ST1706 Worf	2 - 5
ST1707 Ferengi	6 - 12
ST1708 Antican	6 - 12
ST1709 Selay	6 - 12
ST1710 Q	8 - 15

***Star Trek V: The Final Frontier* figures ST1715-19** (Lewis Galoob Toy Co.)

ST1715 Kirk	20 - 40
ST1716 Spock	20 - 40
ST1717 McCoy	20 - 40
ST1718 Klaa	20 - 40
ST1719 Sybok	20 - 40

Action Figure Playsets, Vehicles and Accessories

A vinyl replica of the *U.S.S. Enterprise*'s main bridge was marketed by Mego. A plastic version of the bridge was sold for *Star Trek: The Motion Picture* figures. Two vehicles were later made by the Lewis Galoob Toy Company for "Star Trek: The Next Generation".

ST1750 Vinyl *Enterprise* Bridge (Mego, 1974)	40 - 150
ST1760 Mission to Gamma VI playset (Mego, 1976)	100 - 350

93

ST1522 ST1525 ST1524
ST1520-31

ST1802

ST1825

ST1802

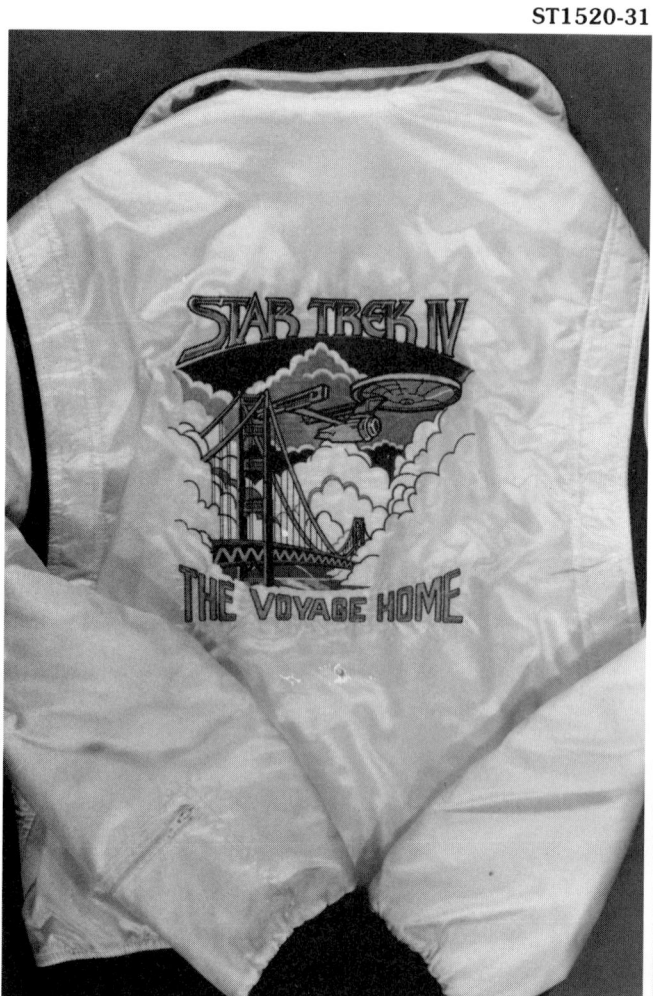

ST1815

ST1855

ST1887

ST1820 ST1820 ST1820 ST1820

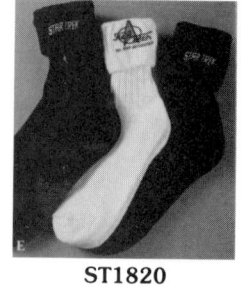

94

ST1761 STTMP Command Bridge	15 - 50	
ST1762 NG *U.S.S. Enterprise* (Lewis Galoob Toy Co.)	15 - 30	
ST1763 NG Shuttlecraft *Galileo* (Lewis Galoob Toy Co.)	10 - 20	
ST1764 NG Ferengi Fighter (Lewis Galoob Toy Co.)	10 - 20	

ActionScape playsets ST1765-67 (Lewis Galoob Toy Co.)

ST1765 #1 Starship Bridge	5 - 15
ST1766 #2 Transporter Room	5 - 15
ST1767 #3 Alien Planet	5 - 15

Advertisements, Print

Star Trek advertisements promote the television show, movies, licensed toys and other products. Celebrity endorsements of Trek products are rare (if they exist at all), and most ads are not strongly character-oriented. Print advertisements include newspapers, magazines, mailings, and similar items. Collecting advertising pieces can be inexpensive, as there are many old magazines and the like in existence, but *Star Trek* advertisements are not as common as some other fields.

ST1800 TV ads	4 - 8
ST1801 Movie ads	4 - 8
ST1802 Toy or merchandise ads	5 - 10
ST1803 Celebrity endorsements	4 - 8

Advertising Signs

This category includes posters, banners, stand-up displays and other items used for promotion of merchandise. These items were provided to merchandisers, and usually were not available to the general public.

ST1806 Paper signs	10+
ST1807 Small cardboard signs	15+
ST1808 Large cardboard signs	25+
ST1809 Plastic signs	15+
ST1810 Other signs	10+

See also: **Inflatables; Posters — Film**

Animation Cels and Backgrounds

An animation celluloid (cel) is one frame of a cartoon. It requires up to 24 of these drawings to photograph one second of animated film, and thousands for an entire episode. Because each picture is slightly different, every cel is a unique item. Cels for the "Star Trek" animated television series were produced by Filmation House. The value of any particular cel must be evaluated on a case-by-case basis, taking into account the character(s) depicted, the pose, and the presence (if at all) of the original background. Backgrounds should be examined carefully, as some modern cels are framed with color photocopies of the original background. Cel collectors with artistic talent have also been known to paint their own backgrounds. Due to the fragile nature of cels, it is not uncommon to find them in damaged condition. Cel collecting is one of the fastest growing collectible fields.

ST1815 Animation Cels. The average cel commands $100-$150, but choice items with original backgrounds must be judged on an individual basis.

Apparel

Star Trek clothing has appeared in many forms, from jackets and T-shirts, to pajamas and socks. Collector interest is lower than in other fields. Apparel is further confused by the prolific T-shirts produced by fans and other independent groups. Crew jackets, available to cast and crew members at the Paramount Studio store, are of special interest to collectors.

ST1820 Miscellaneous apparel	1 - 20
ST1825 Crew jackets, ea	100 - 300

See also: **Costumes and Play Outfits; Iron-On Appliques and Transfers**

Banks

ST1830 Kirk bank, plastic	10 - 35
ST1831 Spock bank, plastic	10 - 35

Belts and Buckles

The *Star Trek* utility belt by Remco was eventually re-issued as a Buck Rogers item, as evidenced by the phaser-like gun design. Assorted brass buckles have been produced by Lee Belts. Make sure to check for the Paramount copyright, as independent and fan-produced items are common.

ST1850 Utility Belt, including disk-shooting phaser, tricorder, and communicator	30 - 100
ST1851 Brass belt buckles	5 - 15
ST1852 Leather belt w/starships, names and insignia	5 - 15
ST1855 Reversible w/coin buckle	35 - 50

Binoculars

Star Trek binoculars were sold as a carded novelty.

ST1860 Binoculars (Larami)	45 - 75

Books

Star Trek has spawned numerous volumes, including original novels, technical manuals, and adaptations of the television shows and films. Publishers vary, ranging from Ballantine to Pocket Books (Simon and Schuster) to independent publications. Books occasionally show up at antique shows and conventions, but lower prices can often be found at a used bookstore or comic shop.

Ballantine ST1875-1985

ST1875 *The Making of Star Trek* (1968)	1 - 5
ST1880 *The Star Trek Interview Book*	3 - 8
ST1885 *The Trek Encyclopedia*	5 - 15
ST1887 *Star Trek The Motion Picture*	5 - 10
ST1890 *Star Trek Trivia Book*	5 - 15
ST1895 *The Trouble with Tribbles* (1973)	1 - 3
ST1900 *The Monsters of Star Trek*	1 - 3
ST1901 *My Enemy, My Ally*	4 - 10
ST1902 *The Vulcan Academy Murders*	4 - 10
ST1903 *The Wounded Sky*	4 - 10
ST1905 *The Klingon Dictionary*	2 - 5

ST2105

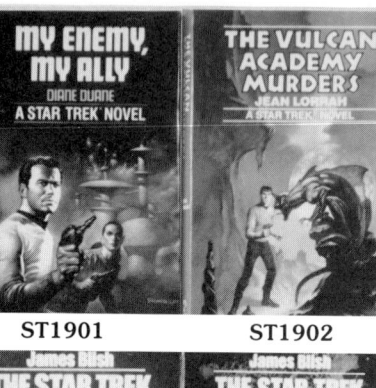

ST1890 
ST1901 
ST1902 
ST1903

ST2079  
ST2080 
ST2081 
ST2082

ST2201
ST2201

ST2070  
ST2202 
ST2209 
ST2213 
ST2217 
ST2240

ST1915  
ST2402

ST2400 
ST2404 
ST2216 
ST2231 
ST2401 
ST2405

ST2074
ST2076

ST2907
ST1920  
ST2100 
ST2101 

96

ID	Title	Price
ST1910	*The Star Trek Compendium*	6 - 11
ST1911	*The Star Trek Compendium*, revised edition	6 - 11
ST1915	*The World of Star Trek*	6 - 12
ST1916	*The World of Star Trek*, revised edition (Bluejay Books)	5 - 10
ST1920	*Star Fleet Technical Manual*	10 - 20
ST1925	*Trek or Treat*	2 - 5
ST1930	*Star Trek Speaks*	2 - 10
ST1935	*Strange and Amazing Facts About Star Trek*	1 - 3
ST1940	*Chekov's Enterprise*	2 - 4

Logbooks ST1950-59 (novelizations of animated series)

ID	Title	Price
ST1950	#1	1 - 3
ST1951	#2	1 - 3
ST1952	#3	1 - 3
ST1953	#4	1 - 3
ST1954	#5	1 - 3
ST1955	#6	1 - 3
ST1956	#7	1 - 3
ST1957	#8	1 - 3
ST1958	#9	1 - 3
ST1959	#10	1 - 3
ST1970	*STII Photostory*	2 - 5
ST1975	*Mr. Scott's Guide to the Enterprise*	
ST1980	*The Worlds of the Federation*	
ST1985	*Captain's Log: William Shatner's Personal Account of the Making of Star Trek V: The Final Frontier*	

Bantam ST2050-64

ID	Title	Price
ST2050	*Death's Angel*	1 - 4
ST2051	*Devil World*	1 - 4
ST2052	*The Fate of the Phoenix*	1 - 4
ST2053	*The Price of the Phoenix*	1 - 4
ST2054	*Mudd's Angels*	1 - 4
ST2055	*Perry's Planet*	1 - 4
ST2056	*Planet of Judgment*	1 - 4
ST2057	*Spock, Messiah!*	1 - 4
ST2058	*Spock Must Die!*	1 - 4
ST2059	*Star Trek: The New Voyages*	1 - 4
ST2060	*Star Trek: The New Voyages 2*	1 - 4
ST2061	*The Starless World*	1 - 4
ST2062	*Trek To Madworld*	1 - 4
ST2063	*Vulcan!*	1 - 4
ST2064	*World Without End*	1 - 4

***Star Trek* adaptations by James Blish** ST2070-79

ID	Title	Price
ST2070	#1	2 - 8
ST2071	#2	2 - 8
ST2072	#3	2 - 8
ST2073	#4	2 - 8
ST2074	#5	2 - 8
ST2075	#6	2 - 8
ST2076	#7	2 - 8
ST2077	#8	2 - 8
ST2078	#9	2 - 8
ST2079-82	*Star Trek Readers* (Compilations of ST2070-78, above), #1-4, ea	5 - 20

Merrigold ST2100-01

ID	Title	Price
ST2100	Color and Activity book: Kirk, Spock, McCoy	1 - 2
ST2101	Color and Activity book: Kirk, Spock, *Enterprise*	1 - 2
ST2105	Punch Out and Play Album (Saalfield, 1975)	30 - 60
ST2110	STTMP Giant Story coloring book	5 - 10

Pocket Books ST2201-2510 (Simon and Schuster)

ID	Title	Price
ST2201	#1 *Star Trek: The Motion Picture*	1 - 4
ST2202	#2 *The Entropy Effect*	1 - 4
ST2203	#3 *The Klingon Gambit*	1 - 4
ST2204	#4 *The Covenant of the Crown*	1 - 4
ST2205	#5 *The Prometheus Design*	1 - 4
ST2206	#6 *The Abode of Life*	1 - 4
ST2207	#7 *Star Trek II: The Wrath of Kahn*	1 - 4
ST2208	#8 *Black Fire*	1 - 4
ST2209	#9 *Triangle*	1 - 4
ST2210	#10 *Web of the Romulans*	1 - 4
ST2211	#11 *Yesterday''s Son*	1 - 4
ST2212	#12 *Mutiny on the Enterprise*	1 - 4
ST2213	#13 *The Wounded Sky*	1 - 4
ST2214	#14 *The Trellisane Confrontation*	1 - 4
ST2215	#15 *Corona*	1 - 4
ST2216	#16 *The Final Reflection*	1 - 4
ST2217	#17 *Star Trek III: The Search for Spock*	1 - 4
ST2218	#18 *My Enemy, My Ally*	1 - 4
ST2219	#19 *The Tears of the Singers*	1 - 4
ST2220	#20 *The Vulcan Academy Murders*	1 - 4
ST2221	#21 *Uhura's Song*	1 - 4
ST2222	#22 *Shadow Lord*	1 - 4
ST2223	#23 *Ishmael*	1 - 4
ST2224	#24 *Killing Time*	1 - 4
ST2225	#25 *Dwellers in the Crucible*	1 - 4
ST2226	#26 *Pawns and Symbols*	1 - 4
ST2227	#27 *Mindshadow*	1 - 4
ST2228	#28 *Crisis on Centaurus*	1 - 4
ST2229	#29 *Dreadnought!*	1 - 4
ST2230	#30 *Demons*	1 - 4
ST2231	#31 *Battlestations!*	1 - 4
ST2232	#32 *Chain of attack*	1 - 4
ST2233	#33 *Deep Domain*	1 - 4
ST2234	#34 *Dreams of the Raven*	1 - 4
ST2235	#35 *The Romulan Way*	1 - 4
ST2236	#36 *How Much for Just the Planet?*	1 - 4
ST2237	#37 *Bloodthirst*	1 - 4
ST2238	#38 *The IDIC Epidemic*	1 - 4
ST2239	#39 *Time for Yesterday*	1 - 4
ST2240	#40 *Timetrap*	1 - 4
ST2241	#41 *The Tree-Minute Universe*	1 - 4
ST2242	#42 *Memory Prime*	1 - 4
ST2243	#43 *The Final Nexus*	1 - 4
ST2244	#44 *Vulcan's Glory*	1 - 4
ST2245	#45 *Double, Double*	1 - 4
ST2246	#46 *The Cry of the Onlies*	1 - 4
ST2247	#47 *The Kobayashi Maru*	1 - 4
ST2248	#48 *Rules of Engagement*	1 - 4
ST2400	*Star Trek IV: The Voyage Home*	1 - 4
ST2401	*Star Trek V: The Final Frontier*	1 - 5
ST2402	*Final Frontier*	1 - 5
ST2403	*Strangers From the Sky*	1 - 5
ST2404	*Enterprise: The First Adventure*	1 - 5
ST2405	*Spock's World*	1 - 5
ST2406	*The Lost Years*	1 - 5

"Star Trek:The Next Generation" novels ST 2500-09 (Pocket)

Encounter at Farpoint

ID	Title	Price
ST2500	#1 *Ghost Ship*	1 - 4
ST2501	#2 *The Peacekeepers*	1 - 4
ST2502	#3 *The Children of Hamlin*	1 - 4
ST2503	#4 *Survivors*	1 - 4

ST2876　　　　　ST2880　　　　　　　　　　　　　　ST2900

　　　　　　　　　　　　　　　　ST2801

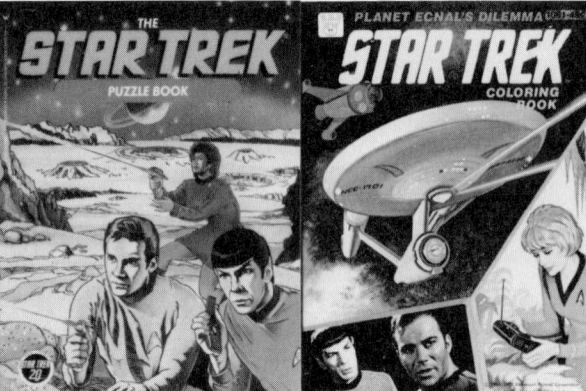

ST2750 　　　　　ST2875 　　　　　ST2825 　　　　　ST2802

ST2910　　　　　　　　　　　　　　ST2110

98

ST2878

ST3001

ST2207

ST3020

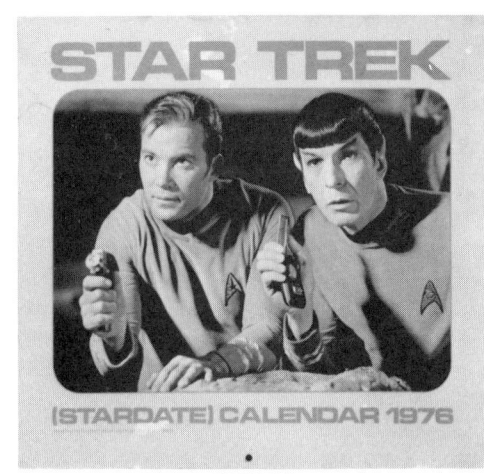

ST3030

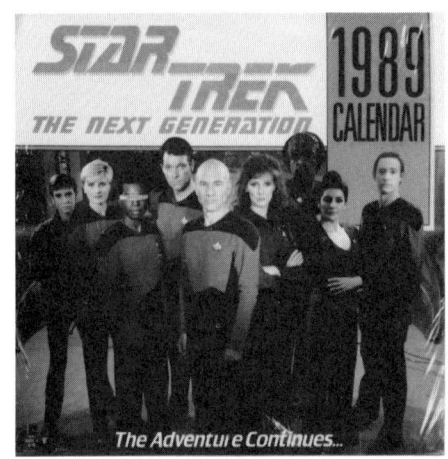

ST3030

ST2504 #5 *Strike Zone*	1 - 4
ST2505 #6 *Power Hungry*	1 - 4
ST2506 #7 *Masks*	1 - 4
ST2507 #8 *The Captains' Honor*	1 - 4
ST2508 #9 *A Call to Darkness*	1 - 4
ST2509 #10 *Gulliver's Fugitives*	1 - 4
ST2650 *Metamorphosis*	1 - 5

Signet ST2701-14
The Best of Trek

ST2701 #1	1 - 4
ST2702 #2	1 - 4
ST2703 #3	4 - 10
ST2704 #4	1 - 4
ST2705 #5	4 - 10
ST2706 #6	1 - 4
ST2707 #7	1 - 4
ST2708 #8	1 - 4
ST2709 #9	4 - 10
ST2710 #10	1 - 4
ST2711 #11	1 - 4
ST2712 #12	1 - 4
ST2713 #13	1 - 4
ST2714 #14	1 - 4

Simon and Schuster

| ST2750 *Star Trek* Puzzle Book (1986) | 5 - 10 |

Wallaby ST2800-03

ST2800 STTMP Make Your Own Costume Book (1979)	5 - 15
ST2801 STTMP Bridge Punch Out Book	8 - 20
ST2802 *Make A Game Book*	5 - 15
ST2803 *Space Flight Chronology* (1980)	10 - 20

Wanderer Books

| ST2825 STTMP pop-up book | 5 - 15 |

Whitman ST2875-76

ST2875 Coloring book: *Planet Ecnal's Dilemma* (1978)	2 - 6
ST2876 Color and Activity Book (1979)	2 - 6
ST2878 *The Truth Machine*	5 - 10
ST2880 Color and activity book *Rescue at Raylo*	2 - 6
ST2900 STIII Storybook	2 - 5
ST2906 *Mission to Horatius*	4 - 10
ST2907 *The Prisoner of Vega*	4 - 10
ST2908 *On the Good Ship Enterprise*	5 - 10
ST2910 *War in Space*, giant color and learn book	10 - 20

See also: **Games; Records, Tapes and Compact Discs**

Bottles and Decanters

A replica of the Saurian Brandy bottle from the television show was made 1968. Grenadier Spirits Corporation produced a Spock bust whiskey decanter, and a large quantity of them were recently found. The decanter is known to have been counterfeited, so be sure to check the bottom — the real ones have the Grenadier logo and Paramount copyright.

| ST3000 Saurian Brandy bottle | 50 - 150 |
| ST3001 Spock decanter (Grenadier) | 10 - 35 |

Bumper Stickers

A licensed bumper sticker was produced in conjunction with *Star Trek: The Motion Picture*. Fan-produced and independent bumper stickers are extremely common, selling for 1-2 dollars each.

ST3010 STTMP bumper sticker   1 - 3

Calculators

The Star Trekulator was produced by Mego in the mid-'70s.

ST3020 Star Trekulator (Mego)   35 - 50

Calendars

Star Trek calendars have been produced for most years since the early '70s. These have ranged from homemade collages to professionally licensed calendars by Ballantine, Wallaby, and Pocket Books. Calendars are not widely collected, and have little investment potential.

ST3030 Calendars, ea   5 - 10

Candy Boxes

Candy by Phoenix Candy Co. was made in the mid-'70s and packaged in several different boxes.

ST3045 Candy boxes, Kirk (two versions), Spock, McCoy, Uhura, Bridge scene, Transporter Room, or Starships (Phoenix Candy Co.), ea   7 - 15
ST3046 Display box for ST2945   60 - 80

Carded Novelties, Miscellaneous

This category includes a variety of items sold on bubble-packed cards which do not fall into any clearly defined category. Most of these items are relatively new, and have little collector interest.

ST3055 Sky diving parachutists, Kirk or Spock (AHI, 1976), ea   5 - 15
ST3057 I.D. set (Larami, 1979)   5 - 15
ST3058 Putty (Larami, 1979)   5 - 15
ST3060 Giant puzzle   3 - 10
ST3061 Wallet   3 - 10

Cereal Boxes

General Mills cereals has featured *Star Trek* offers on several occasions beginning with tie-ins promoting the release of the first feature film. An ID bracelet and T-shirt size iron-on transfers were the first two offers. A contest offering an appearance on an episode of "Star Trek: The Next Generation" TV program was featured in 1988.

ST3100 Bracelet offer box   10 - 30
ST3102 Iron-on offer boxes, 7 dif, each containing a different Starship to be cut out, ea   10 - 30
ST3110 Next Generation Contest   5 - 15

Clocks

Star Trek clocks may have been produced as early as 1974, to coincide with the resurgence in the show's popularity. An alarm clock was made by Zeon in 1984, but there are probably others.

ST3170 Alarm clock (Zeon, 1984)   25 - 50
ST3174 *Enterprise*   20 - 35

100

ST3061   ST3060

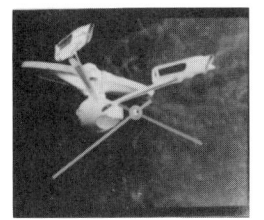

ST3174

ST3303   ST3110

ST3102

ST3252    ST3253

See also: **Watches**

Colorforms
ST3200 Colorforms set   15 - 40

Coins
Collector's edition coins have been issued on several occasions to commemorate the anniversary of *Star Trek* or other events. Collector's coins by Rarities Mint were marketed through the fan club. Some coins included certificates of authenticity.

ST3250 *Enterprise* coin (1974)   25 - 50
ST3251 10th Anniversary (1976)   30 - 75
ST3252 Silver collector's coins, Kirk or
       Spock, *Enterprise* on the reverse,
       (Rarities Mint, 1989), ea   40 - 50
ST3253 Same as ST3252, but gold   150 - 400

Coloring and Painting Sets
ST3300 Pen-A-Poster kit   8 - 22
ST3301 Poster coloring set w/10 pens   5 - 20
ST3303 Paint by Numbers (Hasbro)   10 - 40
See also: **Games**

Comic Books
Gold Key first published *Star Trek* comic books in 1967, and continued to do so for twelve years. Many of the stories printed were later collected into four volumes called *The Enterprise Logs* (not to be confused with the books by Alan Dean Foster), which also included a few pages of new material. Marvel Comics later published an adaptation of *Star Trek: The Motion Picture*. This was used it as a pilot for a new comic series in 1980, but the line only ran for a year and a half. DC picked up the line in 1984, and continued it until 1989. With the release of *Star Trek V: The Final Frontier*, *Star Trek* comics were reset back to issue #1, and simultaneously released with a series based on "Star Trek: The Next Generation". A few other comic projects have been produced, including annuals, DC's *Who's Who in Star Trek*, and a six-issue "Next Generation" mini-series.

Gold Key Comics ST3311-74 (1967-79)
ST3311 #1   15 - 75
ST3312-61 #2-61, ea   5 - 50
ST3371-74 Gold Key *Enterprise Logs*,
       Vol. 1-4, ea   3 - 10
Marvel Comic series ST3381-98 (1980-82)
ST3381 #1   1 - 3
ST3382-98 #2-18, ea   1 - 2
ST3400 *Motion Picture Magazine* (Marvel,
       1979)   2 - 4
First DC Comic series ST3401-56 (1984-89)
ST3401 #1   1 - 3
ST3402-56 #2-56, ea   1 - 2
ST3470 *Star Trek III Movie Special* (DC,1984)   2 - 5
ST3471 *Star Trek IV Movie Special* (DC,
       1987)   1 - 4
ST3481-82 *Who's Who in Star Trek* (DC,
       1987), #1-2, ea   1 - 2
ST3485 *Star Trek V Movie Special* (DC,
       1989)   1 - 4
"Star Trek: The Next Generation" mini-series

ST3371-74 ST3381 ST3470 ST3511

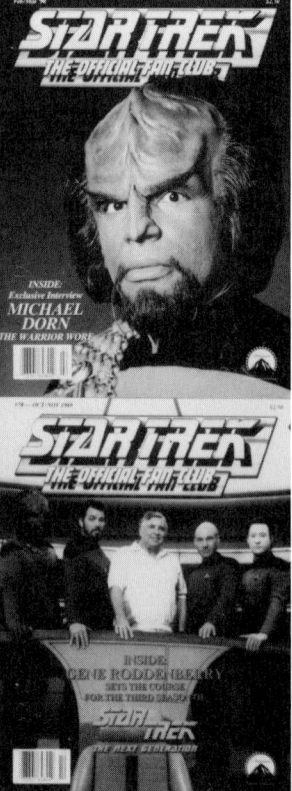

ST3933

ST3402-56 ST3481 ST3482 ST3601

ST3750

ST4000 ST3400

ST4010

ST3951

102

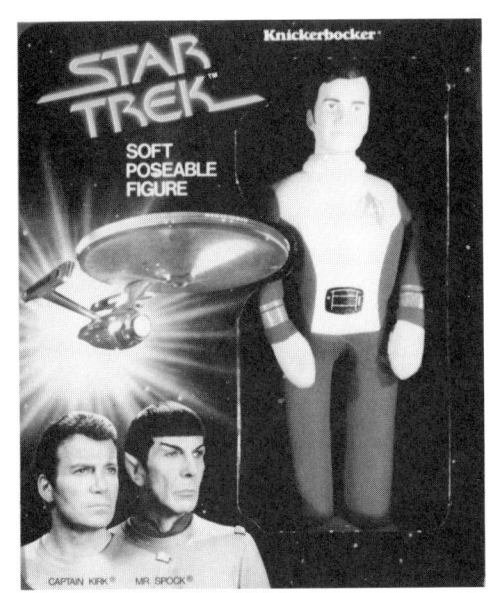

ST3900

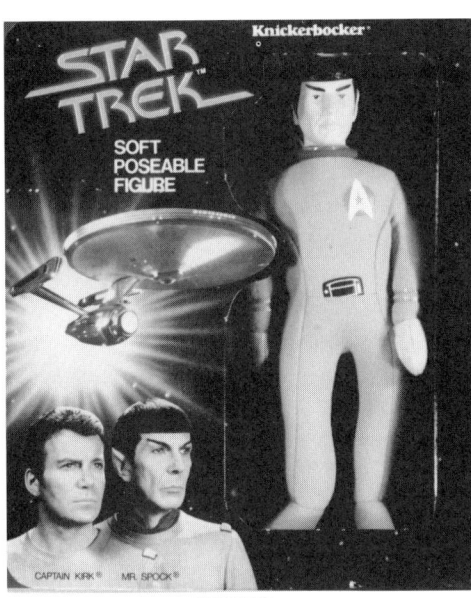

ST3931

ST3951

ST3501-06 (1988)	
ST3501 #1	1 - 3
ST3502-06 #2-6, ea	1 - 2
Second DC Comic series ST 3511-12+ (1989+)	
ST3511 #1	1 - 3
ST3512-? #2+, ea	.80 - 2
"Next Generation" series ST 3601-02+ (1989+)	
ST3601 #1	1 - 3
ST3602-? #2+, ea	.80 - 2

Convention Programs
ST3750 Convention programs　　　　1 - 15

Costumes and Play Outfits
The usual Halloween costumes were produced by Ben Cooper, consisting of of a plastic mask and simple outfit. Later versions were also made with the release of *Star Trek: The Motion Picture*.

ST3795 Mr. Spock (Ben Cooper, 1967)	60 - 120
ST3800 Kirk (1976)	25 - 50
ST3801 Spock (1976)	25 - 70
ST3802 Klingon (1976)	25 - 70
ST3803 Kirk (1979)	10 - 20
ST3804 Spock (1979)	10 - 20
ST3805 Ilia (1979)	10 - 20
ST3806 Klingon (1979)	10 - 20
ST3807 Ferengi (1987)	5 - 10

See also: **Masks; Patterns**

Dolls
Cloth dolls of Kirk and Spock were released with *Star Trek: The Motion Picture*. Two limited edition porcelain dolls of the same characters were produced by The Hamilton Collection in 1988.

ST3900 Large cloth Kirk (Knickerbocker, 1979)	8 - 40
ST3931 Large cloth Spock (Knickerbocker, 1979)	8 - 40
ST3932 Kirk porcelain doll (Hamilton Collection)	50 -100
ST3933 Spock porcelain doll (Hamilton Collection)	50 - 100

See also: **Action Figures and Figures—Other**

Fan Club Kits and Publications
The Official *Star Trek* Fan Club had humble beginnings. Since its formation, its membership has grown from a mere 15 people to more than 35,000. Fan club kits typically included a cardboard membership card, a patch, and cast photo. The fan club magazine has been published bi-monthly.

ST3950 Membership cards	1 - 3
ST3951 Magazines (The first issues were very crude typewritten newsletters. Collectible issues began around issue #20.)	1 - 5

See also: **Patches**

Fanzines
Star Trek has been the subject on an inordinate number of publications produced for and by this special fan group. There were commercial ventures such as

103

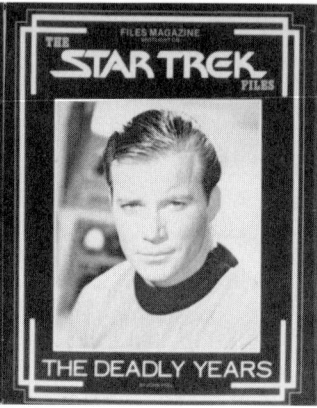

ST4010

Top Row: Kirk, Spock, McCoy   *Bottom Row:* Uhura, Sulu, Chekov

ST4030

104

Trek and *Files Magazine* featuring the *Star Trek* files and art portfolios such as the one by Kelly Freas.

Then there are hundreds of fan-produced publications on all aspects of *Star Trek*. The focus ranges from fans of a specific character or the *Enterprise* spaceship to poems and essays on the *Star Trek* phenomenon. Most fan produced fanzines had printings of less than 1000 copies. Many are well done, others contain information for the fans who can't find enough to read about *Star Trek*. The collectible value of these largely self-published works is more personal than negotiable, particularly where a photocopy is just as good as an original.

ST4000	*Trek* magazines, ea	3 - 6
ST4010	*Star Trek Files Magazines*, ea	2 - 5
ST4030	Kelly Freas art portfolio	5 - 10
ST4035	Fan produced publications	?
ST4036	"Next Generation" magazines, ea	1 - 3

Films, Slides and Viewers

ST4050	Movie viewer (1967)	8 - 20
ST4052	The Omega Glory (View-Master packet)	8 - 12
ST4054	Talking View-Master packet	8 - 12
ST4056	Show Beam cartridge	8 - 12
ST4058	NG View-Master packet	3 - 6

Frisbees

ST4075 Frisbee (Remco, 1967)   5 - 15

Fun Meal Boxes and Prizes

McDonald's fun meal boxes were used as a movie tie-in promotion in Dec 1979. Six different colorfully illustrated boxes were used. An exceptional group of prizes were found inside. Several different point-of-purchase signs and tray placemats were part of the promotion.

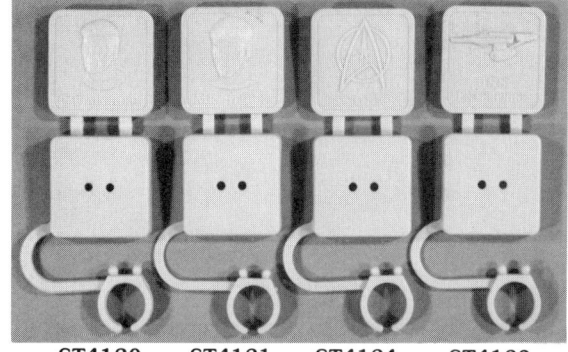

105

ST4100

ST4101

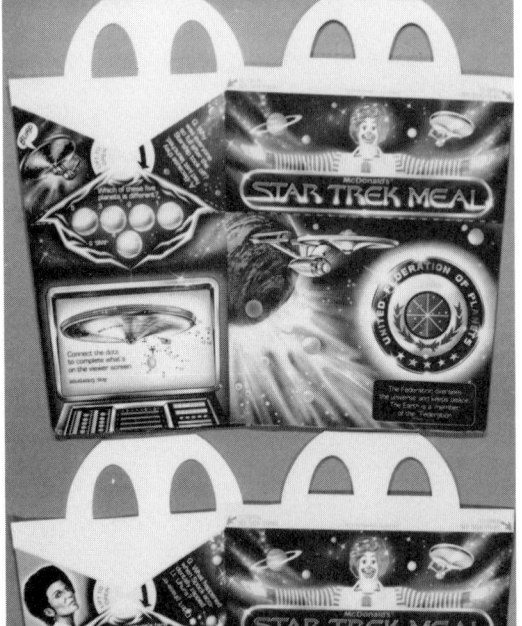

ST4102

ST4103

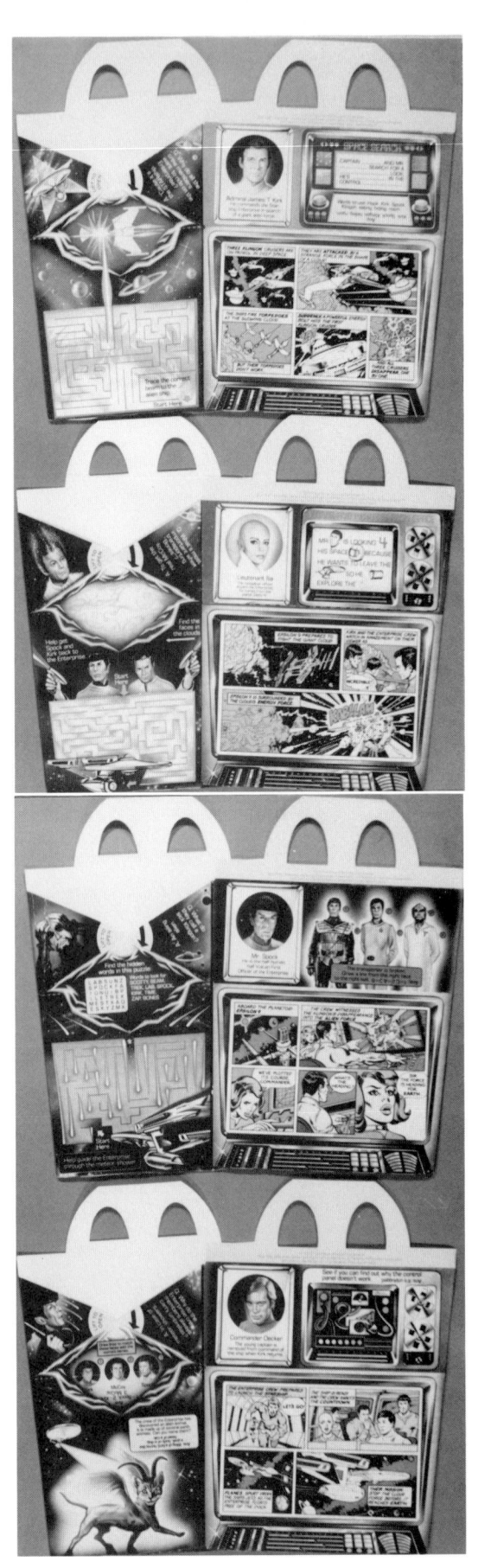

106

ST4100-05 Fun Meal boxes, 6 different, ea	2 - 5
ST4111 Starfleet paperboard game w/unpunched pieces	2 - 5
ST4112 Iron-on transfer of McCoy or Ilia, ea	1 - 2
ST4114 Video Communicator w/5 strips	2 - 5

Rings ST4120-24, 5 different in light blue or yellow plastic, snap together

ST4120 Kirk	2 - 5
ST4121 Spock	2 - 5
ST4122 McCoy	2 - 5
ST4123 *Enterprise*	2 - 5
ST4124 *Star Trek* logo	2 - 5
ST4130 Wrist bracelet	2 - 6
ST4131 Placemat	1 - 3
ST4132 *Enterprise* mobile	2 - 5

ST4104

Games

Board and card games have been manufactured throughout the years by Ideal, Hasbro, Milton Bradley, and Mego. The phaser games by Mego are also popular collector's items. Sega manufactured a full-sized arcade game in regular and cockpit-style sizes. Sar Fleet Battles by Task Force Games and *Star Trek* Role-Playing Game by FASA have also been

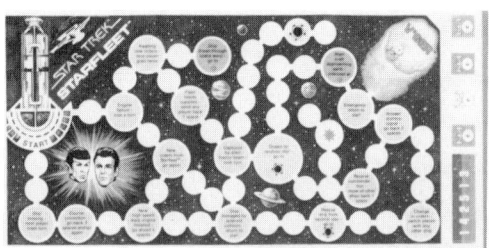

ST4105

107

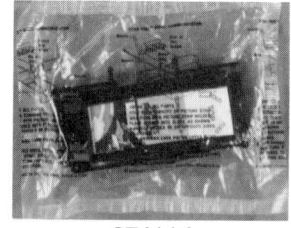

ST4180  ST4175

ST4165 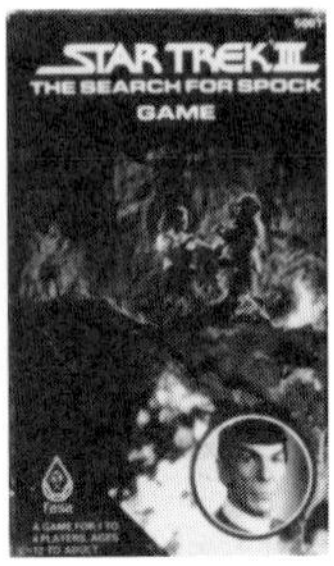 ST4450  ST4155

ST4338  ST4338  ST4341

ST4311  ST4231  ST4252  ST4242

a major source of games.

ST4150	Board game (Ideal, 1967)	60 - 125
ST4155	Board game (Hasbro, 1974)	15 - 50
ST4160	Phaser battle game (Mego)	20 - 65
ST4165	Phaser II target game (Mego, 1976)	20 - 65
ST4170	Fizzbin card game (1976)	15 - 35
ST4175	STTMP board game (Milton Bradley, 1979)	15 - 30
ST4178	Game cloth (Avalon)	10 - 20
ST4180	Trivia game	10 - 20
ST4185-86	Arcade game, 2 sizes (Sega), ea	400 - 1000
ST4187	Computer game	5 - 15

Star Fleet Battles ST4205-25 (Task Force)

ST4205	Pouch game, first edition	20 - 30
ST4206	Original boxed set	20 - 30

Supplements to boxed set ST4207-25

ST4207	Volume 1 (1983)	22 - 25
ST4208	Volume 2 (1984)	22 - 25
ST4209	Volume 3 (1985)	22 - 25
ST4210	Federation and Empire (1986)	30 - 36
ST4211	Battlecards	8 - 10
ST4212	Terrain maps	13 - 15
ST4213	Commander's SSD books, #1-9, ea	6 - 8
ST4214	Star Fleet Battle Update #2, #3032	7 - 9
ST4215	Megahex, #3033	13 - 15
ST4216	Megahex II, #3034	13 - 15
ST4217	Captain's Log #1, #3004	5 - 7
ST4218	Introduction to Star Fleet Battles, #3000	6 - 8
ST4219	Star Fleet Battles Reinforcements, #3024	7 - 8
ST4220	Captain's Logs #2-4, ea	5 - 7
ST4221	Captain's Log #5, #3026	5 - 7
ST4222	Captain's Log #6, #3027	5 - 7
ST4223	Captain's Log #7, #3028	5 - 7
ST4224	Federation and Empire, second edition, 1990	35 - 40
ST4225	Federation and Empire Conversion, for first to second edition	13 - 15

Role-playing games ST4230-4302 (FASA)

ST4230	Basic set, original edition	15 - 25
ST4231	Basic set, second edition	10 - 15
ST4232	Deluxe edition	15 - 30
ST4233	*U.S.S. Enterprise* deck plans	8 - 18
ST4234	Klingon D-7 deck plans	10 - 15
ST4236	*The Triangle*	5 - 10
ST4237	*The Triangle Campaign*	5 - 10
ST4238	*The Vanished*	3 - 7
ST4240	*Witness for the Defense*	3 - 7
ST4242	*Denial of Destiny*	3 - 7
ST4244	*Termination: 1456*	5 - 12
ST4246	*Demand of Honor*	3 - 10
ST4248	*The Orion Ruse*	3 - 7
ST4250	*Margin of Profit*	3 - 7
ST4252	*The Outcasts*	3 - 7
ST4254	*A Matter of Priorities*	3 - 7
ST4256	*A Doomsday Like Any Other*	3 - 8
ST4258	*The Mines of Selka*	3 - 8
ST4260	*Graduation Exercise*	3 - 8
ST4262	*Where Has All the Glory Gone?*	3 - 8
ST4264	*Return to Axanar/The Four Years War*	6 - 12

ST4160

ST4176

ST4187

ST4236

ST4272

ST4312

ST4237

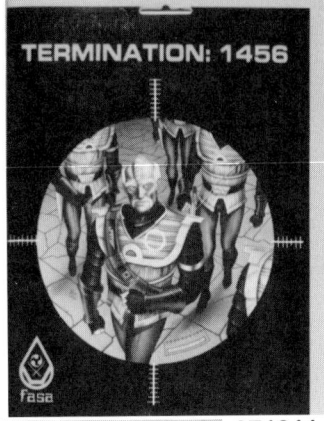

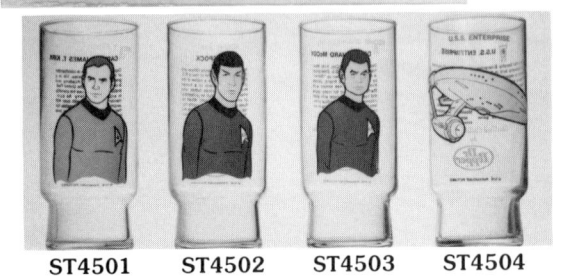

ST4266 *Decision at Midnight*	3 - 8
ST4268 *Imbalance of Power*	6 - 12
ST4270 *A Conflict of Interests/Klingon Intelligence Briefing*	6 - 12
ST4272 *The Dixie Gambit*	3 - 8
ST4274 *The White Flame*	3 - 8
ST4276 *The Strider Incident/Regula I* deck plans	6 - 12
ST4300 "Next Generation" First Year Sourcebook	5 - 10
ST4302 "Star Trek: The Next Generation" U.S.S. Enterprise blueprints	5 - 10

Ship recognition manuals ST4310-13

ST4310 Klingon	4 - 8
ST4311 Federation	4 - 8
ST4312 Romulan	4 - 8
ST4313 The Gorn and Minor Races	10 - 25
ST4320 *Trader Captains and Merchant Princes*, 1st ed	4 - 12
ST4321 *Trader Captains and Merchant Princes*, 2nd ed	7 - 18
ST4325 *Ship Construction Manual*, 1st ed	3 - 12
ST4326 *Ship Construction Manual*, 2nd ed	6 - 12
ST4330 Starship Combat Hex Grid	3 - 8
ST4332 Gamemaster's kit	5 - 10
ST4334 Tricorder/Sensors Interactive Display	3 - 10
ST4336 Tactical Combat Simulator	10 - 20
ST4338 Star Trek III: Starship Combat role-playing game	8 - 15
ST4340 *Star Trek III Sourcebook*	5 - 10
ST4341 *Star Trek III Sourcebook Update*	5 - 9
ST4342 *Star Trek IV Sourcebook*	5 - 10
ST4350 *The Klingons*, 1st ed	8 - 20
ST4351 *The Klingons*, 2nd ed	6 - 15
ST4355 *The Romulans*, 1st ed	8 - 15
ST4356 *The Romulans*, 2nd ed	6 - 12
ST4360 *The Orions*	10 - 15
ST4365 *The Federation*	6 - 14
ST4370 *Next Generation Officer's Manual*	6 - 12
ST4375 *Star Fleet Intelligence Manual*	8 - 15

Micro adventure games ST4450-53

ST4450 The Search for Spock	5 - 8
ST4451 Struggle for the Throne	5 - 8
ST4452 Starship Duel #1	5 - 8
ST4453 Starship Duel #2	5 - 8

See also: **Lead Miniatures**

Glasses

Glass collecting can be a rewarding hobby, as many good looking pieces are relatively inexpensive. The first *Star Trek* glasses were made by Dr. Pepper in 1976, with more detailed versions of the same characters appearing on a set two years later. The first and third film were accompanied by glass giveaways through fast food chains.

ST4500 Cartoon series (Dr. Pepper, 1976), Kirk, Spock, McCoy or *Enterprise*, set in presentation box	80 - 150

Individual glasses ST4501-04

ST4501 Kirk	20 - 30
ST4502 Spock	20 - 30
ST4503 McCoy	20 - 30
ST4504 *Enterprise*	20 - 30

TV series ST4505-08 (Dr. Pepper, 1978)

110

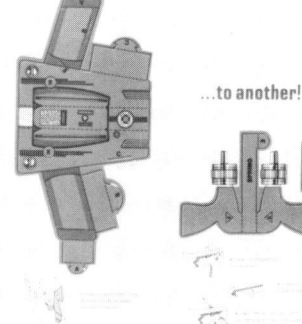

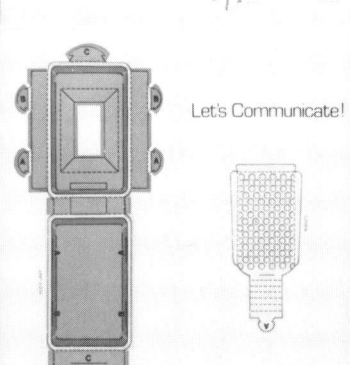

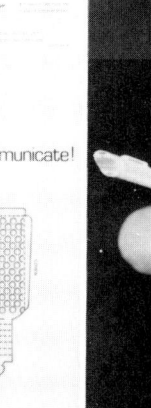

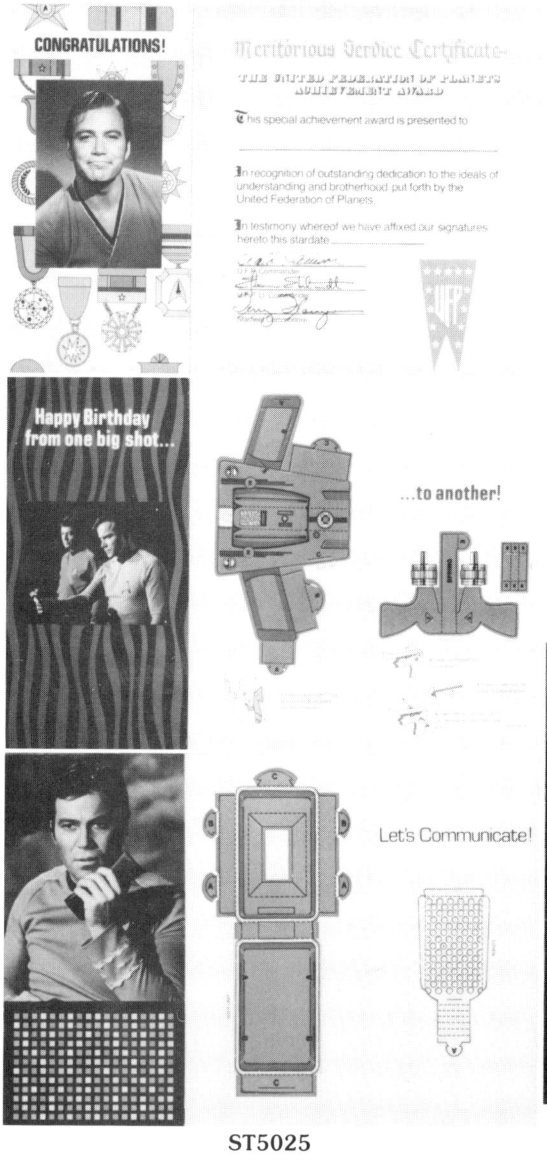

ST4505 Kirk	35 - 50
ST4506 Spock	35 - 50
ST4507 McCoy	35 - 50
ST4508 *Enterprise*	35 - 50

STTMP ST4509-11 (Coca-Cola, 1980)

ST4509 Kirk/Spock/McCoy	12 - 20
ST4510 Decker/Ilia	12 - 20
ST4511 *Enterprise*	12 - 20
ST4512 STTMP plastic tumbler	12 - 20

STIII ST4513-16 (Taco Bell, 1984)

ST4513 Lord Kruge	3 - 6
ST4514 *Enterprise* Destroyed	3 - 6
ST4515 Fal-Tor-Pan	3 - 6
ST4516 Spock Lives	3 - 6

See also: **Household Goods, Products and Miscellaneous**

Greeting Cards

A series of 24 greeting cards with *Star Trek* characters and scenes was published by Random House in 1976. The cards come in two sizes, the larger ones having punch-out items ranging from Spock's ears to paper toys.

ST5000 Small greeting cards, ea	1 - 2
ST5025 Medium greeting cards, ea	3 - 6
ST5051 Large greeting cards, unpunched, ea	4 - 8

Gum Cards, Gum Wrappers and Trading Cards

This section includes trading cards and related items offered in stores, as well as premium cards found in bread or similar offers. The Leaf black and white gum

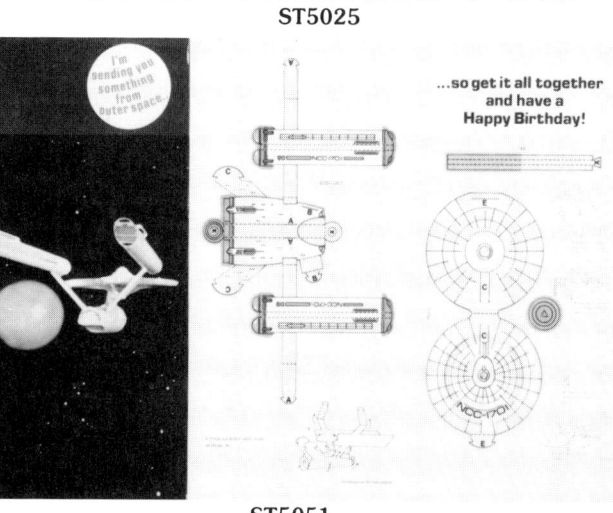

ST5100

ST5102

ST5112

ST5142

ST5154

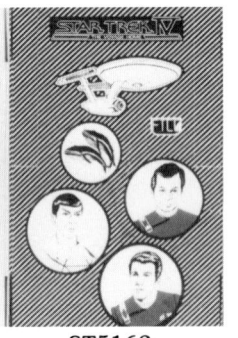

ST5162

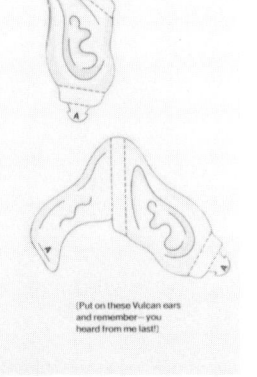

ST5051

ST5130

112

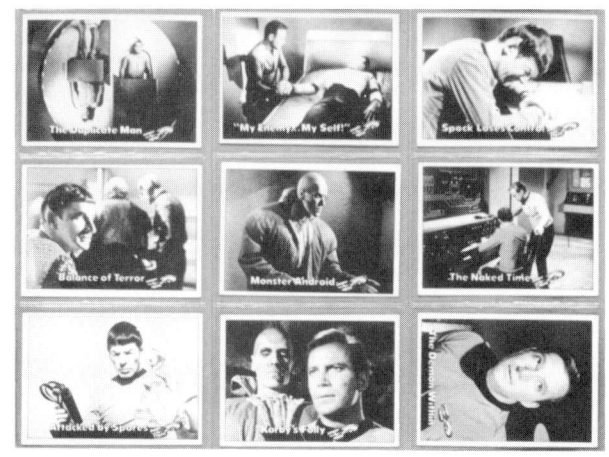

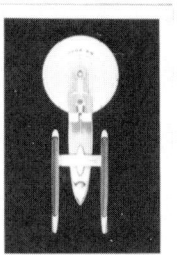

card set is one of the most sought-after items by *Star Trek* and card collectors. Topps published a set of card for the TV series during the popularity resurgence of the mid-seventies, as well as a set for the movie. *Star Trek II: The Wrath of Khan* inspired an oversized set of 5" x 7" photocards. Instead of stickers, the *Star Trek III* set included 20 laminated cards depicting various views of starships from the film, which are prized by collectors. In addition to the cards themselves, some people also collect the original boxes and wrappers, as well as unopened packages. Cards and stickers from the same set are listed separately.

ST5100	Black and white trading cards, set of 72 (Leaf, 1967)	250 - 700
ST5101	Individual cards, ea	5 - 10
ST5102	Box for ST5100	500 - 750
ST5103	Wrappers for ST5100	20 - 100
ST5104	Unopened waxpacks for ST5100	100 - 200
ST5110	TV trading cards, set of 88 (Topps, 1976)	15 - 45
ST5111	Individual TV trading cards, ea	.25 - .80
ST5112	Stickers for ST4360, set of 22 (Topps, 1976)	12 - 25
ST5113	Individual stickers, ea	.50 - 1
ST5114	Box for ST5110	5 - 15
ST5115	Wrappers for ST5110	1 - 2
ST5116	Unopened waxpacks for ST5110	2 - 5
ST5130	STTMP trading cards, set of 88 (Topps, 1979)	5 - 10
ST5131	Individual trading cards, ea	.05 - .10
ST5132	Stickers for ST5130, set of 22 (Topps, 1979)	9 - 11
ST5133	Individual stickers, ea	.25 - .50
ST5134	Box for ST5130	3 - 5
ST5135	Wrappers for ST5130	.55 - 1
ST5136	Unopened waxpacks for ST5130	1 - 2
ST5140	STII 5" x 7" cards, set of 30 (FTCC)	15 - 35
ST5141	Individual cards, ea	.50 - .75
ST5142	Box for ST5140	2 - 5
ST5143	Plastic bag wrappers for ST5140	.50 - 1
ST5144	Unopened packs for ST5140	1 - 2
ST5150	STIII trading cards, set of 60 (FTCC)	10 - 20
ST5151	Individual trading cards, ea	.05 - .50
ST5152	STIII laminated ship cards, set of 20 (FTCC)	5 - 12
ST5153	Individual ship cards, ea	.07 - .15
ST5154	Box for ST5150-53	3 - 6
ST5155	Plastic bag wrappers for ST5150-53	.50 - 1
ST5156	Unopened packs for ST5150-53	2 - 4
ST5160	STIV trading cards, set of 60	5 - 10
ST5161	Individual trading cards, ea	.07 - .15
ST5162	Box for ST5160	2 - 6
ST5163	Wrappers for ST5160	1 - 2
ST5164	Unopened waxpacks for ST5160	1 - 3

Guns — see Phasers, Guns, and Other Play Weapons

Hats and Caps

ST5200	Helmet (Enco)	30 - 75

ST5300

ST5410

ST5340

Household Goods, Products and Miscellaneous

This category includes household items and other goods not listed elsewhere. If you have an oddball item, this is a good place to start.

ST5300	Freezicle set (1975)	25 - 40
ST5301	Bowl, mug, and glass set (Deka, 1975)	10 - 20
ST5302	STTMP bandages	5 - 10
ST5303	STTMP first aid kit	6 - 15
ST5304	STTMP beanbag chair	20 - 35
ST5305	ST5 marshmallow dispenser	10 - 20

Inflatables
ST5325	Spock bop bag (AHI, 1975)	20 - 45
ST5326	STIV *Enterprise* display	10 - 20

Iron-On Appliques and Transfers

Four iron-on transfers were offered as premiums by General Mills in 1979. There were also iron-on fun meal premiums (see Fun Meal Boxes and Prizes).

General Mills transfers ST4480-83
ST5330	Kirk	1 - 3
ST5331	Spock	1 - 3
ST5332	Kirk and Spock	1 - 3
ST5333	*Enterprise*	1 - 3

Jewelry (except rings)

This is an area where there are many fan-produced items. Many pins and uniform decorations might also be considered jewelry by some. Of the licensed jewelry, the General Mills I.D. bracelet is probably the most common.

ST5340	I.D. bracelet (General Mills premium)	5 - 10
ST5342	*Enterprise* pendant	5 - 15
ST5350	Coin pendant, gold plate (Rarities Mint, 1989)	15 - 30
ST5351	Coin pendant, sterling silver (Rarities Mint, 1989)	10 - 25

Keychains and Cases

A set of Lucite keychains was made for *Star Trek: The Motion Picture*. A coin-style keychain was later

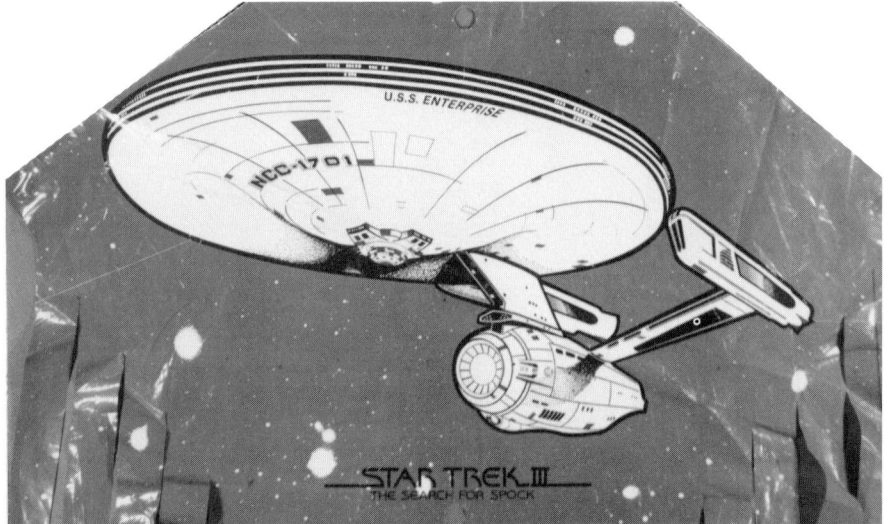

ST5435

ST5507

114

ST5508 **ST5521**

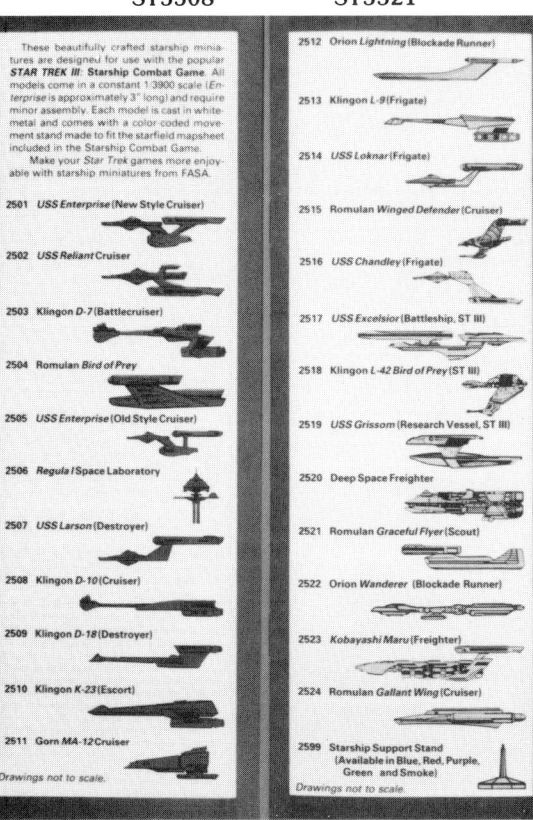

ST5500-23

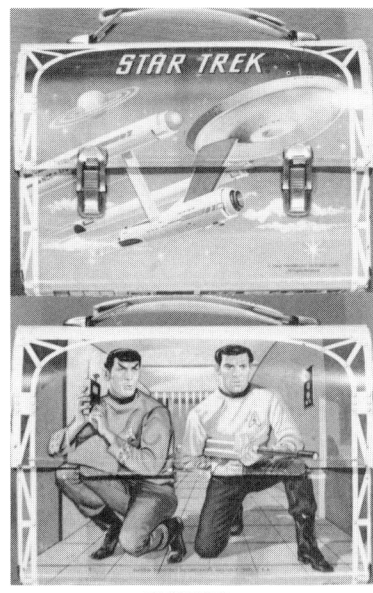

ST5600

offered through the fan club.

STTMP lucite keychains ST5410-5415
ST5410	"Live Long and Prosper"	1 - 4
ST5411	Spock/STTMP	1 - 4
ST5412	Kirk/Spock/*Enterprise*	1 - 4
ST5413	Spock/Insignia	1 - 4
ST5414	Vulcan Salute	1 - 4
ST5415	*Enterprise*	1 - 4
ST5420	Spock/*Enterprise* gold plate coin keyholder (Rarities Mint, 1989)	15 - 30
ST5421	Spock/*Enterprise* rhodium plate coin keyholder (Rarities Mint, 1989)	10 - 20

Kites
ST5435	STIII kite	10 - 20

Lead Miniatures

Heritage Models made a line of 25mm crew and alien figures in 1978-79. Citidal Miniatures made 25mm and 54mm lead figures the same years in conjunction with STTMP.

Minatures of *Star Trek* ships were produced by Task Force and FASA for use with each company's role-playing game. Part of the Task Force line was plastic (*Enterprise*, Scount, 3 engine Dreadnought and tug), but the Kingon, Romulan, Orion and ISC Races ship were lead.

Task Force figures were discontinued in 1988. FASA apparently acquired all rights to miniature figures at that time and produced 1/3900 scale reproductions. Each miniature has a hexagonal plastic base ded for the same scale Tactical Combat Simulator grid.

ST5450	Crew figures, 25mm (Heritage Models) ea	8 - 10
ST5460	Alien figures, 25mm (Heritage Models) ea	8 - 10
ST5464	STTMP 25mm figures (Citidal Miniatures)	10 - 20
ST5470	Kirk, 54mm (Citidal Miniatures)	10 - 20
ST5471	Spock, 54mm (Citidal Miniatures)	10 - 20
ST5472	Ilia, 54mm (Citidal Miniatures)	10 - 20
ST5473	Klingon warrior, 54mm (Citidal Miniatures)	10 - 20
ST5480	*Enterprise*, plastic (Task Force)	6 - 10
ST5481	Scout, plastic (Task Force)	6 - 10
ST5482	3 engine Dreadnought, plastic (Task Force)	6 - 10
ST5483	Tug, plastic (Task Force)	6 - 10
ST5484	Klingon ship, lead (Task Force)	6 - 10
ST5485	Romulan ship, lead (Task Force)	6 - 10
ST5486	Orion ship, lead (Task Force)	6 - 10
ST5487	Ship for ISC Races, lead (Task Force)	6 - 10
ST5500	*U.S.S. Enterprise* (movie version)	3 - 5
ST5501	*U.S.S. Reliant*	3 - 5
ST5502	Klingon D-7	3 - 5
ST5503	Romulan Bird of Prey	3 - 5
ST5504	*U.S.S. Enterprise* (TV)	3 - 5
ST5505	*Regula I* Space Lab/Defense Outpost	3 - 5
ST5506	*U.S.S. Larson*	3 - 5
ST5507	Klingon D-10	3 - 5
ST5508	Klingon D-18	3 - 5
ST5509	Klingon K-23	3 - 5
ST5510	Gorn MA-12	3 - 5

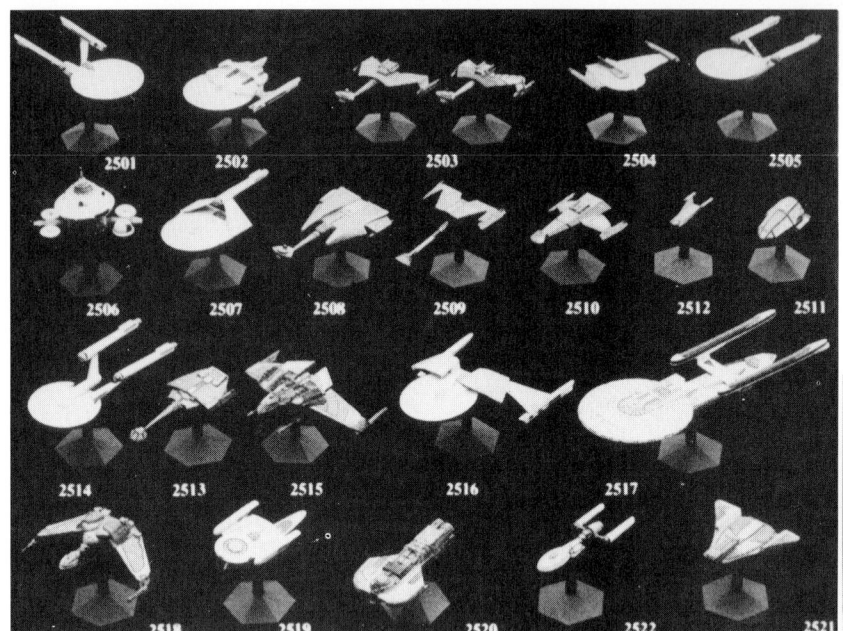

ST5500-23

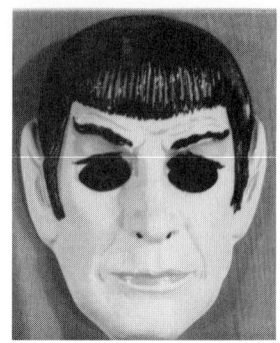

ST5676

ST5651

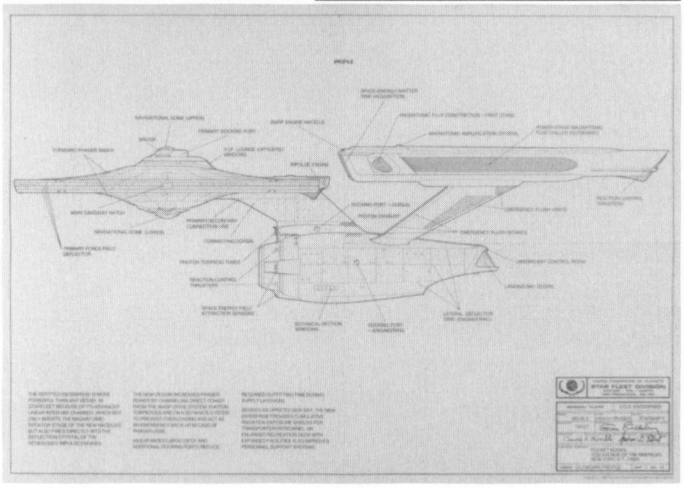

ST5650

ST5511	Orion Blockade Runner	3 - 5
ST5512	Klingon L-9	3 - 5
ST5513	U.S.S. Loknar	3 - 5
ST5514	Romulan Winged Defender	3 - 5
ST5515	U.S.S. Chandley	3 - 5
ST5516	U.S.S. Excelsior	6 - 12
ST5517	Klingon L-42	3 - 5
ST5518	U.S.S. Grissom	3 - 5
ST5519	Deep Space Freighter	3 - 5
ST5520	Romulan Graceful Flyer	3 - 5
ST5521	Orion Wanderer	3 - 5
ST5522	Kobayashi Maru	3 - 5
ST5523	Romulan Gallant Wing	3 - 5
ST5524	Gorn Battleship	6 - 12
ST5525	U.S.S. Baker	3 - 5
ST5526	Romulan Nova	6 - 12
ST5527	Romulan Bright One	3 - 5
ST5528	Klingon L-24	6 - 12
ST5529	Klingon D-2	3 - 5
ST5530	Romulan Whitewind	3 - 5
ST5531	U.S.S. Andor	3 - 5
ST5532	U.S.S. Enterprise (Galaxy Class)	6 - 12
ST5533	Ferengi Cruiser	3 - 5

License Plates

ST5545	*Enterprise* license plate	10 - 30

Lunch Boxes

Lunch box collecting is a popular but expensive field. Boxes and bottles were originally sold as a set, but these items tend to become separated.

ST5600	TV lunch box (Aladdin, 1968)	100 - 400
ST5601	Bottle for ST5600	40 - 100
ST5610	STTMP lunch box (King Seely Thermos, 1980)	25 - 50
ST5611	Bottle for ST5610	15 - 30
ST5620	NG lunch box (Halsey Taylor/ Thermos)	5 - 10
ST5621	Bottle for ST5620	2 - 4

Magazines with *Star Trek* Articles

This category includes magazine articles appearing in various periodicals, as well as licensed *Star Trek* magazines. It does not include fanzines or other non-licensed publications. In the case of non-Trek periodicals, cover stories bring a higher value.

116

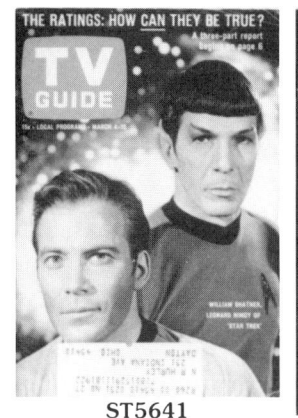

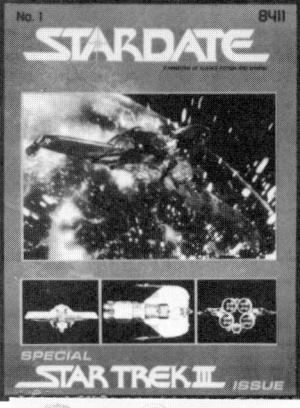

ST5640 Licensed Trek magazines   2 - 10
ST5641 Magazines w/Trek covers   2 - 10
ST5642 Magazines w/Trek articles   1 - 2
See also: **Fan Club Kits and Publications**

Maps
ST5650 Blueprints   8 - 12
ST5651 *Star Trek* map set (Bantam, 1980) 5 - 15
See also: **Games**

Masks
ST5675 Adult Spock mask   25 - 50
ST5676 Ben Cooper masks   2 - 5
See also: **Costumes and Play Outfits**

Mobile
The Action Fleet mobile was a mail-in and store distributed premium in 1979. It was a cardboard punch-out kit consisting of the *U.S.S. Enterprise*, Klingon Cruiser, Vulcan Shuttle, Work Bee, and Travel Pod space vehicles. A Fleet Specification Guide poster was also included.

ST5750 Action Fleet, complete in envelope   5 - 20
See also: **Fun Meal Boxes and Prizes for McDonald's display mobile**

Model Kits
AMT is the only known licensee for *Star Trek* model kits. Most of the older kits are rare (especially the alien vessels), but those including the *Enterprise* are

117

ST6088

ST6084

ST6087

ST6090

ST6091

ST6110

ST6092

ST6130

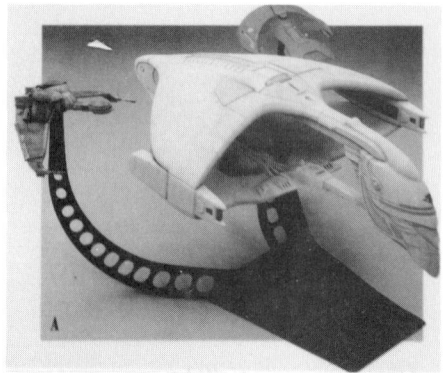

ST6181

118

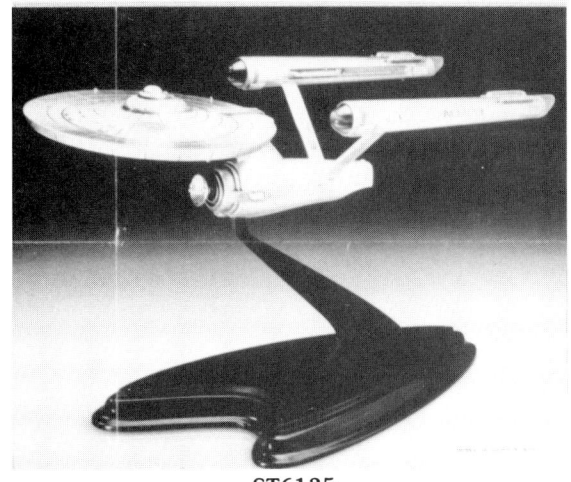

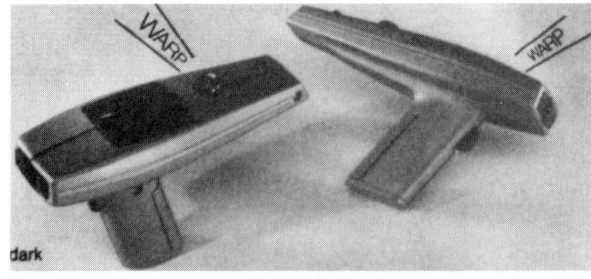

very common. The Starship set is the most common, and continued to be sold for many years after its first appearance in 1976. The film version of the *Enterprise* was re-released in an upgraded box with each new movie. The decals were changed to read NCC-1701A for the *Star Trek IV* version, and a shuttlecraft was added for *Star Trek V*.

ST6070	*U.S.S. Enterprise*, TV version w/lights (AMT, 1967)	60 - 125
ST6071	Klingon Battle Cruiser w/lights (1967)	50 - 75
ST6072	Mr. Spock, large box (1968)	50 - 100
ST6073	Mr. Spock, small box (1968)	25 - 65
ST6077	Exploration set, large box (1974)	20 - 35
ST6078	Exploration set, small box (1974)	15 - 35
ST6080	Romulan Bird of Prey (1974)	15 - 35
ST6082	Galileo Shuttlecraft	15 - 35
ST6084	*U.S.S. Enterprise* bridge (1975)	25 - 50
ST6086	K-7 Space Station (1976)	25 - 50
ST6087	*U.S.S. Enterprise*	15 - 30
ST6088	Starship Set: *Enterprise*, Klingon D-7, and Romulan Bird of Prey (1976)	4 - 10
ST6089	ST6088, revised box (1989)	3 - 6
ST6090	STTMP *Enterprise* (1979)	40 - 80
ST6091	STTMP Vulcan Shuttle (1979)	15 - 35
ST6092	STTMP Klingon Cruiser (1979)	15 - 35
ST6093	STTMP Mr. Spock (1979)	10 - 25
ST6100	STII *Enterprise* (1982)	10 - 20
ST6110	STIII *Enterprise* (1984)	5 - 15
ST6120	STIV *Enterprise* (1986)	5 - 15
ST6130	ST5 *Enterprise* and Shuttle (1989)	5 - 15
ST6135	*Enterprise* pewter model	100 - 150
ST6175	NG *Enterprise*	5 - 15
ST6180	3 Piece *U.S.S. Enterprise* set	5 - 15
ST6181	3 Piece Adversary set	5 - 15

See also: **Rocket Kits**

Molding Kits

ST6220	Mix 'N Mold casting sets: Kirk, Spock, or McCoy, ea	20 - 45

Mugs

ST6275	Ceramic steins (Image Products) Kirk or Spock, ea	10 - 40
ST6279	STII mugs: Kirk, Spock, Khan or crew, ea	3 - 5
ST6283	Mugs reprinting scenes from collector's plates: Kirk, Spock, McCoy, Scotty, Sulu, Uhura, Chekov or crew, ea	3 - 5
ST6290	Transporter magic mug	6 - 12

See also: **Household Goods, Products and Miscellaneous**

Party Supplies and Hats

Matching party supplies based on the animated series were produced by Party Creations/Tuttle Press in 1976.

ST6350	Plates, 6-3/4"	2 - 5
ST6351	Plates, 9"	2 - 5
ST6352	Paper cups	2 - 5
ST6353	Napkins	2 - 5

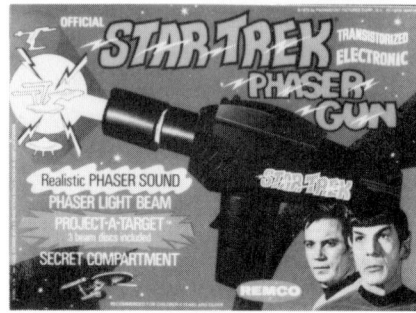

ST6354	Table cover	5 - 10
ST6355	Candy cake decorations	2 - 5

Patches
Licensed patches were produced in 1975, based on the animated series, and in conjunction with *Star Trek: The Motion Picture*. In addition, there are many fan-produced and independent patches. Many continue to be produced.

Emblem patches ST6370-77 (1975)
ST6370	Kirk	15 - 35
ST6371-72	Spock (2 versions)	15 - 35
ST6373	Uhura	15 - 35
ST6374	Federation emblem	15 - 35
ST6375	Phaser	15 - 35
ST6376	NCC-1701	15 - 35
ST6377	Uniform stripe	15 - 35

STTMP patches ST6390-95 (1979)
ST6390-91	Kirk (2 versions)	10 - 30
ST6392-93	Spock (2 versions)	10 - 30
ST6394	Kirk and Spock	10 - 30
ST6395	Kirk/Spock/McCoy	10 - 30
ST6400	Fan club patches	5 - 15

Patterns
Patterns have been produced for every version of the *Star Trek* uniforms, although many of these are independent productions. Licensed patterns for "Next Generation" jumpsuits were printed by Simplicity.

ST6450	Patterns, ea	4 - 10

Phasers, Guns and Other Play Weapons
The famous phaser gun has been reproduced numerous times. If you can't find a particular piece here, it may be part of a game or playset. This section includes only officially licensed merchandise, not homemade replicas.

ST6460	Tracer gun (1966)	10 - 50
ST6461	Tracer scope (1966)	20 - 65
ST6462	Jet Discs blister pack (1966)	12 - 25
ST6465	Projection Phaser	50 - 150
ST6468	Phaser Saucer gun (AHI, 1975)	15 - 35
ST6469	Phaser Ray gun	15 - 35
ST6475	"U.S.S. Enterprise" water gun	15 - 35
ST6478	STTMP Dual Phaser II set (South Bend, 1979)	20 - 45
ST6480	STTMP Signal gun	20 - 45
ST6482	STTMP water pistol	20 - 40
ST6495	NG Phasers (Lewis Galoob Toy Co.)	10 - 25

See also: **Belts and Buckles; Games**

Pinback Buttons, Badges and Tabs
Licensed *Star Trek* buttons were produced in conjunction with several of the films. Button collecting has been confounded by the spread of inexpensive button-making machines, enabling a large variety of fan-produced items. Photographic reproduction is the most common means of producing counterfeit buttons, and can sometimes be detected by small developing flaws. Color photocopies are less common, as they are easily spotted by their muddier image. A num-

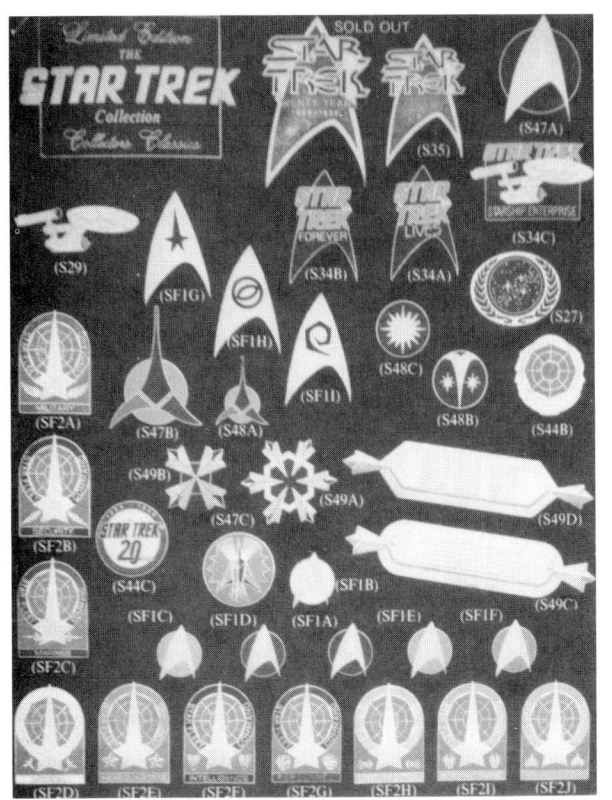

ber of insignia pins have been produced by assorted independent companies, but these are of little interest to most collectors, as their continual manufacture make them poor investments. A limited edition set of pins made by Collector's Classics was marketed through the fan club.

STTMP buttons ST6600-06 (Aviva, 1979)
ST6600-02 Kirk (3 versions)	1 - 3
ST6603-04 Spock (2 versions)	1 - 3
ST6605 Kirk/Spock/McCoy	1 - 3
ST6606 Crew	1 - 3

STTMP metal pins ST6607-14 (Aviva, 1979)
ST6607 Kirk	3 - 6
ST6608 Spock	3 - 6
ST6609 McCoy	3 - 6
ST6610-11 *Enterprise* (2 versions)	3 - 6
ST6612-13 Vulcan Salute (2 versions)	3 - 6
ST6614 Insignia	3 - 6

STII buttons ST6620-24 (Image Products, 1982)
ST6620 Kirk	1 - 3
ST6621 Spock	1 - 3
ST6622 Crew	1 - 3
ST6623 Khan	1 - 3
ST6624 *Enterprise*	1 - 3

STIII buttons ST6630-42 (Button-Up Co., 1984)
ST6630-31 Kirk (2 versions)	1 - 3
ST6632-33 Spock (2 versions)	1 - 3
ST6634 McCoy	1 - 3
ST6635 Sulu	1 - 3
ST6636 Uhura	1 - 3
ST6637 Chekov	1 - 3
ST6638 Savvik	1 - 3
ST6639 David	1 - 3
ST6640-41 Kruge (2 versions)	1 - 3
ST6642 Logo	1 - 3

Collector's classics pins ST6660-6727 (1989)
ST6660 Communicator pin	10 - 15
ST6661 Communicator pin (half size)	5 - 10
ST6662 NCC-1701D call letters pin	4 - 8
ST6663 United Federation of Planets pin (NG)	3 - 6
ST6664 *Enterprise* cut-out pin (NG)	4 - 8
ST6665 *Enterprise* cut-out pin (TV)	3 - 6
ST6666 Next Generation logo pin, blue	3 - 6
ST6667 Next Generation logo pin, red	3 - 6
ST6668 Star Trek Lives pin	4 - 8
ST6669 Star Trek Forever pin	4 - 8
ST6670 Star Trek w/*Enterprise*	4 - 8
ST6671 Star Trek Twenty Years insignia pin	4 - 8
ST6672 Star Trek theme pin	5 - 10
ST6673 Next Generation cast and crew pin	3 - 6
ST6674 Command pin, green	3 - 6
ST6675 Command pin, dark maroon	3 - 6
ST6676 Command pin, yellow	3 - 6
ST6677 Starbase 74 pin	3 - 6
ST6678 *Star Trek V* on symbol	4 - 8
ST6679 *Star Trek V* w/*Enterprise* in triangle	4 - 8
ST6680 *Star Trek V* w/*Enterprise* on top	5 - 10
ST6681 *Star Trek V* w/Galileo on top	5 - 10
ST6682 *Star Trek V* logo pin	3 - 6
ST6683 *Star Trek V* symbol	3 - 6
ST6684 Galileo lettering	3 - 6
ST6685 Galileo name w/ship	5 - 10
ST6686 Special UFP—Starfleet Command	4 - 8
ST6687 United Federation of Planets Crest	4 - 8
ST6688 *Star Trek* 20th Anniversary, round	3 - 6
ST6689 Ferengi symbol	1 - 4
ST6690 Ferengi DaiMon symbol	3 - 6
ST6691 Starfleet Command symbol	4 - 8
ST6692 Klingon symbol, large	4 - 8
ST6693 Romulan Crest, large	4 - 8
ST6694 Klingon symbol, small	3 - 6
ST6695 Klingon ranks "Admiral" (2 star)	3 - 6
ST6696 Klingon ranks "Captain" (1 large star)	3 - 6
ST6697 Klingon ranks "Flag Admiral"	4 - 8
ST6698 Klingon ranks "Admiral"	3 - 6
ST6700 Klingon ranks "Commodore"	4 - 8
ST6701 Klingon ranks "Captain"	4 - 8
ST6702 Star Fleet Command Exec. Insignia, Command Div., maroon	3 - 6
ST6703 Star Fleet Command Exec. Insignia, Command Div., white	3 - 6
ST6704 Star Fleet Command Exec. Insignia, Engineering Div., yellow	3 - 6
ST6705 Star Fleet Command Exec. Insignia, Security Div., red	3 - 6
ST6706 Star Fleet Command Exec. Insignia, Medical Div., green	3 - 6
ST6707 Star Fleet Command Exec. Insignia, Science Div., blue	3 - 6
ST6708 Star Fleet Command Gold Symbol Executive (black star)	3 - 6
ST6709 Star Fleet Command Gold Symbol Science (black symbol)	3 - 6
ST6710 Star Fleet Command Gold Symbol Eng. (black symbol)	3 - 6
ST6711 Starfleet Branch pin, "Military"	4 - 8
ST6712 Starfleet Branch pin, "Security"	4 - 8
ST6713 Starfleet Branch pin, "Marines"	4 - 8
ST6714 Starfleet Branch pin, "Medical"	4 - 8

ST6715 Starfleet Branch pin, "Headquarters" 4 - 8
ST6716 Starfleet Branch pin, "Intelligence" 4 - 8
ST6717 Starfleet Branch pin, "Personnel" 4 - 8
ST6718 Starfleet Branch pin, "Communications" 4 - 8
ST6719 Starfleet Branch pin, "Merchant Marine" 4 - 8
ST6720 Starfleet Branch pin, "Engineering" 4 - 8
ST6721 Caution Force Field pin 3 - 6
ST6722 Caution Anti Matter pin 3 - 6
ST6723 "Make It So" pin 3 - 6
ST6724 "Fully Functional" pin 3 - 6
ST6725 Borg Emblem 3 - 6
ST6726 Phaser Gun (TV) 4 - 8
ST6727 Communicator (TV) 4 - 8

ST6905   ST6902

ST6908

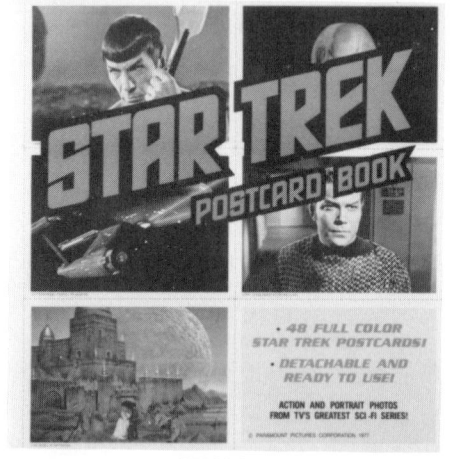

ST6980

Plates

A set of collector's plates was produced by Ernst Enterprises depicting assorted characters from the series. A second set depicting scenes from original episodes was also made, and a "Next Generation" set was recently announced.

Collector's plates ST6900-08 (Ernst Enterprises)
ST6900 Kirk 15 - 30
ST6901 Spock 15 - 30
ST6902 McCoy 15 - 30
ST6903 Scotty 15 - 30
ST6904 Sulu 15 - 30
ST6905 Uhura 15 - 30
ST6906 Chekov 15 - 30
ST6907 Crew on Transporter 15 - 30
ST6908 10-1/4" plate w/crew and
       Enterprise 25 - 45

Second series plates ST6910-17
ST6910 The Trouble With Tribbles 15 - 30
ST6911 Mirror, Mirror 30 - 75
ST6912 A Piece of the Action 15 - 30
ST6913 The Devil in the Dark 15 - 30
ST6914 Amok Time 15 - 30
ST6915 The City on the Edge of Forever 30 - 75
ST6916 Journey to Babel 15 - 30
ST6917 The Menagerie 15 - 30
ST6919 Star Trek V 40 - 50
ST6920 NG: Picard, Data or others, ea 15 - 30

See also: **Party Supplies and Hats for paper plates**

Playing Cards

A deck of regular playing cards was produced for *Star Trek: The Wrath of Khan*, using a different photo from the movie on the face of ea card.

ST6952 STII playing cards 4 - 10

ST7029

122

ST6952

ST6990 ST6992 ST6994 ST7002 ST7004

ST7030

ST7029

ST6984

123

Playsets

A few playsets were manufactured by Mego, and are fairly difficult to find. The Command Communications Console is compatible with the communicators (see **Walkie Talkies**).

ST6960	Telescreen Console	50 - 135
ST6961	Transporter Room	50 - 135
ST6962	Command Communications Console (Mego, 1976)	75 - 150

Postcards

ST6980	TV postcard book (1977)	5 - 15
ST6982	STTMP postcard set (1979)	25 - 35
ST6984	STIII postcard book	2 - 5

Posters - Film

Movie posters were issued for the original release of the film, reprints from the original plates, smaller versions of the release posters, video store versions, and collector reprints for sale in Paramount's mail order memorabilia catalog. The art is the same on all versions, but the original release poster commands a bit more from those who can tell the difference.

ST6990	*Star Trek: The Motion Picture*	20 - 40
ST6992	*Star Trek II: The Wrath of Khan*	18 - 35
ST6994	*Star Trek III: The Search For Spock*	15 - 30
ST7000	*Star Trek IV: The Voyage Home* Teaser	15 - 30
ST7002	*Star Trek IV: The Voyage Home*	15 - 30
ST7004	*Star Trek V: The Final Frontier*	10 - 25

Posters - Other

There have been many *Star Trek* premium, art, and personality posters. Some licensed, some not. None are in great demand by collectors.

ST7029	Retail posters	5 - 15
ST7030	Premium posters	5 - 15
ST7031	Art prints	5 - 10
ST7032	Fan posters	2 - 5
ST7033	Novelty or gag posters	2 - 5

Press Kits

A press kit included news releases, background information, and b&w photos generally designed for newspaper use. Electronic media also received film clips on video tape or an audio tape with soundbites designed for radio use.

ST7150	Original "Star Trek" TV press kit	30 - 75
ST7155	*Star Trek: The Motion Picture* press kit	15 - 30
ST7156	*Star Trek II: The Wrath of Khan* press kit	10 - 20
ST7157	*Star Trek III: The Search For Spock* press kit	10 - 20
ST7158	*Star Trek IV: The Voyage Home* press kit	8 - 15
ST7159	*Star Trek V: The Final Frontier* press kit	5 - 10
ST7160	"Star Trek: The Next Generation"	8 - 15

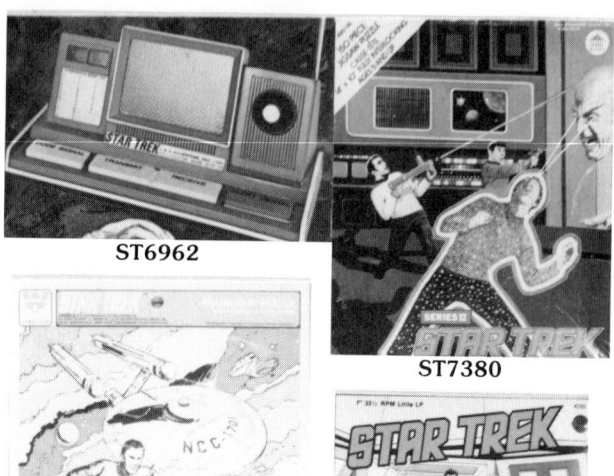

124

ST7620

ST7527

ST7532   ST7533

ST7570-7682

Programs and Official Collector's Editions
ST7270	*Star Trek: The Motion Picture* program	10 - 25
ST7271	*Star Trek II: The Wrath of Khan* program	10 - 25
ST7272	*Star Trek III: The Search For Spock* program	10 - 25
ST7273	*Star Trek IV: The Voyage Home* program	8 - 20
ST7274	*Star Trek V: The Final Frontier* program	8 - 10

Puzzles and Puzzle Sets
A number of puzzles were produced by Milton Bradley and Whitman for *Star Trek: The Motion Picture*.

ST7380	Jigsaw puzzles (H-G, 1976), ea	8 - 18

STTMP puzzles ST7390-92 (Milton Bradley, 1979)
ST7390	*Enterprise*	5 - 15
ST7391	*Faces of the Future*	5 - 15
ST7392	*Sick Bay*	5 - 15
ST7395	Tray puzzles (Whitman, 1979), ea	3 - 10

Radios, Phonographs, and Tape Players
Mego produced a cassette player "tricorder" in 1976, which included a tape of sound effects.

ST7400	Tricorder, w/cassette (Mego, 1976)	50 - 100

Records, Tapes and Compact Discs
Star Trek book and record sets were made by Peter Pan Records, and later by Buena Vista Records. In addition to film scores, several of the Pocket novels were dramatized on tape.

Power Records ST7525-27 (Peter Pan, 1975)
ST7525	Passage to Moauv	3 - 6
ST7526	The Time Stealer	3 - 6
ST7527	Large Record: A Mirror For Futility/The Time Stealer	5 - 10

Book and record sets ST7530-66
ST7530	*Star Trek* Volume I (Peter Pan, 1979)	2 - 6
ST7531	*Star Trek* Volume II: The Crier in Emptiness (Peter Pan, 1979)	2 - 5
ST7532	*Dinosaur Planet* (Peter Pan, 1979)	2 - 5
ST7533	*The Robot Masters* (Peter Pan, 1979)	2 - 5
ST7550	*Star Trek: The Motion Picture* (Buena Vista Records)	2 - 5
ST7551	Same as ST7550, but w/cassette	2 - 5
ST7555	*Star Trek II: The Wrath of Khan*	2 - 5
ST7556	Same as ST7555, but w/cassette	2 - 5
ST7560	*Star Trek III: The Search for Spock*	2 - 5
ST7561	Same as ST7560, but w/cassette	2 - 5
ST7565	*Star Trek IV: The Voyage Home*	2 - 5
ST7566	Same as ST7565, but w/cassette	2 - 5

TV and film soundtracks ST7570-7682
TV soundtrack recording: The Cage/Where No Man Has Gone Before
ST7570	Picture disc	10 - 20
ST7571	Cassette	5 - 10
ST7572	Compact disc	10 - 20

ST7555
ST7560 
ST7531
ST9010-89
ST8100
ST7850 
ST7851

Star Trek volume one: Is There In Truth No Beauty?/The Paradise Syndrome
ST7573 Record	5 - 10
ST7574 Cassette	5 - 10
ST7575 Compact disc	10 - 20

Star Trek volume two: I, Mudd/Spectre of the Gun/The Conscience of the King
ST7576 Record	5 - 10
ST7577 Cassette	5 - 10
ST7578 Compact disc	10 - 20

TV series music, volume one
ST7600 Record	5 - 10
ST7601 Cassette	5 - 10
ST7602 Compact disc	10 - 20

TV series music, volume two
ST7605 Record	5 - 10
ST7606 Cassette	5 - 10
ST7607 Compact disc	10 - 20

Star Trek: The Motion Picture
ST7620 Record	5 - 10
ST7621 Cassette	5 - 10
ST7622 Compact disc	10 - 20

Star Trek II: The Wrath of Khan
ST7630 Record	5 - 10
ST7631 Cassette	5 - 10
ST7632 Compact disc	10 - 20

Star Trek III: The Search For Spock
ST7640 Record	5 - 10
ST7641 Cassette	5 - 10
ST7642 Compact disc	10 - 20

Star Trek IV: The Voyage Home
ST7651 Record	5 - 10
ST7652 Cassette	5 - 10
ST7653 Compact disc	10 - 20

Star Trek V: The Final Frontier
ST7661 Record	5 - 10
ST7662 Cassette	5 - 10
ST7663 Compact disc	10 - 20

"Next Generation: Encounter at Farpoint" soundtrack
ST7680 Record	5 - 10
ST7681 Cassette	5 - 10
ST7682 Compact disc	10 - 20

Taped novels ST7710-20 (Pocket)
ST7710 *The Entropy Effect*	5 - 10
ST7711 *Yesterday's Son*	5 - 10
ST7712 *Strangers From the Sky*	5 - 10
ST7713 *Enterprise: The First Aventure*	5 - 10
ST7714 *Star Trek IV: The Voyage Home*	5 - 10
ST7715 *Final Frontier*	5 - 10
ST7716 *Web of the Romulans*	5 - 10
ST7717 *Star Trek V: The Final Frontier*	5 - 10
ST7718 *Time For Yesterday*	5 - 10
ST7719 *Spock's World*	5 - 10
ST7720 *The Lost Years*	5 - 10

Rocket Kits
ST7850 Starship *Enterprise* (Estes)	15 - 30
ST7851 Klingon Ship (Estes)	15 - 30

School Supplies

A set of molded erasers was produced for *Star Trek III: The Search For Spock*. Small 40 page notebooks by Reed Productions were sold through the fan club.

ST7900 STIII erasers: Kirk, Spock, McCoy,
    Scotty, Kruge, *Enterprise*, or
    Excelsior (Diener Enterprises, 1984)   3 - 7
Notebooks ST7910-13 (Reed Productions, 1989)
ST7910 Kirk and Spock   1 - 3
ST7911 Kirk and Spock/Transporter   1 - 3
ST7912 ST5 *Enterprise*   1 - 3
ST7913 ST5 crew   1 - 3

Sheets, Pillows, Bedspreads, Sleeping Bags and Drapes
ST8000 Sleeping bag   5 - 10
ST8001 Drapes   5 - 10

Spock Ears
"Original Spock Ears" come a dime a dozen—let the buyer beware. Authentic ears are not full-ear covers, but custom-designed make-up pieces to give existing ears a pointed look. Plastic costume ears are even more common, but an officially licensed version is not known.

Stamps, Collector's
ST8100 *Star Trek* stamp book   2 - 4
ST8111-16 Stamp sets for ST8100, ea   2 - 4

Stamps, Rubber
ST8120 STTMP rubber stamp   2 - 6

Stickers and Sticker Books
Panini produced a sticker set and album for "Star Trek: The Next Generation". Although these items were never officially sold in the United States, they were made available to fan club members.

ST8140 STTMP puffy stickers   1 - 3
"Instant Stained Glass" stickers ST8141-46
ST8141 "Live Long and Prosper"   1 - 3
ST8142 Spock/STTMP   1 - 3
ST8143 Kirk/Spock/*Enterprise*   1 - 3
ST8144 Spock/Insignia   1 - 3
ST8145 Vulcan Salute   1 - 3
ST8146 *Enterprise*   1 - 3
ST8155 "Next Generation" sticker series,
    set of 240   12 - 70
ST8156 Individual stickers, ea   .05 - .08
ST8157 Album for ST8155   4 - 8
ST8158 Unopened packs, ea   1 - 2
See Also: **Gum Cards, Gum Wrappers and Trading Cards**

String Art
ST8275 Battle scene   5 - 10

Towels
ST8580 Beach towel   5 - 10

Tribbles
"The Trouble With Tribbles" was one of the most popular *Star Trek* episodes. Tribbles are adorable, purring balls of fur with overactive reproductive tendencies. Homemade fan-produced tribbles seem to reproduce even faster than those which appeared on the show. Only one officially licensed version exists, produced by Mego.

ST8111-16

ST8275

ST8825   ST8827

127

ST8650 Tribble (Mego)   50 - 75

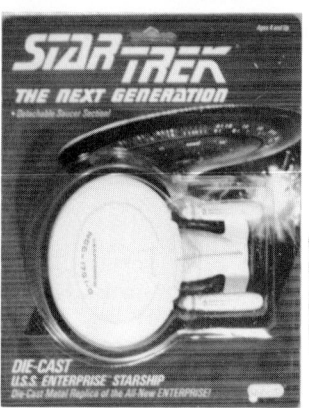

Vehicles

This category is comprised of vehicle replicas not listed elsewhere.

ST8800	Controlled Space Flight *Enterprise* (Remco, 1976)	35 - 75
ST8805	Dinky *Enterprise* (Micano)	30 - 50
ST8810	Small Dinky *Enterprise* (1979)	30 - 50
ST8811	Dinky Klingon Battlecruiser	30 - 50
ST8812	STTMP Electronic *Enterprise* (Milton Bradley/Southbend, 1979)	40 - 80
ST8813	Action Fleet Mobile (unpunched)	10 - 35
ST8815	STII Mini *Enterprise* (Corgi)	35 - 75
ST8820	STII Klingon ship (Corgi)	35 - 75
ST8825	STIII die cast *Enterprise*	35 - 75
ST8826	STIII die cast *Excelsior*	35 - 75
ST8827	STIII die cast Klingon Bird of Prey	35 - 75
ST8840	Pewter *Enterprise*	150 - 250
ST8850	NG die cast *Enterprise*	5 - 15

See also: **Action Figure Playsets, Vehicles and Accessories; Model Kits**

Video Tapes and Discs

In addition to the films, every original and animated *Star Trek* episode produced was sold commercially on video tape. Color and black & white versions of "The Cage" were also sold.

Films ST9000-09

ST9000	*Star Trek: The Motion Picture*, videocassette	10 - 20
ST9001	*Star Trek: The Motion Picture*, laser disc	15 - 30
ST9002	*Star Trek II: The Wrath of Khan*, videocassette	10 - 20
ST9003	*Star Trek II: The Wrath of Khan*, laser disc	15 - 30
ST9004	*Star Trek III: The Search For Spock*, videocassette	10 - 20
ST9005	*Star Trek III: The Search For Spock*, laser disc	15 - 30
ST9006	*Star Trek IV: The Voyage Home*, videocassette	10 - 20
ST9007	*Star Trek IV: The Voyage Home*, laser disc	15 - 30
ST9008	*Star Trek V: The Final Frontier*, videocassette	10 - 20
ST9009	*Star Trek V: The Final Frontier*, laser disc	15 - 30

Original TV series ST9010-89

ST9010	The Cage, black and white	10 - 15
ST9011	The Cage, color	10 - 15
ST9012	Where No Man Has Gone Before	10 - 15
ST9013	The Corbomite Maneuver	10 - 15
ST9014	Mudd's Women	10 - 15
ST9015	The Enemy Within	10 - 15
ST9016	The Man Trap	10 - 15
ST9017	The Naked Time	10 - 15
ST9018	Charlie X	10 - 15
ST9019	Balance of Terror	10 - 15
ST9020	What Are Little Girls Made Of?	10 - 15
ST9021	Dagger of the Mind	10 - 15
ST9022	Miri	10 - 15

ST9023	The Conscience of the King	10 - 15
ST9024	Galileo 7	10 - 15
ST9025	Court Martial	10 - 15
ST9026	The Menagerie, part 1 and 2	10 - 15
ST9027	Shore Leave	10 - 15
ST9028	The Squire of Gothos	10 - 15
ST9029	Arena	10 - 15
ST9030	The Alternative Factor	10 - 15
ST9031	All Our Yesterdays	10 - 15
ST9032	Return of the Archons	10 - 15
ST9033	A Taste of Armageddon	10 - 15
ST9034	Space Seed	10 - 15
ST9035	This Side of Paradise	10 - 15
ST9036	The Devil in the Dark	10 - 15
ST9037	Errand of Mercy	10 - 15
ST9038	The City on the Edge of Forever	10 - 15
ST9039	Operation Annihilate	10 - 15
ST9040	Catspaw	10 - 15
ST9041	Metamorphosis	10 - 15
ST9042	Friday's Child	10 - 15
ST9043	Who Mourns for Adonis?	10 - 15
ST9044	Amok Time	10 - 15
ST9045	The Doomsday Machine	10 - 15
ST9046	Wolf in the Fold	10 - 15
ST9047	The Changeling	10 - 15
ST9048	The Apple	10 - 15
ST9049	Mirror, Mirror	10 - 15
ST9050	The Deadly Years	10 - 15
ST9051	I, Mudd	10 - 15
ST9052	The Trouble With Tribbles	10 - 15
ST9053	Bread and Circuses	10 - 15
ST9054	Journey to Babel	10 - 15
ST9055	A Private Little War	10 - 15
ST9056	The Gamesters of Triskelion	10 - 15
ST9057	Obsession	10 - 15
ST9058	The Immunity Syndrome	10 - 15
ST9059	A Piece of the Action	10 - 15
ST9060	By any Other Name	10 - 15
ST9061	Return to Tomorrow	10 - 15
ST9062	Patterns of Force	10 - 15
ST9063	The Ultimate Computer	10 - 15
ST9064	Omega Glory	10 - 15
ST9065	Assignment: Earth	10 - 15
ST9066	Spectre of the Gun	10 - 15
ST9067	Elian of Troyus	10 - 15
ST9068	The Paradise Syndrome	10 - 15
ST9069	The Enterprise Incident	10 - 15
ST9070	The Children Shall Lead Them	10 - 15
ST9071	Spock's Brain	10 - 15
ST9072	Is There in Truth No Beauty?	10 - 15
ST9073	The Empath	10 - 15
ST9074	The Tholian Web	10 - 15
ST9075	For the World is Hollow and I Have Touched the Sky	10 - 15
ST9076	Day of the Dove	10 - 15
ST9077	Plato's Stepchildren	10 - 15
ST9078	Wink of an Eye	10 - 15
ST9079	That Which Survives	10 - 15
ST9080	Let That Be Your Last Battlefield	10 - 15
ST9081	Whom Gods Destroy	10 - 15
ST9082	The Mark of Gideon	10 - 15
ST9083	The Lights of Zetar	10 - 15
ST9084	The Cloud Minders	10 - 15
ST9085	The Way to Eden	10 - 15
ST9086	Requiem for Methuselah	10 - 15
ST9087	The Savage Curtain	10 - 15
ST9088	All Our Yesterdays	10 - 15
ST9089	Turnabout Intruder	10 - 15

Animated Series ST9090-9100

ST9090	More Tribbles/Infinite Vulcan	8 - 12
ST9091	Yesteryear/Beyond the Farthest Star	8 - 12
ST9092	The Survivor/The Lorelei Signal	8 - 12
ST9093	One of Our Planets is Missing/Mudd's Passion	8 - 12
ST9094	Megas-Tu/Time Trap	8 - 12
ST9095	The Slaver Weapon/The Ambergris Element	8 - 12
ST9096	Jihad/The Terratin Incident	8 - 12
ST9097	Eye of the Beholder/Once Upon a Planet	8 - 12
ST9098	Bem/Albatross	8 - 12
ST9099	Pirates of Orion/The Practical Joker	8 - 12
ST9100	Sharper than a Serpent's Tooth/Counter Clock	8 - 12

COMMUNICATORS

ST9300

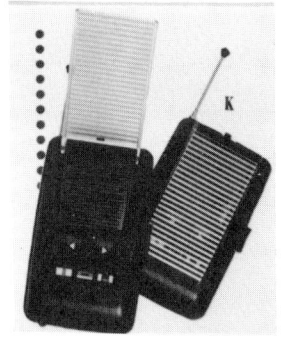

ST9305

ST9400

Walkie-Talkies

Communicator walkie-talkies were produced by Mego, sold either in a box or on a bubble-pack card. They are compatible with a larger console (see **Playsets**).

ST9300	Communicator set (Mego, 1974)	50 - 100
ST9303	STTMP Wrist Communicators	35 - 85
ST9305	Working comunicators (1989)	30 - 40

Wastebaskets

ST9320	TV wastebasket	20 - 50
ST9321	STTMP wastebasket	10 - 30

Watches

Star Trek watches were produced by Bradley. Be wary of photo watches, which can be assembled by nearly anyone.

ST9400	Spock, round face (Bradley, 1979)	60 - 125
ST9401	*U.S.S. Enterprise*, round face (Bradley, 1980)	50 - 100
ST9402	Kirk and Spock digital (Bradley, 1980)	35 - 65
ST9405	STII game watch	50 - 100
ST9410	Spock/20 Years of *Star Trek*, dimensional Spock and *Enterprise*	15 - 25
ST9417	Handpainted *Enterprise*	60 - 80
ST9418	*U.S.S. Enterprise* coin watch	50 - 100

ST9417

ST9418

STAR WARS

A short time ago, in a galaxy not too far away, a man named George Lucas created *Star Wars*. This new film revived the cliff-hanger style of early movie serials, and inspired a renewed interest in space adventure.

The *Star Wars* saga is actually comprised of three trilogies. The first film produced was episode four, *A New Hope*, released in 1977. To the world's surprise, the film was a smash hit which set new quality standards for special effects and space adventure. Despite a slow start, *Star Wars* merchandise was produced in enormous quantities. Approximately 80% of the original items were manufactured by Kenner products. *The Empire Strikes Back* (episode five, 1980) and *Return of the Jedi* (episode six, 1983) renewed interest in *Star Wars*, and inspired merchandise of their own.

Episode six was originally titled *Revenge of the Jedi*. Though the title was changed early on, several items and advance merchandise were released using the *Revenge* name. These items were quickly pulled from circulation and re-released with the new title.

The film logo shown on the box of a given item is a good indication of when it was produced. All original *Star Wars* merchandise was licensed by 20th Century Fox. Lucasfilm Ltd. retained rights to all sequels and regained merchandise rights to the *Star Wars* name prior to releasing *The Empire Strikes Back* through 20th Century Fox. Older toys were often released in new packages with the most recent film title. Although six more films were planned, the *Star Wars* saga was put on hold in favor of other projects.

In January of 1987, Star Tours opened at Disneyland in California. New merchandise was created in conjunction with this exhibit. Similar attractions were later built at Tokyo Disneyland and the Disney-MGM Studio Tour at Walt Disney World. Lucasfilm Ltd. runs shops adjacent to the Star Tours attraction at each theme park.

Due to the vast amount of merchandise produced in connection with the *Star Wars* saga, items listed here have been broken down into alphabetical categories. Code numbers begin with "SW" instead of "S". Abbreviations are often used in this section for *Star Wars* (SW), *The Empire Strikes Back* (ESB) and *Return of the Jedi* (ROTJ).

Original *Star Wars* merchandise was licensed by and copyrighted in the name of 20th Century Fox. They in turn granted a broad license to the Kenner Toy Company of Cincinnati to make toys, games, puzzles, and books. Kenner produced about 80% of all merchandise sold in the U.S. and Canada.

Virtually all Kenner *Star Wars* products were made available in England, Europe, and other English speaking countries through Palitoy of London. Palitoy also made fine items which were not available in the U.S. — a Death Star cardboard playset, Droid Factory (different bases), Creature Cantina, Jawa playset, and a talking R2-D2. Products were licensed for many other countries, most notably, Japan, which produced larger action figures and a different line of toys. Many non-Kenner products have been imported by collectors and dealers. A few examples are given, but in keeping to the scope of this guide, values are given only for items regularly sold in the U.S.

Prior to the release of the *Empire Strikes Back*, George Lucas re-acquired merchandise rights to *Star Wars* and all subsequent properties. Products produced after this period are copyrighted in the Lucasfilm name.

Action Figures

Action figures are molded plastic figurines designed for use with playsets and other accessories related to the *Star Wars* genre. They were produced by Kenner. Although similar figures had appeared before, (in connection with *Planet of the Apes*, *Space:1999*, *Star Trek* and others) none of these had matched the popularity of the *Star Wars* line.

Initially, there were complications. The original figures were not available in time for Christmas. In response to the demand, Kenner introduced the "early bird" kits. The kits came in a large cardboard envelope and contained the following items: a cardboard display stand with detachable cards and a sheet of stickers. Most important, however, was the early bird certificate. This last item was mailed to Kenner. In return, the company would send four of the original figures (Luke Skywalker, Princess Leia, Chewbacca and R2-D2) "as soon as they are ready!", and plastic pegs to complete the display stand. The sets were to be mailed between Feb 1 and June 1.

Almost all of the figures came with tiny plastic guns or other accessories which were easily lost. Prices listed here assume all accessories are intact.

High-end values for action figures always include the card the figure was packaged on. These packages were regularly updated to include advertisements for new merchandise, and the *Star Wars* logo was always that of the most recent film. Fifty cards were printed with the *Revenge of the Jedi* logo. Although figures were never packaged or sold on these cards, a number of them found their way to the collector's market. Packages with *Revenge of the Jedi* stickers or advertisements can occasionally be found. Later packages were marked "The Power of the Force", and some included a collector's coin. Proof of purchase seals could be sent in to obtain new figures not yet available in stores. These included Boba Fett, Yoda, Nein Nunb, Admiral Ackbar, the Emperor and Anakin Skywalker.

The figures were occasionally redesigned. Following the release of The Empire Strikes Back, R2-D2 figures came with a pop-up sensorscope. C-3PO figures could be taken apart and carried around by other figures in a special pack. Boba Fett was originally advertised as a mail-in premium with a working rocket launcher, but legislation prohibiting such toys was passed during production. Advertisements for the figure, already printed on other action figure packages, were covered with a sticker promoting the offer that did not mention the rocket launcher. The figure itself arrived with a glued-in rocket and a letter explaining the situation. In conjunction with *Return of the Jedi*, the R2-D2 figure was redesigned again, this time with a pop-up light saber.

Separate action figure lines were produced for the Droids and Ewoks animated television shows. Collector's coins were included with each figure. A few characters from the main line are repeated here, but are cast in a cartoon-like style as they appeared in the show. A second series of Droids/Ewok figures was planned, but never went beyond the prototype stage.

With the success of *Star Wars*, action figures became a standard form of character merchandise for space adventure. Similar figures were later produced for *Battlestar Galactica*, the 1979 revival of *Buck Rogers*, *Star Trek: The Motion Picture* and many others. All figures were commercially available in the United States with the exception of Yak Face.

Virtually all Kenner Star Wars products made by Kenner were available in Europe and the rest of the English-speaking world by Palitoy of London. Palitoy also made five items which were not available in the U.S. – a talking R2-D2 and four cardboard playsets.

SW1000 Early Bird kit	100 - 300
SW1001 Early Bird figures in mailing box w/12 pegs	75 - 200

Original 12 SW1101-12 (SW1101-04 comprised "early bird" set), 1977

SW1101 Chewbacca	15 - 30
SW1102 Luke Skywalker	15 - 30
SW1103 Artoo-Detoo (R2-D2)	15 - 30
SW1104 Princess Leia Organa	20 - 30
SW1105 Han Solo	20 - 30
SW1106 See-Threepio (C-3PO)	15 - 30

SW1107	Stormtrooper	20 - 30
SW1108	Darth Vader	20 - 30
SW1109	Ben (Obi-Wan) Kenobi	15 - 30
SW1110	Jawa	15 - 30
SW1111	Sand People (Tusken Raider)	20 - 30
SW1112	Death Squad Commander (later called Star Destroyer Commander)	20 - 30

Later *Star Wars* figures SW1113-23 (1978-79)

SW1113	Hammerhead	10 - 20
SW1114	Power Droid	10 - 20
SW1115	R5-D4	10 - 20
SW1116	Snaggletooth	15 - 20
SW1117	Blue Snaggletooth (Sears exclusive)	25 - 60
SW1118	Greedo	15 - 20
SW1119	Death Star Droid	10 - 20
SW1120	Walrus Man	10 - 20
SW1121	Luke Skywalker X-Wing Pilot	10 - 20
SW1122	Boba Fett	15 - 20
SW1123	Boba Fett w/working Rocket Launcher (mail offer)	100 - 200

***The Empire Strikes Back* SW1124-52** (1980-82)

SW1124	Luke Skywalker (Bespin fatigues)	10 - 20
SW1125	Bespin Security Guard (white)	10 - 20
SW1126	Rebel Soldier (Hoth battle gear)	10 - 20
SW1127	FX-7 Medical Droid	10 - 20
SW1128	Han Solo (Hoth outfit)	10 - 20
SW1129	Lando Calrissian	10 - 20
SW1130	Imperial Stormtrooper (Hoth battle gear)	10 - 20
SW1131	Leia Organa (Bespin gown)	10 - 20
SW1132	Bossk (Bounty Hunter)	10 - 20
SW1133	IG-88 (Bounty Hunter)	10 - 20
SW1134	2-1B	10 - 20
SW1135	Yoda	10 - 20
SW1136	Ugnaught	10 - 20
SW1137	AT-AT Driver	10 - 20
SW1138	Lobot	10 - 20
SW1139	Dengar	15 - 25
SW1140	Han Solo (Bespin outfit)	10 - 20
SW1141	Rebel Commander	10 - 20
SW1142	Imperial Commander	10 - 20
SW1143	Leia Organa (Hoth outfit)	10 - 20
SW1144	Artoo-Detoo (R2-D2) (w/sensorscope)	10 - 20
SW1145	See-Threepio (C-3PO) (w/removable limbs)	10 - 20
SW1146	4-Lom	10 - 20
SW1147	Zuckuss	10 - 20
SW1148	Imperial TIE Fighter Pilot	10 - 20
SW1149	Bespin Security Guard (black)	10 - 20
SW1150	Cloud Car Pilot	10 - 20
SW1151	AT-AT Commander	10 - 20
SW1152	Luke Skywalker (Hoth battle gear)	10 - 20

***Return of the Jedi* SW1153-99** (1983)

SW1153	Bib Fortuna	8 - 15
SW1154	Ree-Yees	8 - 15
SW1155	Weequay	10 - 20
SW1156	Emperor's Royal Guard	8 - 15
SW1157	Chief Chirpa	8 - 15
SW1158	Lando Calrissian (Skiff guard disguise)	8 - 15
SW1159	Luke Skywalker (Jedi knight outfit)	8 - 15
SW1160	Leia Organa (Boush disguise)	8 - 15
SW1161	Logray (Ewok medicine man)	8 - 15
SW1162	Squid Head	10 - 20
SW1163	Klaatu	10 - 20
SW1164	Gamorrean Guard	10 - 20

132

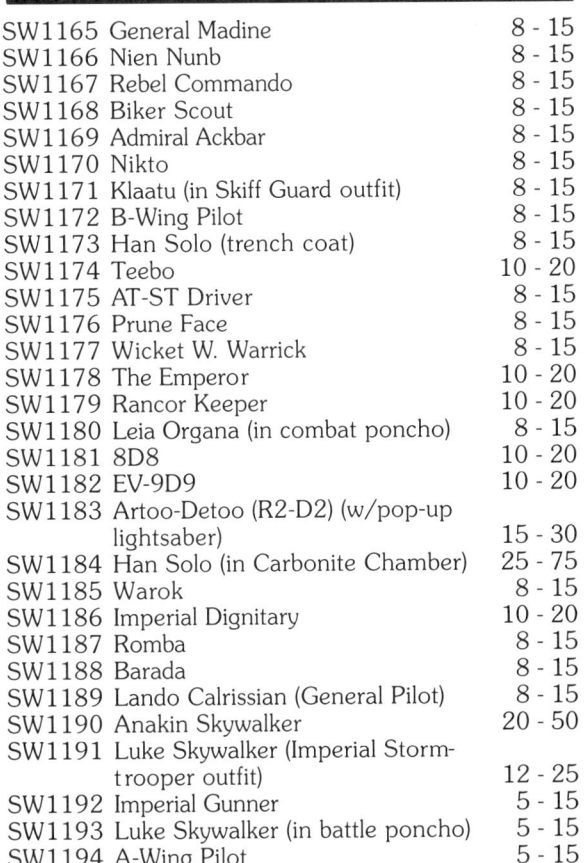

SW1165	General Madine	8 - 15
SW1166	Nien Nunb	8 - 15
SW1167	Rebel Commando	8 - 15
SW1168	Biker Scout	8 - 15
SW1169	Admiral Ackbar	8 - 15
SW1170	Nikto	8 - 15
SW1171	Klaatu (in Skiff Guard outfit)	8 - 15
SW1172	B-Wing Pilot	8 - 15
SW1173	Han Solo (trench coat)	8 - 15
SW1174	Teebo	10 - 20
SW1175	AT-ST Driver	8 - 15
SW1176	Prune Face	8 - 15
SW1177	Wicket W. Warrick	8 - 15
SW1178	The Emperor	10 - 20
SW1179	Rancor Keeper	10 - 20
SW1180	Leia Organa (in combat poncho)	8 - 15
SW1181	8D8	10 - 20
SW1182	EV-9D9	10 - 20
SW1183	Artoo-Detoo (R2-D2) (w/pop-up lightsaber)	15 - 30
SW1184	Han Solo (in Carbonite Chamber)	25 - 75
SW1185	Warok	8 - 15
SW1186	Imperial Dignitary	10 - 20
SW1187	Romba	8 - 15
SW1188	Barada	8 - 15
SW1189	Lando Calrissian (General Pilot)	8 - 15
SW1190	Anakin Skywalker	20 - 50
SW1191	Luke Skywalker (Imperial Stormtrooper outfit)	12 - 25
SW1192	Imperial Gunner	5 - 15
SW1193	Luke Skywalker (in battle poncho)	5 - 15
SW1194	A-Wing Pilot	5 - 15
SW1195	Paploo	5 - 15
SW1196	Amanaman	10 - 20
SW1197	Lumat	12 - 22
SW1198	Yak Face, w/coin	50 - 150
SW1199	Sy Snootles and the Rebo Band (boxed set)	20 - 35
SW1200	*Revenge of the Jedi* cards, ea	10 - 20

133

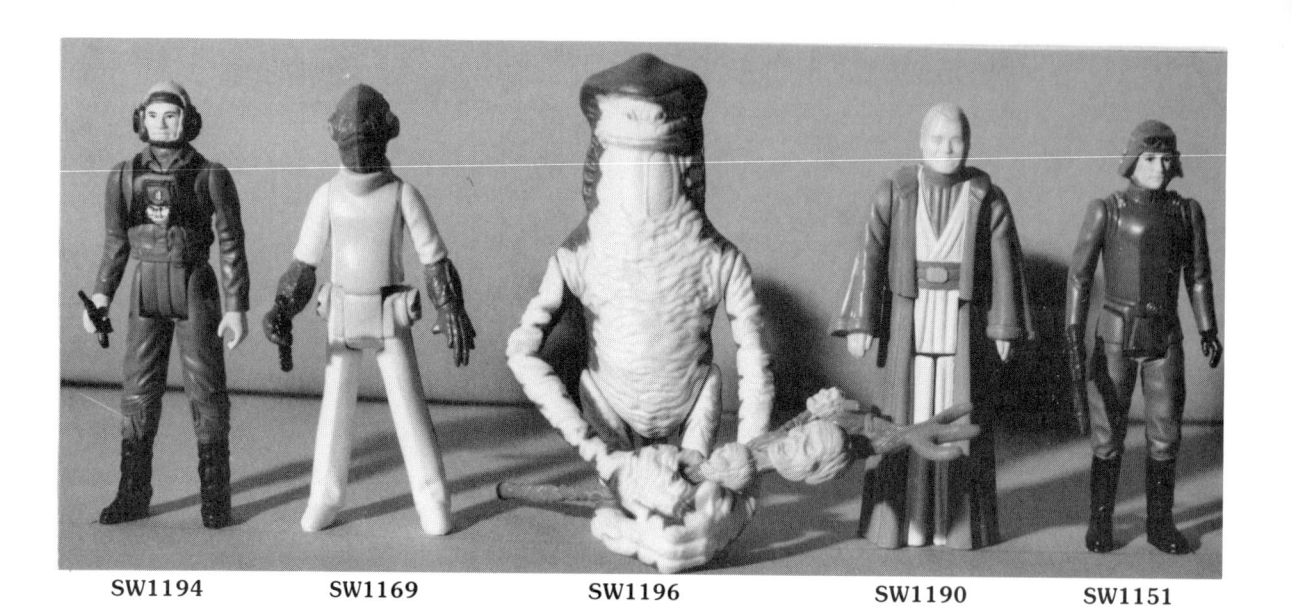

| SW1194 | SW1169 | SW1196 | SW1190 | SW1151 |

| SW1137 | SW1175 | SW1172 | SW1188 | SW1149 |

| SW1125 | SW1153 | SW1168 | SW1122 | SW1132 |

| SW1106 | SW1145 | SW1101 | SW1157 | SW1150 |

| SW1108 | SW1119 | SW1139 | SW1181 | SW1182 |

| SW1178 | SW1156 | SW1146 | SW1127 | SW1164 |

SW1165	SW1118	SW1113	SW1105	SW1128
SW1140	SW1184	SW1173	SW1133	SW1142
SW1186	SW1192	SW1130	SW1148	SW1110

STAR WARS
TWELVE EXCITING ACTION FIGURES FROM THE SMASH HIT MOVIE STAR WARS!
AUTHENTIC COSTUMES
MOVABLE ARMS AND LEGS FOR GREAT ACTION POSES
DESIGNED FOR STAR WARS SPACESHIPS AND ACTION TOYS
STAR WARS HANG GLIDERS
ONE INSIDE
STAR WARS MOVIE PHOTO CARDS BUBBLE GUM
LAND OF THE JAWAS ACTION PLAYSET
STAR WARS ACTION FIGURES
Kenner
DEATH STAR SPACE STATION
DESTROY DEATH STAR GAME
First one to Destroy DEATH STAR wins!
MILLENNIUM FALCON SPACESHIP
WITH BATTLE ALERT SOUND
PRINCESS LEIA ORGANA
RADIO CONTROLLED R2-D2
CAUTION: ELECTRIC TOY
ELECTRONIC LASER BATTLE GAME
PATROL DEWBACK
COLLECTOR SERIES
ADVENTURES OF R2-D2 GAME
STAR WARS A NEW HOPE

STAR WARS
ACTION FIGURES
COLLECT ALL
21
ORIGINAL 12
9 NEW
STAR WARS
TOY GALAXY
STAR WARS
JIGSAW PUZZLE
500
Dixie
Dixie
STAR WARS
STAR WARS
SPECIAL EARLY BIRD CERTIFICATE PACKAGE
GOOD FOR 4 STAR WARS ACTION FIGURES:
TO GET YOUR SET OF STAR WARS FIGURES
1. BUY
2. MAIL-IN
3. RECEIVE
Power Passers
STAR WARS
DUEL AT DEATH STAR RACING SET
Hours of slotless racing excitement in a Star Wars setting.
STAR WARS
DROID FACTORY
STAR WARS
EARLY BIRD CERTIFICATE PACKAGE
STAR WARS
CREATURE CANTINA
STAR WARS
ACTION DISPLAY STAND
FOR STAR WARS FIGURES
STAR WARS
ESCAPE FROM DEATH STAR GAME
STAR WARS POSTAGE STAMP COLLECTING KIT
THE STAR WARS STORYBOOK
STAR WARS
X-WING FIGHTER
STAR WARS
STAR WARS BLUEPRINTS
GEORGE LUCAS' STAR WARS
STAR WARS
STAR WARS
OFFICIAL LCD WRIST WATCH
STAR WARS
FUN'N GAMES BOOKLET
Burger Chef
STAR WARS
STAR WARS
PRINCESS LEIA ORGANA
HAN SOLO
LUKE SKYWALKER

STAR WARS
STRUCTORS
AT-ST
STAR WARS
RECORD TOTE
STAR WARS MICRO COLLECTION
HOTH ION CANNON
STAR WARS THE EMPIRE STRIKES BACK
IMPERIAL ATTACK BASE
YODA
HAND PUPPET
DAGOBAH
ACTION PLAYSET
THE EMPIRE STRIKES BACK
REBEL BASE
SNAP ACTION SCENE
ENCOUNTER WITH YODA... ON DAGOBAH
STAR WARS
The Empire Strikes Back Storybook
Dixie
HOTH ICE PLANET ADVENTURE GAME
figurine
Craft Master
Kenner
YODA
THE JEDI MASTER GAME
HOTH TURRET DEFENSE
STAR WARS
STRUCTORS
AT-AT
STAR WARS COLLECTIONS
STAR WARS
THE EMPIRE STRIKES BACK
FREE! REVENGE OF THE JEDI

STAR WARS
RETURN OF THE JEDI
LASER RIFLE
CARRY CASE
IMPERIAL
SHUTTLE
VEHICLE
SEE-THREEPIO
(C-3PO)
COLLECTOR'S
CASE
Holds 40 STAR WARS Action Figures
Includes a special chamber to store accessories
EMPEROR'S
ROYAL GUARD
BANK
Dixie
5 OZ. Kitchen Cups
C-3PO
Speeder Bike
EWOK
VILLAGE
ACTION PLAYSET
CHEWBACCA
BANDOLIER
STRAP
JABBA
THE HUTT
ACTION PLAYSET
B-Wing Fighter
A POP-UP BOOK
RETURN OF THE JEDI
SPEEDER
BIKE
VEHICLE
RETURN OF THE JEDI
PENCIL TABLET
Han Solo's Rescue
The Play-For-Power Card Games
MOVIE PHOTO CARDS
BUBBLE GUM
36 STICKS OF GUM

STAR TREK IV
STAR TREK THE MOTION PICTURE
GENE RODDENBERRY
STAR TREK III STARSHIP COMBAT ROLE PLAYING GAME
STAR TREK V THE FINAL FRONTIER
Over 22" Long Assembled
Display Stand Included
Authentic Decals
STAR TREK III
U.S.S. ENTERPRISE
Knickerbocker
STAR TREK
SOFT POSEABLE FIGURE
CAPTAIN KIRK
MR. SPOCK
STAR TREK III THE SEARCH FOR SPOCK
STAR TREK V THE FINAL FRONTIER
U.S.S. ENTERPRISE AND SHUTTLECRAFT
To seek out new life and new civilizations ...To boldly go where no man has gone before!
STAR TREK
GAME
NEW!
STAR TREK THE MOTION PICTURE
KLINGON CRUISER
VULCAN
Avalon
STAR TREK
color 'n recolor
GAME CLOTH
STAR TREK III THE SEARCH FOR SPOCK
STORYBOOK
ASSEMBLE THE VITAL CENTER OF THE GREATEST SPACESHIP OF ALL TIME-WITHOUT SCISSORS OR GLUE!
STAR TREK THE MOTION PICTURE
THE U.S.S. ENTERPRISE
BRIDGE PUNCH-OUT
Vectrex
STAR TREK II THE WRATH OF KHAN
STAR TREK III THE SEARCH FOR SPOCK
STAR TREK III SOURCEBOOK UPDATE
BOOK & RECORD
STAR TREK THE POP-UP BOOK
STAR TREK THE MOTION PICTURE
STAR TREK III
SCOTTY

THE ORIGINAL TELEVISION SOUNDTRACK
STAR TREK
"THE CAGE" & "WHERE NO MAN HAS GONE BEFORE"
STAR TREK
Capt. Kirk
Mr. Spock
ESTES
STAR TREK
FLYING MODEL ROCKET
KLINGON
BATTLE CRUISER
I'm sending you something from outer space...
...so get it all together and have a Happy Birthday!
STAR TREK
MAPS
THE NAVIGATIONAL CHARTS OF THE FIVE-YEAR VOYAGE OF THE STARSHIP ENTERPRISE
STAR TREK
POSTCARD BOOK
48 FULL COLOR STAR TREK POSTCARDS!
DETACHABLE AND READY TO USE!
View-Master 3-D Reels
STAR TREK
FLYING MODEL ROCKET
STARSHIP ENTERPRISE
I must be hard of hearing.
SPACE SHIP SET
STAR TREK
Klingon
STAR TREK
U.S.S. ENTERPRISE
WIN AN APPEARANCE ON
STAR TREK
THE NEXT GENERATION
Hasbro
STAR TREK
GAME
ACTION AND ADVENTURE IN OUTER SPACE
BASIC GAME
STAR TREK
THE ROLE PLAYING GAME
SECOND EDITION
The Original
STAR TREK
FREEZICLES
EASY TO MAKE YOURSELF
FRUIT CONCENTRATE
STAR TREK
Kirk, Spock and McCoy must foil the take-over of Star Fleet's Jutterdon space station!
GOLDEN
TRIVIA GAME
STAR TREK EDITION
STAR TREK
STAR TREK
THE NEXT GENERATION
U.S.S. ENTERPRISE
STARSHIP
STAR TREK
TRANSISTORIZED ELECTRONIC
PHASER GUN
Realistic PHASER SOUND
PHASER LIGHT BEAM
STAR TREK
Super Phaser II
Target Game
TRIANGLE
STAR TREK
COLORING BOOK
ROMULAN SHIP
RECOGNITION MANUAL
STAR TREK
Color and Activity Book
THE STAR TREK
PUZZLE BOOK
STAR TREK
THE OFFICIAL FAN CLUB
EXCLUSIVE INTERVIEW
GEORGE TAKEI
PLUS WILLIAM SHATNER
STAR TREK
THE NEXT GENERATION
STAR TREK
THE NEXT GENERATION
STAR TREK
THE NEXT GENERATION
STAR TREK
THE NEXT GENERATION
STAR TREK
THE NEXT GENERATION
STAR TREK
STAR FLEET
TECHNICAL MANUAL
THE OFFICIAL
STAR TREK
TRIVIA BOOK
Star Trek

PLANET OF THE APES
PICTURE ACTIVITY ALBUM
PLANET OF THE APES ADVENTURE SET
AMSCO
Quick Draw Cartoons
Action Stallion
Remote Control
MIX 'N MOLD
CORNELIUS
DR. ZAIUS
Beneath The Planet of The Apes
"CONQUEST OF BLOOD!"
JIGSAW PUZZLE
OFFICIAL PLANET OF THE APES
SKY DIVING PARACHUTIST
GALEN

CLOSE ENCOUNTERS OF THE THIRD KIND
MARVEL SPECIAL EDITION
CLOSE ENCOUNTERS OF THE THIRD KIND
A MARVEL SUPER SPEC
Battlestar GALACTIC
THE OFFICIAL ADAPTATION
IN FULL MARVELCOLOR!
Battlestar GALACTICA
COLORFORMS ADVENTURE SET
Battlestar GALACTICA GALACTIC CRUISER
Battlestar GALACTICA COSTUME with MASK
Battlestar GALACTICA
CLOSE ENCOUNTERS OF THE THIRD KIND
A PARKER BROTHERS GAME
COLONIAL VIPER
From BATTLESTAR GALACTICA
MONOGRAM
BATTLESTAR GALACTICA
A PARKER BROTHERS JIGSAW PUZZLE
140
CLOSE ENCOUNTERS OF THE THIRD KIND
POSTCARD BOOK
FREE Battlestar GALACTICA 21 PIECE KIT
BATTLESTAR GALACTICA
COLONIAL WARRIOR
CYLON CENTURIAN
TV GUIDE
BATTLESTAR GALACTICA
A PARKER BROTHERS GAME
Original Motion Picture Soundtrack
CLOSE ENCOUNTERS OF THE THIRD KIND
Music by JOHN WILLIAMS
From The Movie CLOSE ENCOUNTERS
Authentic Bendable Extra Terrestrial Figure
WE ARE NOT ALONE
Battlestar GALACTICA
CYLON BUBBLE MACHINE
GALACTICA
BATTLESTAR GALACTICA
A GAME OF STARFIGHTER COMBAT
fasa
OFFICIAL COLLECTORS EDITION
CLOSE ENCOUNTERS OF THE THIRD KIND
CLOSE ENCOUNTERS
BATTLESTAR GALACTICA
Commander ADAMA
Battlestar GALACTICA
PHOTON BLASTER
MARVEL COMICS GROUP
BATTLESTAR GALACTICA
BATTLESTAR GALACTICA
Battlestar GALACTICA

| SW1163 | SW1171 | SW1129 | SW1158 | SW1189 |

| SW1102 | SW1121 | SW1191 | SW1152 | SW1124 |

| SW1159 | SW1193 | SW1138 | SW1161 | SW1197 |

SW1166	SW1170	SW1109	SW1195	SW1114

SW1104	SW1143	SW1131	SW1160	SW1180

SW1176	SW1103	SW1144	SW1183	SW1115

146

| SW1179 | SW1141 | SW1167 | SW1126 | SW1154 |

| SW1187 | SW1116 | SW1162 | SW1112 | SW1107 |

| SW1134 | SW1174 | SW1111 | SW1136 | SW1120 |

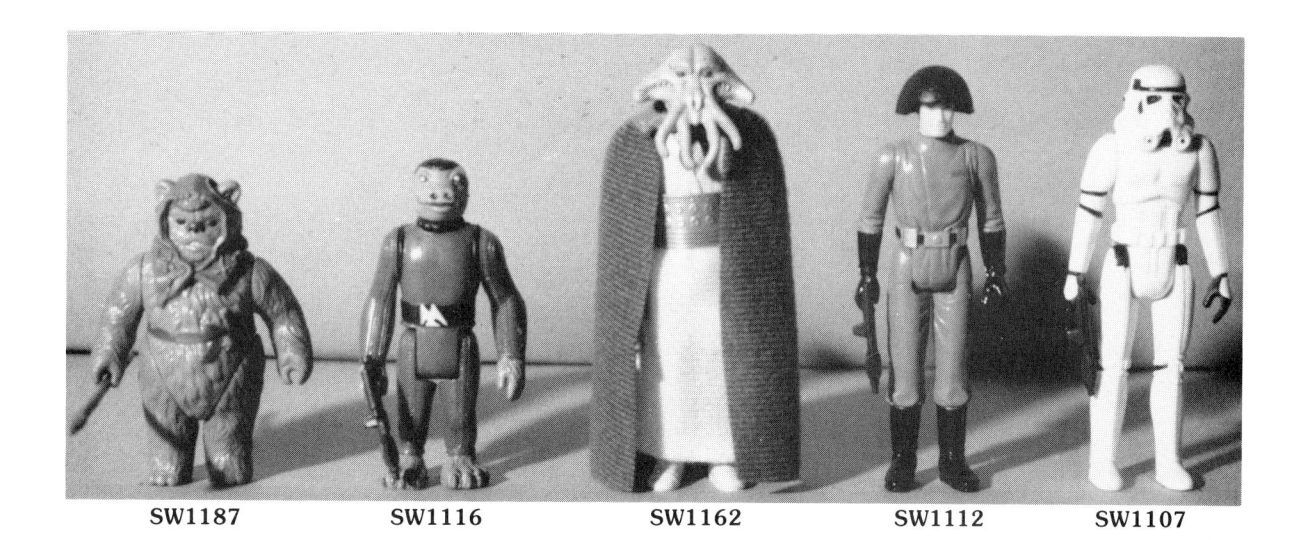

SW1185　　SW1155　　SW1177　　SW1135　　SW1198　　SW1147

SW1199

WICKET W. WARRICK™　　LOGRAY™　　KING GORNEESH™

URGAH LADY GORNEESH™　　DULOK SCOUT™　　DULOK SHAMAN™

SW1200　　　　　　　　SW1220-25 *plus unproduced figures*

148

Droids action figures SW1201-12

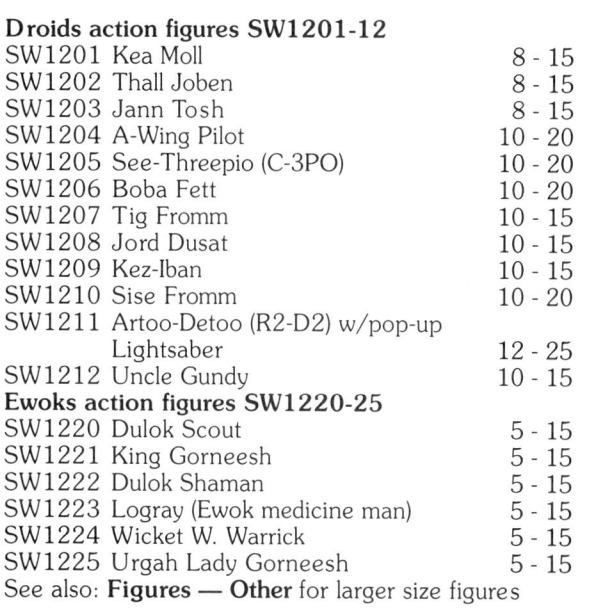

SW1201	Kea Moll	8 - 15
SW1202	Thall Joben	8 - 15
SW1203	Jann Tosh	8 - 15
SW1204	A-Wing Pilot	10 - 20
SW1205	See-Threepio (C-3PO)	10 - 20
SW1206	Boba Fett	10 - 20
SW1207	Tig Fromm	10 - 15
SW1208	Jord Dusat	10 - 15
SW1209	Kez-Iban	10 - 15
SW1210	Sise Fromm	10 - 20
SW1211	Artoo-Detoo (R2-D2) w/pop-up Lightsaber	12 - 25
SW1212	Uncle Gundy	10 - 15

Ewoks action figures SW1220-25

SW1220	Dulok Scout	5 - 15
SW1221	King Gorneesh	5 - 15
SW1222	Dulok Shaman	5 - 15
SW1223	Logray (Ewok medicine man)	5 - 15
SW1224	Wicket W. Warrick	5 - 15
SW1225	Urgah Lady Gorneesh	5 - 15

See also: **Figures — Other** for larger size figures

SW1225 SW1220 SW1224

SW1222 SW1221 SW1223

SW1210 SW1203 SW1201

SW1211 SW1205

SW1202

SW1201-12 *plus unproduced figures*

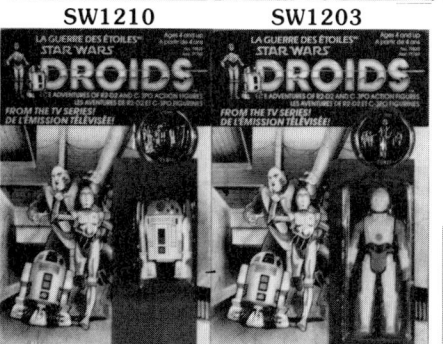

SW1201-12

149

Palitoy cardboard playset

SW1504

SW1519

SW1514

SW1568

SW1501

SW1545

150

Action Figure Playsets, Vehicles and Accessories

This category includes the various toys designed for use with the figures listed above. In addition, it includes large creatures (such as the Wampa and Rancor monster) intended for use with such figures. Like the figures, older items were often continued in new boxes with the current film logo. Some items also changed slightly, such as the "battle-damaged" X-Wing fighters released with the second film. The original Tauntaun was molded in solid plastic, but was later released with a split rubber belly.

The Ice Planet Hoth playset was almost identical to the Land of the Jawas playset. The base was cast from the same mold, but in white plastic, and packaged with a new cardboard background. (A real disappointment to at least one young fan.) Jabba's Prison was a slightly revised version of the Droid Factory.

Star Wars SW1500-45 (1977-1979)

SW1500	X-Wing Fighter	20 - 40
SW1501	X-Wing Fighter w/"battle-damage" stickers	20 - 40
SW1504	Imperial TIE Fighter	20 - 40
SW1506	Darth Vader TIE Fighter	20 - 40
SW1508	Imperial Troop Transporter	25 - 50
SW1510	*Millennium Falcon* Spaceship	50 - 125
SW1512	Patrol Dewback	10 - 20
SW1514	Death Star Space Station	50 - 100
SW1516	Droid Factory	25 - 50
SW1518	Creature Cantina	20 - 40
SW1519	Cantina Adventure Set (Sears exclusive)	50 - 75
SW1520	Land Speeder	15 - 30
SW1522	Sonic Land Speeder (J.C. Penney exclusive)	100 - 200
SW1524	Land of the Jawas Playset	75 - 125
SW1545	Display stand for action figures	45 - 75

The Empire Strikes Back SW1550-75 (1980-1982)

SW1550	All-Terrain Armored Transport (AT-AT)	35 - 95
SW1552	Scout Walker	20 - 30
SW1554	Wampa	10 - 20
SW1556	Tauntaun, solid belly (1980)	10 - 20
SW1558	Same as SW1556, but w/split belly (1982)	10 - 25

SW1500

SW1506

SW1508

SW1520

SW1522

151

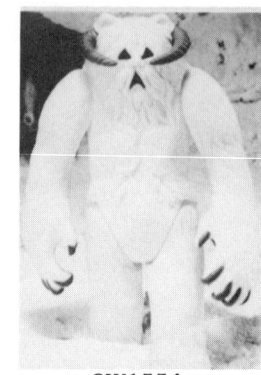

SW1554

SW1510

SW1558

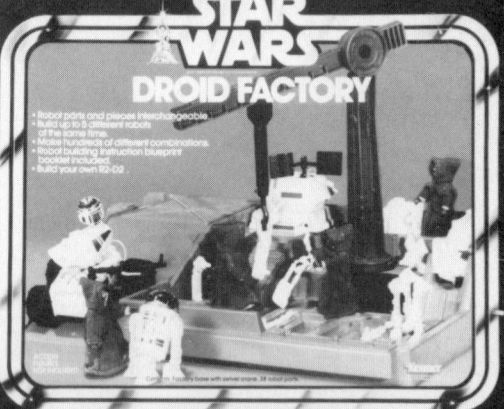

SW1512

SW1516

SW1575

SW1572

SW1556

152

SW1518

SW1560	Turret and Probot playset (J.C. Penney exclusive)	50 - 125
SW1561	Rebel Command Center	90 - 175
SW1562	Imperial Attack Base	30 - 75
SW1563	Star Destroyer	30 - 60
SW1564	Rebel Armored Snowspeeder	20 - 40
SW1566	Rebel Transport	20 - 40
SW1568	Degobah playset	25 - 35
SW1570	Twin-Pod Cloud Car	20 - 35
SW1572	Slave I	25 - 45
SW1574	Ice Planet Hoth playset	75 - 100
SW1575	Display Arena	20 - 40

***Return of the Jedi* SW1580-1642 (1983+)**

SW1580	Imperial Shuttle	30 - 60

SW1574

SW1564

SW1562

SW1552

SW1566

153

SW1608

SW1618
SW1610

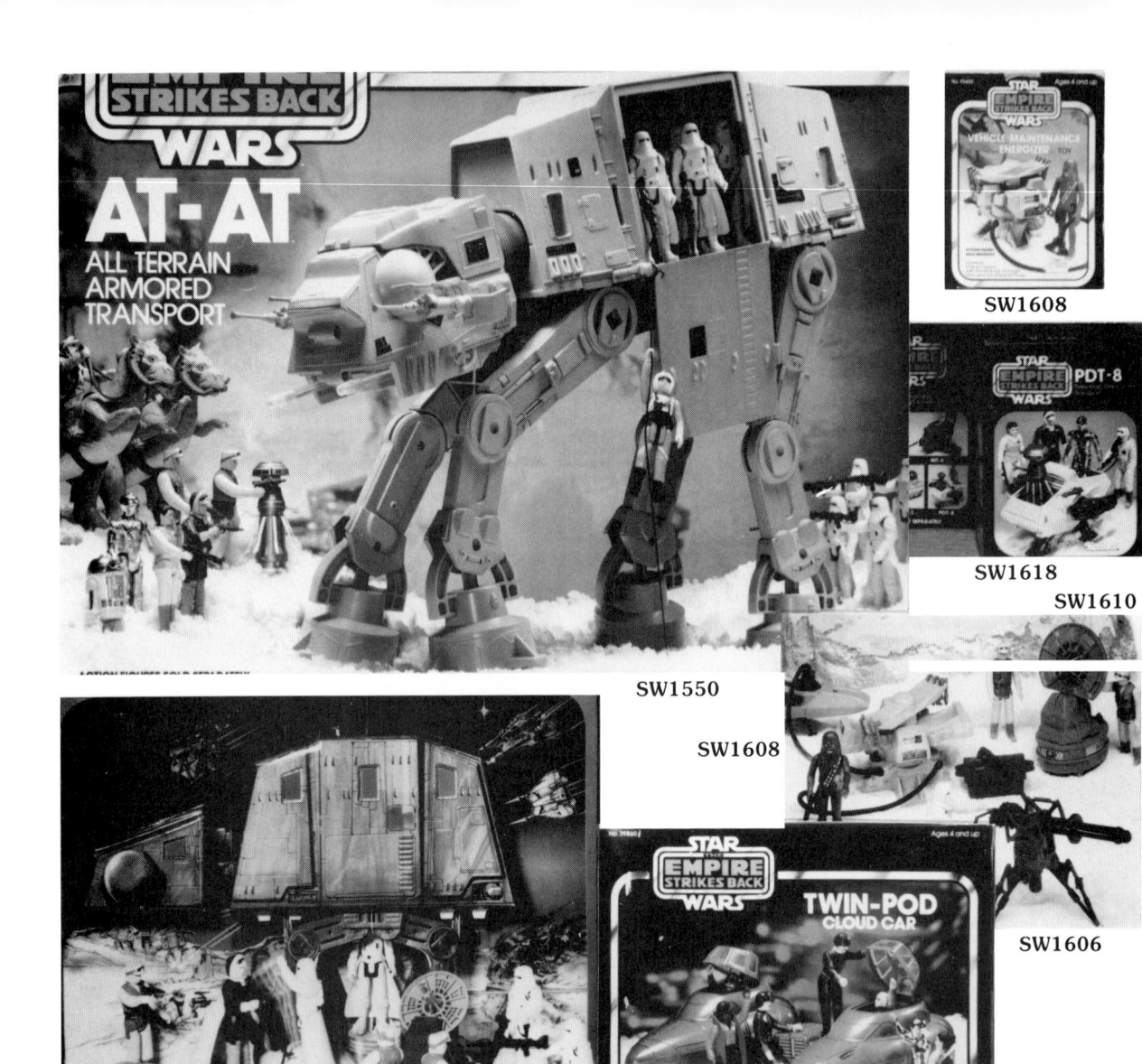

SW1550

SW1608

SW1606

SW1574

SW1570

SW1524

SW1613   SW1617   SW1618

154

SW1614

SW1586

SW1580

SW1594

SW1590

SW1592

SW1615

155

SW1582

SW1621-23

SW1634

SW1600

SW1604

SW1630

SW1602

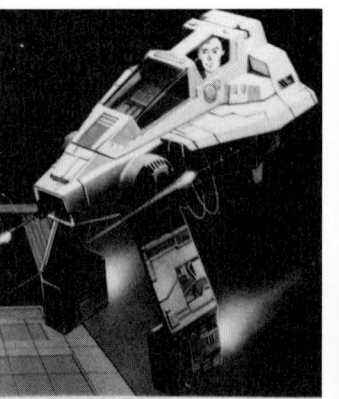

SW1632

156

SW1596

SW1582	Jabba the Hutt action playset	30 - 60
SW1583	Jabba's Prison (Sears exclusive)	35 - 65
SW1586	Rancor Monster	15 - 30
SW1590	Speeder Bike	10 - 20
SW1592	Ewok Village	25 - 50
SW1593	Ewok Assault Catapult	10 - 20
SW1594	Ewok Combat Glider	10 - 20
SW1596	Ewok Battle Wagon	20 - 40
SW1598	TIE Interceptor	15 - 30
SW1600	A-Wing Fighter	15 - 30
SW1602	B-Wing Fighter	15 - 35
SW1604	Y-Wing Fighter	15 - 35
SW1606	Tri-Pod Cannon	10 - 18
SW1608	Vehicle Maintenance Energizer	10 - 18
SW1610	Battle Action Radar Laser Cannon	10 - 18

Mini-Rigs SW1612-23

SW1612	Captivator (CAP-2)	10 - 25
SW1613	Mobile Laser Cannon (MLC-3)	10 - 25
SW1614	Interceptor (INT-4)	10 - 25
SW1615	Armored Sentinel Transport (AST-5)	10 - 25
SW1616	Imperial Shuttle Pod (ISP-6)	10 - 25
SW1617	Multi-Terrain Vehicle (MTV-7)	10 - 25
SW1618	Personnel Deployment Transport (PDT-8)	15 - 20
SW1619	Desert Sail Skiff	15 - 35
SW1620	Endor Forest Ranger	20 - 40
SW1621	One-Man Sand Skimmer	20 - 40
SW1622	Imperial Sniper	20 - 45
SW1623	Security Scout	15 - 25
SW1630	Droids Side Gunner	15 - 25
SW1632	Droids ATL Interceptor	15 - 25
SW1634	Droids Tatooine Skiff	35 - 50
SW1640	Ewoks Woodland Wagon	15 - 35
SW1641	Ewoks Treehouse	20 - 40
SW1642	Ewoks Firecart	10 - 25

See also: **Micro Collection Sets**

SW1616   SW1615

SW1642

SW1641

SW1821 SW1819

SW1815

SW1900

SW1818

SW1619

158

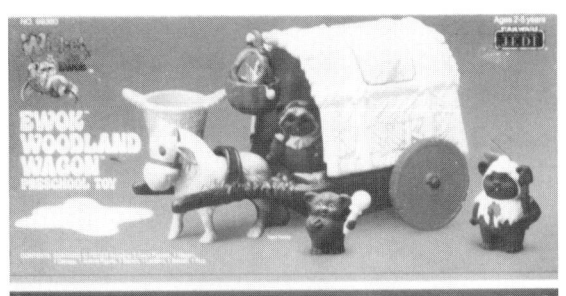

SW1640

SW1810

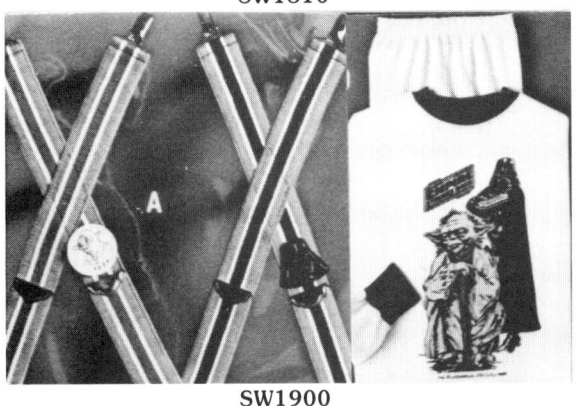

SW1900

SW2150-55

Action Figure Storage Cases

These were initially simple cases containing trays with figure-sized compartments. The trays could be flipped and used as a playing surface with foot pegs for the figures. Later cases were more elaborate, and were molded like characters or items from the films. These had a greater storage capacity, and included special compartments for the easily-lost accessories.

SW1800 SW vinyl storage case	10 - 35
SW1810 ESB vinyl storage case, 2 styles, ea	10 - 35
SW1815 Darth Vader bust case (plastic)	8 - 25
SW1818 Chewbacca bandolier strap	5 - 15
SW1819 C-3PO bust case	8 - 20
SW1821 Laser rifle case	10 - 25

Animation Cels and Backgrounds

An animation celluloid (cel) is one frame of a cartoon. It requires up to 24 of these drawings to photograph one second of animated film, and thousands for an entire cartoon. Because each picture is slightly different, every cel is a unique item. *Star Wars* cels are either from the Droids and Ewoks television shows, or from a holiday special produced in 1978. Most of the special was live-action, but included an animated sequence which first introduced Boba Fett. The value of any particular cel must be evaluated on a case-by-case basis, taking into account the character(s) depicted, the pose, and the presence (if at all) of the original background. Backgrounds should be examined carefully, as some modern cels are framed with color photocopies of the original background. Cel collectors with artistic talent have also been known to paint their own backgrounds. Due to the fragile nature of cels, it is not uncommon to find them in damaged condition. Animation cel collecting is one of the fastest growing collectible fields.

SW1850 Animation cels. The average cel commands $100-$150, but choice items with original backgrounds must be judged on an individual basis.

Apparel

T-shirts, pajamas, underwear, socks and other apparel items were sold commercially in stores, and special items were made available exclusively through the *Star Wars* and Lucasfilm fan clubs. Other items were later sold at Lucasfilm shops in the Disney theme parks in conjunction with the Star Tours attraction. Few apparel items spark much collector interest and resulting values are lower.

SW1900 General apparel item	1 - 15
SW1901 Commemorative item	5 - 20
SW1902 Crew jackets	25 - 100

See also: **Costumes and Play Outfits; Iron-On Appliques and Transfers**

Art Portfolios

Pre-production artwork for the *Star Wars* saga by artist Ralph McQuarrie was published by Ballantine Books after the release of each film. In addition, much of it was used for pre-release promotion. The blueprint set is a series of drawings related to the design and

159

construction of sets for the first film.

SW2000 SW portfolio	10 - 20
SW2001 SW blueprint set	8 - 20
SW2010 ESB promotional art portfolio	25 - 50
SW2011 ESB portfolio	8 - 12
SW2020 ROTJ portfolio	8 - 12

See also: **Books**

Banks

Early banks were made by Roman Ceramics Corporation in 1977, in the shape of R2-D2, C-3PO or a Darth Vader bust. Sigma also made ceramic banks for ROTJ in 1983. A series of rubber banks were made by Adam Joseph Industries in 1983.

SW2130-32 Roman Ceramics, 1977
SW2130 R2-D2 ceramic bank	25 - 40
SW2131 Darth Vader ceramic bank	25 - 40
SW2132 C-3PO ceramic bank	25 - 40
SW2133 Darth Vader anodized silver plated (Leonard Silver, 1981)	40 - 70
SW2134 Jabba the Hutt	15 - 25
SW2135 Yoda	10 - 20
SW2136 Chewbacca	15 - 25
SW2140 Yoda bank (lithographed tin w/combination dials)	8 - 12

SW2140-42 Sigma, 1983-84
SW2140 Chewbacca figure bank	15 - 35
SW2141 Yoda figure bank	15 - 35
SW2142 Jabba the Hutt figure bank	15 - 35

ROTJ Banks SW2150-55 (Adam Joseph Industries, 1983)
SW2150 Gamorrean Guard	8 - 12
SW2151 Emperor's Royal Guard	10 - 20
SW2152 Darth Vader	10 - 20
SW2153 R2-D2	8 - 12
SW2154 Wicket	8 - 12
SW2155 Kneesaa	8 - 12

Belts and Buckles

Four buckles were produced in 1977 by Leather Shop Inc. A black and white belt was made in 1979.

Belt buckles SW2200-03
SW2200 *Star Wars* logo	10 - 20
SW2201 R2-D2	10 - 20
SW2202 R2-D2 and C-3PO	10 - 20
SW2203 Darth Vader	10 - 20
SW2210 SW belt	2 - 8
SW2212 SW stretch belt	2 - 5
SW2230 ROTJ belt	1 - 4

Book Marks

A series of 16 bookmarks was produced by Random House in 1983.

SW2251 #1 Luke	2 - 5

160

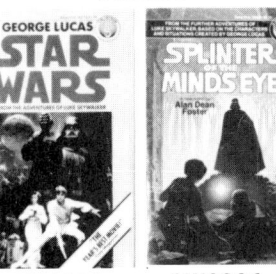

SW2252	#2 Darth Vader	2 - 5
SW2253	#3 Princess Leia, Boushh disguise	2 - 5
SW2254	#4 R2-D2	2 - 5
SW2255	#5 C-3PO	2 - 5
SW2256	#6 Lando, Skiff disguise	2 - 5
SW2257	#7 Chewbacca	2 - 5
SW2258	#8 Yoda	2 - 5
SW2259	#9 Obi-Wan	2 - 5
SW2260	#10 Han Solo	2 - 5
SW2261	#11 Boba Fett	2 - 5
SW2262	#12 Wicket the Ewok	2 - 5
SW2263	#13 Emperor's Royal Guard	2 - 5
SW2264	#14 Imperial Stormtrooper	2 - 5
SW2265	#15 Jabba the Hutt	2 - 5
SW2266	#16 Admiral Ackbar	2 - 5

Book Plates

SW2290	Book plates: C-3PO and R2-D2, Wicket or Darth Vader, (Random House, 1983) ea	2 - 5

Bookends

SW2295	Chewbacca/Darth Vader bookends (Sigma)	30 - 60

Books

In addition to novelized adaptations of the films, new stories have been written by Alan Dean Foster, Brian Daley, and L. Neil Smith. There have also been numerous coloring, activity, and information books. The major publishers were Random House (including its subsidiaries Ballantine and Del Rey books), and Paradise Press. Comic, stamp, and sticker books are listed elsewhere.

SW2300	*Star Wars* novel, hardcover (Del Rey, 1976)	10 - 20
SW2301	*Star Wars* novel, paperback	1 - 3
SW2305	SW Storybook, hardcover (Random House)	10 - 15
SW2306	SW Storybook, softcover (Scholastic Book Service)	7 - 10
SW2310	SW Sketchbook (Ballantine, 1977)	10 - 20
SW2315	SW Album (Ballantine, 1977)	10 - 20
SW2320	SW Pop-up book (Random House, 1978)	10 - 15
SW2325	*Splinter of the Mind's Eye*, hardcover (Ballantine, 1978)	4 - 8
SW2326	*Splinter of the Mind's Eye*, paperback (Del Rey, 1978)	8 - 18
SW2330	SW Compendium (Paradise Press)	8 - 18
SW2335	*The Art of Star Wars*, hardcover (1979)	25 - 35
SW2340	*The Art of Star Wars*, softcover	20 - 25
SW2345	Artoo Detoo's Activity Book (Random House, 1979)	5 - 10
SW2350	*Han Solo at Star's End*, hardcover (Ballantine, 1979)	4 - 7
SW2355	*Han Solo at Star's End*, paperback (Del Rey, 1979)	5 - 10
SW2360	*Han Solo's Revenge*, hardcover (Ballantine, 1979)	4 - 7
SW2365	*Han Solo's Revenge*, paperback (Del Rey, 1979)	5 - 10
SW2370	*The Wookiee Storybook* (Random	

SW2390

SW2395

SW2391

SW2423

SW2400 SW2435  SW2436

SW2445

SW2440

SW2466  SW2465 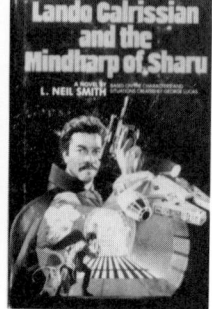 SW2464

SW2380

SW2379

ID	Title	Price
	House, 1979)	5 - 10
SW2379	*The Mystery of the Rebellious Robot* (Random House)	1 - 3
SW2380	*The Maverick Moon* (Random House, 1979)	1 - 3
SW2381	*The Droid Dilemma* (Random House, 1979)	1 - 3
SW2385	*Han Solo and the Lost Legacy*, hardcover (Ballantine, 1980)	4 - 7
SW2386	*Han Solo and the Lost Legacy*, paperback (Del Rey, 1980)	5 - 10
SW2390	*The Empire Strikes Back* novel, hardcover (Ballantine, 1983)	4 - 8
SW2391	*The Empire Strikes Back* novel, paperback (Del Rey, 1983)	5 - 10
SW2395	ESB Storybook, hardcover (Random House, 1980)	8 - 12
SW2396	ESB Storybook, softcover (Scholastic Book Service, 1980)	3 - 6
SW2400	ESB Pop-up book (Random House, 1980)	10 - 15
SW2405	*Art of The Empire Strikes Back* (Ballantine, 1980)	15 - 35
SW2408	*The Jedi Master's Quizbook*	4 - 8
SW2410	ESB Sketchbook (Ballantine, 1980)	8 - 15

ESB coloring books SW2415-22 (Kenner)

ID	Title	Price
SW2415	Darth Vader and Stormtroopers	3 - 5
SW2416	Yoda	3 - 5
SW2417	R2-D2	3 - 5
SW2418	Luke	3 - 5
SW2419	Chewbacca and Leia	3 - 5
SW2420	Chewbacca, Han, Leia and Lando	3 - 5
SW2421	Chewbacca and C-3PO	3 - 5
SW2422	Cast	3 - 5
SW2423	ESB Panorama Book	10 - 20
SW2430	*The World of Star Wars* (Paradise Press, 1981)	5 - 10
SW2435	*Return of the Jedi* novel, hardcover (Ballantine, 1983)	3 - 6
SW2436	*Return of the Jedi* novel, paperback (Del Rey, 1983)	5 - 10
SW2440	ROTJ Storybook, hardcover (Random House, 1983)	8 - 10
SW2441	ROTJ Storybook, softcover (Scholastic Book Service)	2 - 5
SW2445	ROTJ Pop-up book (Random House, 1983)	8 - 12
SW2450	*Art of Return of the Jedi* (Ballantine, 1983)	15 - 25
SW2455	ROTJ Sketchbook (Ballantine, 1983)	8 - 15
SW2460	ROTJ of the Jedi Giant Collector's Compendium (Paradise Press, 1983)	4 - 12

SW2455

SW2470

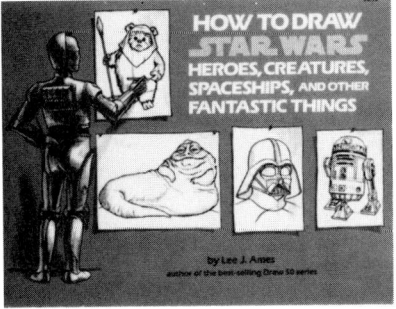

SW2505

SW2467

SW2500

SW2494

SW2521

SW2408

SW2510

SW2464	*Lando Calrissian and the Mindharp of Sharu*, hardcover (Ballantine)	1 - 3
SW2465	*Lando Calrissian and the Mindharp of Sharu*, paperback (Del Rey, 1983)	2 - 5
SW2466	*Lando Calrissian and the Flamewind of Oseon* (Del Rey, 1983)	1 - 3
SW2467	*Lando Calrissian and the Starcave of ThonBoka* (Del Rey)	1 - 3
SW2470	*My Jedi Journal* (Ballantine)	3 - 6

ROTJ coloring books SW2481-87 (Kenner, 1983)

SW2481	Luke	2 - 5
SW2482	Lando fighting skiff guard	2 - 5
SW2483	Lando in Falcon cockpit	2 - 5
SW2484	Max Rebo	2 - 5
SW2485	Ewoks Wicket on vine	2 - 5
SW2486	Ewoks Wicket, Kneesa and Logray	2 - 5
SW2487	Ewoks Wicket and Kneesa on hang gliders	2 - 5

ROTJ activity books SW2490-94 (Happy House, 1983)

SW2490	Activity Book	2 - 5
SW2491	Monster Activity Book	2 - 5
SW2492	Word Puzzle Book	2 - 5
SW2493	Picture Puzzle Book	2 - 5
SW2494	Maze Book	2 - 5
SW2500	ROTJ Punch-out and Make It book	10 - 20
SW2505	*How to Draw* Star Wars *Heroes, Creatures, Spaceships, and other Fantastic Things*	5 - 15
SW2510	*Han Solo's Rescue*	8 - 12
SW2520	*The Star Wars Question and Answer Book about Space*	3 - 7
SW2521	*The Star Wars Question and Answer Book about Computers*	3 - 7
SW2530	Movie Storybook Trilogy	5 - 15
SW2535	*Guide to the Star Wars Universe*	4 - 10

Droids books SW2550-55 (Random House, 1985-86)

SW2550	*The Pirates of Tarnoonga*	2 - 8
SW2551	*The Red Ghost*	2 - 8
SW2552	*The Lost Prince*	2 - 8
SW2553	*Escape from the Monster Ship*	2 - 8
SW2555	*Shiny as a Droid*	2 - 8

Ewoks books SW2571-80 (Random House, 1985-86)

SW2571	*Wicket Goes Fishing*	2 - 8
SW2572	*Wicket and the Dandelion Warriors*	2 - 8
SW2573	*Learn-to-Read Activity Book*	2 - 8
SW2574	*ABC Fun*	2 - 8
SW2575	*School Days*	2 - 8
SW2576	*How the Ewoks Saved the Trees*	2 - 5
SW2580	*Fuzzy as an Ewok*	3 - 8

See also: **Comic Books; Games; Records, Tapes and Compact Discs; Stickers & Sticker Books**

Bumper Stickers

Bumper stickers were sold in conjunction with the Star Tours exhibit at the Disney theme parks. In addition there have been many fan-produced bumper stickers with *Star Wars*-related messages.

SW3000 Star Tours bumper sticker   1 - 3

Calendars

Star Wars calendars have been produced each year since 1978. Calendars are not widely sought, but

SW3100　　　　　　　　　　SW3100　　　　　　　　　　　　　SW3300

SW3200 　　　　　　　　　　　　　　　　　　　　SW3404

SW3300

164

some collectors seek to own the entire run.

SW3100 Calendars, ea 5 - 10

Candy Containers
SW3200 ROTJ dimensional candy containers Darth Vader, Jabba the Hutt, Sy Snootles, Admiral Ackbar, Wicket or Ewo ,(Topps, 1983), ea 1 - 2
SW3210 Box of 18 containers (SW3200) 30 - 50

Cereal Boxes
Star Wars advertisements and premiums appeared in conjunction with General Mills cereals in 1978. C-3POs was a short-lived cereal which appeared in 1984. Prices are for complete boxes.

SW3300 Boxes w/SW advertisements 20 - 50
SW3305 C-3PO's boxes 15 - 30
See SW7214 for masks which came on C-3PO cereal boxes.

Clocks
One of the most common *Star Wars* items is the C-3PO and R2-D2 talking alarm clock made by Bradley in 1980. (Blurb RE 3-D clock)

SW3400 Talking alarm clock, C-3PO and R2-D2 15 - 25
SW3404 3-D electronic quartz sceni-clock (Bradley, 1982) 15 - 25
SW3405 Droid wall clock (Bradley) 15 - 30
SW3406 ESB wall clock (Bradley) 15 - 25
SW3415 Portable clock/radio (Bradley, 1984) 10 - 15
SW3420 Ewok teaching clock 15 - 30
See also: **Watches**

Coins
Sixty-two aluminum coins associated with the action figures were produced in 1984. Each coin was available by mail in exchange for a proof-of-purchase seal. Coins were distributed at random. Later 23 of the coins were included on matching "Power of the Force" action figure packages. Coins which were only available by mail bring higher values. The Droids and Ewoks figures were also packaged with similar coins, but were gold toned.

Action figure coins SW3501-62
SW3501 Amanaman 5 - 10
SW3502 Anakin Skywalker 5 - 10
SW3503 AT-AT 5 - 10
SW3504 AT-ST Driver 2 - 4
SW3505 A-Wing Pilot 5 - 10
SW3506 Barada 5 - 10
SW3507 Bib Fortuna 5 - 10
SW3508 Biker Scout 5 - 10
SW3509 Boba Fett 2 - 4
SW3510 B-Wing Pilot 2 - 4
SW3511 Chewbacca 2 - 4
SW3512 Chief Chirpa 5 - 10
SW3513 Creatures: Hammerhead, Snaggletooth, and Greedo, ea 2 - 4
SW3514 C-3PO 5 - 10
SW3515 Darth Vader 5 - 10

SW3300

SW3305

SW3400

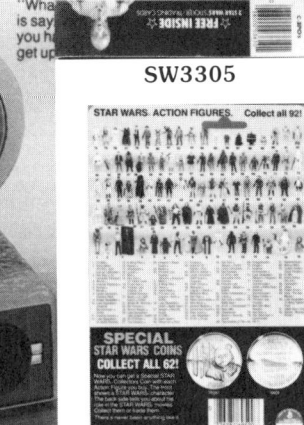

Coin offer

SW3405 *SW3406*

Coins on action figure cards

SW3516 Droids	5 - 10
SW3517 Emperor	2 - 4
SW3518 Emperor's Royal Guard	2 - 4
SW3519 EV-9D9, torture droid	5 - 10
SW3520 FX-7, medical droid	2 - 4
SW3521 Gammorrean Guard	5 - 10
SW3522 Greedo	2 - 4
SW3523 Han Solo, carbon freeze	5 - 10
SW3524 Han Solo, rebel	5 - 10
SW3525 Han Solo, rebel fighter	5 - 10
SW3526 Han Solo, rebel hero	5 - 10
SW3527 Hoth Stormtrooper	2 - 4
SW3528 Imperial Commander	5 - 10
SW3529 Imperial Dignitary	5 - 10
SW3530 Imperial Gunner	5 - 10
SW3531 Jawas	5 - 10
SW3532 Lando Calrissian w/ *Millennium Falcon*	2 - 4
SW3533 Lando Calrisian w/Cloud City	2 - 4
SW3534 Luke Skywalker	5 - 10
SW3535 Luke Skywalker on Tauntaun	2 - 4
SW3536 Luke Skywalker w/landspeeder	5 - 10
SW3537 Luke Skywalker on scout bike	5 - 10
SW3538 Luke Skywalker, Jedi	5 - 10
SW3539 Luke Skywalker, Jedi knight-head	5 - 10
SW3540 Luke Skywalker, Jedi knight-bust	2 - 4
SW3541 Logray	5 - 10
SW3542 Lumat	5 - 10
SW3543 *Millennium Falcon*	5 - 10
SW3544 Obi-Wan Kenobi	5 - 10
SW3545 Paploo	5 - 10
SW3546 Princess Leia	2 - 4
SW3547 Princess Leia in Endor outfit	5 - 10
SW3548 Princess Leia, head and w/R2-D2	5 - 10
SW3549 Romba	5 - 10
SW3550 R2-D2	3 - 7
SW3551 Sail Skiff	5 - 10
SW3552 Star Destroyer Commander	5 - 10
SW3553 Stormtrooper	5 - 10
SW3554 Teebo	5 - 10
SW3555 TIE Fighter Pilot	5 - 10
SW3556 Too-One Bee	2 - 4
SW3557 Tusken Raider	2 - 4
SW3558 Warok	5 - 10
SW3559 Wicket	5 - 10
SW3560 Yak Face	10 - 20
SW3561 Yoda	5 - 10
SW3562 Zuckuss	2 - 4

Droids coins SW3601-12
SW3601 Kea Moll	1 - 3
SW3602 Thall Joben	1 - 3
SW3603 Jann Tosh	1 - 3
SW3604 A-Wing Pilot	1 - 3
SW3605 See-Threepio (C-3PO)	1 - 3
SW3606 Boba Fett	1 - 3
SW3607 Tig Fromm	1 - 3
SW3608 Jord Dusat	1 - 3
SW3609 Kez-Iban	1 - 3
SW3610 Sise Fromm	1 - 3
SW3611 Artoo-Detoo (R2-D2)	1 - 3
SW3612 Uncle Gundy	1 - 3

Ewoks coins SW3621-26
SW3621 Dulok Scout	1 - 3
SW3622 King Gorneesh	1 - 3
SW3623 Dulok Shaman	1 - 3
SW3624 Logray (Ewok medicine man)	1 - 3
SW3625 Wicket W. Warrick	1 - 3
SW3626 Urgah Lady Gorneesh	1 - 3

Coloring and Painting Sets

Poster sets for coloring and painting were among the earliest *Star Wars* merchandise. One set featured a dimensional Darth Vader mask which was assembled from cardboard and attached to the finished poster. A later set, released with *The Empire Strikes Back*, used glow-in-the-dark paint.

Plastic figurine paint sets were produced by Craft Master.

SW3800 Dip Dots painting set	10 - 20
SW3801 Poster set (Playnts)	10 - 20
SW3805 *Star Wars* Poster Art coloring set (Craft Master, 1978)	10 - 20
SW3807 Darth Vader Dimensional Mask poster set	10 - 20
SW3820 Battle on Hoth paint set	5 - 15

ESB Glow-in-the-Dark paint sets SW3830-33
SW3830 Luke	5 - 10
SW3831 Leia and Han Solo	5 - 10
SW3832 Darth Vader	5 - 10
SW3833 Yoda	5 - 10

ESB figurine paint sets SW3840-43 (Craft Master)
SW3840 Leia	5 - 15
SW3841 Luke and Tauntaun	5 - 15
SW3842 Yoda	5 - 15
SW3843 Han Solo	5 - 15

SW3801

ROTJ figurine paint sets SW3860-63 (Craft Master)
SW3860 Admiral Ackbar	4 - 12
SW3861 Wicket	4 - 12
SW3862 C-3PO	4 - 12
SW3863 Other	4 - 12

Comic Books

Comic adaptations of the *Star Wars* films and further adventures of its heroes were published by Marvel Comics Group. The series ran 107 issues from July, 1977-Sept 1986. Reprints were made of the first nine issues, and are distinguished from the originals by the word "reprint" in the upper left corner or a listing inside. *The Empire Strikes Back* appeared in issues 39-44, and was also produced in a larger format as a Marvel Special Edition. *Return of the Jedi* was published as a four-issue limited series. Star Comics (a division of Marvel) published comics based on the Droids and Ewoks animated series. Three 3-D comic books were released by Blackthorne Publishing, beginning Nov 1987.

Star Wars **comic series SW4001-4129** (Marvel)
SW4001 #1	5 - 10
SW4002 #2	3 - 5
SW4003 #3	3 - 5
SW4004 #4	3 - 5
SW4005 #5	3 - 5
SW4006 #6	1 - 3
SW4007 #7	1 - 3
SW4008 #8	1 - 3

SW4006	SW4007	SW4008	SW4009	SW4010
SW4011	SW4012	SW4013	SW4014	SW4202

SW4191

SW4160	SW4170	SW4175

SW4198

SW4171	SW4172	SW4173	SW4174

168

SW4221 SW4223

SW4305

SW4548 SW4543

SW4548 SW4545 SW4542 SW4543

SW4009 #9	1 - 3
SW4010-SW4107 #10-107, ea	1 - 2
SW4110 Packaged set (#1-3 reprints)	4 - 8
SW4121-29 Reprints of #1-9, ea	1 - 2
SW4150 *Star Wars* (Marvel Special Edition)	3 - 5
SW4155 *The Empire Strikes Back* (Marvel Special Edition)	2 - 4
SW4160 *The Empire Strikes Back* comic paperback	1 - 3
SW4170 *Return of the Jedi* (Marvel Super Special)	2 - 4
SW4171-74 *Return of the Jedi* Limited Series, #1-4, ea	1 - 2
SW4175 *Return of the Jedi* comic paperback	1 - 3
SW4191-98 Droids comics, #1-8, ea	1 - 2
SW4201-15 Ewoks comics, #1-15, ea	1 - 2
SW4221-23 *Star Wars* in 3-D (Blackthorne), #1-3, ea	2 - 4

Cookie Jars

Ceramic cookie jars were manufactured by Roman Ceramics Corporation in 1977. The Sigma jar shows Darth Vader, C-3PO and R2-D2.

SW4300 C-3PO ceramic cookie jar	40 - 125
SW4301 R2-D2 ceramic cookie jar	40 - 125
SW4302 Darth Vader ceramic cookie jar	40 - 125
SW4305 Hexagon jar (Sigma)	25 - 75

Cork Boards

Bulletin boards were manufactured by Manton Cork for all three films. The boards made for *The Empire Strikes Back* have glow-in-the-dark features.

SW4420 SW cork board (1979)	10 - 15
SW4421 Yoda, 16-3/8" x 22-3/4"	10 - 15
SW4422 AT-ATs, 11" x 17"	8 - 12
SW4423 Chewbacca, 11" x 17"	8 - 12
SW4424 Darth Vader, 11" x 17"	8 - 12
SW4425 Luke on Tauntaun, 11" x 17"	8 - 12
SW4426 R2-D2 and C-3PO, 11" x 17"	8 - 12
SW4427 Yoda, 11" x 17"	8 - 12
SW4430 Max Rebo Band	5 - 9

Costumes and Play Outfits

Ben Cooper manufactured Halloween costumes. These typically consisted of a molded plastic mask and 2-piece apparel set. The Klaatu costume has *Revenge of the Jedi* printed on the chestplate.

SW4540 Darth Vader picture poncho	5 - 10
SW4541 C-3PO picture poncho	5 - 10
SW4542 Chewbacca #746	10 - 30
SW4543 C-3PO #742	10 - 30
SW4544 Boba Fett #748	10 - 30
SW4545 Stormtrooper #747	10 - 30
SW4546 R2-D2 #744	8 - 25
SW4547 Yoda #749 (1980)	8 - 25
SW4548 Darth Vader #740	10 - 30
SW4549 Princess Leia	10 - 30
SW4550 Luke Skywalker #741	10 - 30
SW4551 Gamorrean Guard	10 - 30
SW4552 Wicket the Ewok	10 - 30
SW4553 Admiral Ackbar	10 - 30
SW4554 Klaatu	15 - 40

| SW4803 | SW4804 | SW4805 | SW4800 | SW4801 | SW4802 |

| SW4806 | SW4807 | SW4828 | SW4829 | SW4830 | SW4825 |

| SW4826 | SW4827 |

SW4740

SW4974

SW4700

SW4760

170

See also: **Masks; Patterns**

Decals
Two paintings by Ralph McQuarrie were printed on 4" x 5" decals. These were originally given away as renewal premiums through the *Star Wars* fan club, and were later sold as merchandise. A glow-in-the-dark decal bearing the Star Tours logo was sold at the Disney theme parks.

SW4660	4" x 5" decals: Yoda or Bounty Hunters, ea	2 - 5
SW4663	Star Tours decal (1986)	1 - 3

See also: **Stickers and Sticker Books**

Dinnerware
SW4700	SW sets	10 - 30
SW4720	ESB sets	8 - 25
SW4740	ROTJ sets	5 - 20
SW4760	Wicket the Ewok sets	4 - 18
SW4770	Droids sets	4 - 18

Dixie Cups and Boxes
The Dixie Cup Co. remained a licensee throughout the complete Star Wars saga issuing four major designs throughout the years. Several different premiums were offered as well. Boxes featured contests, games and cut-outs. As many as 60 different cup designs were included in each issue.

Star Wars **boxes SW4800-07**
SW4800	Droids	8 - 15
SW4801	Obi-Wan Kenobi	8 - 15
SW4802	Princess Leia	10 - 20
SW4803	Han and Chewbacca	8 - 15
SW4804	Luke Skywalker	8 - 15
SW4805	Strormtrooper	8 - 15
SW4806	TIE Fighter/X-Wing/Death Star	8 - 15
SW4807	Darth Vader	8 - 15

ESB boxes SW4825-32
SW4825	Yoda	6 - 12
SW4826	X-Wing in Swamp	6 - 12
SW4827	Luke on Tauntaun	6 - 12
SW4828	Twin-Pod Cloud Car	6 - 12
SW4829	AT-ATs and Snowspeeder	6 - 12
SW4830	*Millennium Falcon*	6 - 12
SW4831	Star Destroyer	6 - 12
SW4832	Darth Vader	6 - 12

ROTJ boxes SW4850-53
SW4850	Luke/Yoda/B-Wing	5 - 10
SW4851	Jabba/Princess Leia	5 - 10
SW4852	Ewoks	5 - 10
SW4853	Emperor/Guard/Darth Vader	5 - 10

Star Wars **Saga boxes SW4860-62**
SW4860	Droids	8 - 15
SW4861	Leia/Han/Strormtroopers	8 - 15
SW4862	**Darth Vader**	8 - 15

Fan Club Kits and Publications
The official *Star Wars* Fan Club produced a small line of merchandise. Subscribers to the club received a newsletter, Bantha Tracks, four times yearly.

The club folded in 1987, but was soon replaced by the Lucasfilm Fan Club. New merchandise was offered through the club, and occasional finds of older items

| SW4853 | SW4852 | SW4850 | SW4851 |

SW5209

SW5208

SW5225

SW5227

SW5203

SW5200-12

172

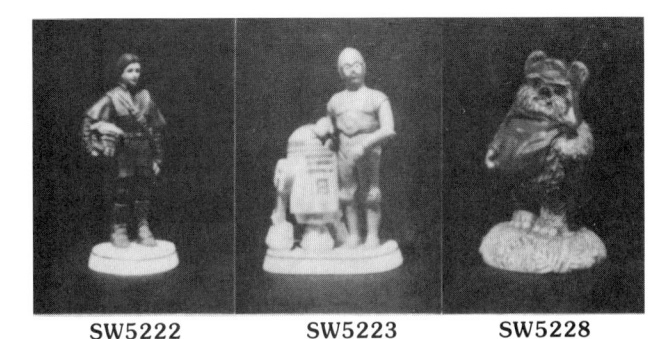

were sometimes made available.

Back issues of earlier newsletters were usually available. The highlights of *Bantha Tracks* 1-4 were assembled into a compilation issue. *Bantha Tracks* #34 included a record from Sprocket Systems, the Lucasfilm post-production department.

SW4900 Original Fan Club kit	15 - 35
SW4910 ESB kit	10 - 25
SW4920 ROTJ kit	6 - 15
SW4931-34 *Bantha Tracks*, #1-4, ea	3 - 12
SW4935 *Bantha Tracks* compilation, highlights of #1-4	2 - 8
SW4945-74 *Bantha Tracks*, #5-34, ea	5 - 10
SW4981-89 Lucasfilm Fan Club Magazine, #1-9, ea	2 - 5
SW4990+ Lucasfilm Fan Club Magazine, #10+, ea	2 - 4

Figures — Other

Kenner marketed a larger set of poseable figures in 1979, ranging in size from 7-1/2"-15" tall. Like the smaller figures, they came with plastic accessories which were frequently lost. Without them, the value of the figures drops drastically. Boba Fett and IG-88 were the only characters from *The Empire Strikes Back* produced in this size. The Princess Leia figure brings higher values if the original hairdo is intact. Listed prices assume the figure is in its original box.

"Yoda the Jedi Master" was a fortune-telling figure which gave random answers to yes/no questions.

A series of twelve bisque figures was produced by Towle/Sigma in 1983.

Large figures SW5200-12

SW5200 C-3PO	50 - 75
SW5201 Ben Kenobi	75 - 100
SW5202 Jawa	75 - 100
SW5203 R2-D2	45 - 60
SW5204 Darth Vader	75 - 100
SW5205 Princess Leia	75 - 150
SW5206 Chewbacca	50 - 75
SW5207 Luke Skywalker	100 - 125
SW5208 Stormtrooper	75 - 100
SW5209 Han Solo	80 - 175
SW5210 Boba Fett	75 - 150
SW5211 SW5210 in ESB box	90 - 200
SW5212 IG-88	50 - 225
SW5215 Yoda the Jedi Master	10 - 25

Bisque figures SW5220-31 (Towle/Sigma, 1983)

SW5220 Han Solo	20 - 50
SW5221 Luke Skywalker	20 - 50
SW5222 Princess Leia	20 - 50
SW5223 C-3PO/R2-D2	25 - 55
SW5224 Darth Vader	20 - 50
SW5225 Klaato	20 - 50
SW5226 Bib Fortuna	20 - 50
SW5227 Gammorean Guard	20 - 50
SW5228 Wicket W. Warrick	20 - 50
SW5229 Lando Calrissian	20 - 50
SW5230 Boba Fett	20 - 50
SW5231 Galactic Emperor	25 - 55

See also: **Coloring and Painting Sets**

Films, Slides and Viewers

173

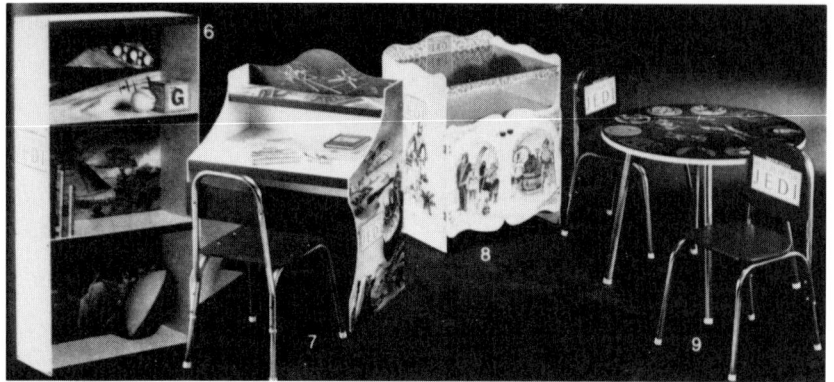

SW5504 SW5505 SW5506 SW5507

SW5463

SW5515

SW5500 SW5501 SW5502 SW5503

SW5640

SW5626

SW5635  SW5629

174

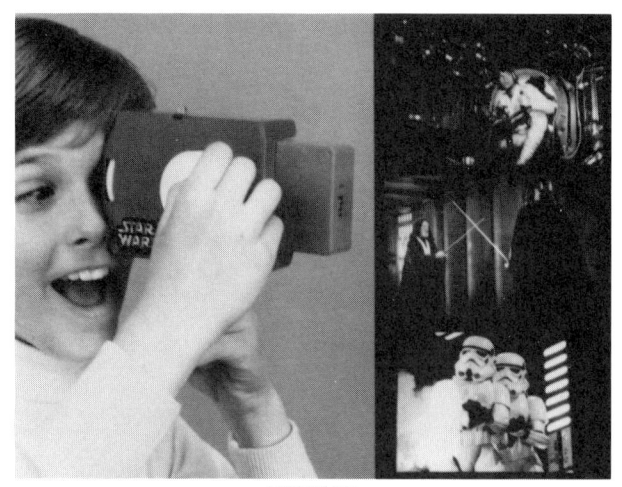

The *Star Wars* movie viewer was crank-operated and designed for special cartridges containing Super-8 film. There were several different cartridges. Home movie Super-8 clips of *Star Wars* were sold in black and white, color, and color with sound.

SW5450 Movie viewer (Kenner, 1978)	15 - 30
Movie viewer cartridges SW5451-55	
SW5451 "May the Force Be With You"	8 - 12
SW5452 Destroy Death Star	10 - 20
SW5453 Danger at the Cantina	10 - 20
SW5454 Battle in Hyperspace	10 - 20
SW5455 Assault on Death Star	10 - 20
Super-8 films SW5460-64	
SW5460 Black and white	15 - 20
SW5461 Color	20 - 30
SW5462 Color w/sound, 4 min	25 - 40
SW5463 Color w/sound, 8 min	30 - 45
SW5464 Color w/sound, 15 min	35 - 50

See also: **Projection Equipment**

Furniture

A number of interesting children's furniture pieces were sold in conjunction with the release of ROTJ.

SW5500 Darth Vader clothes rack	30 - 50
SW5501 Bookcase/toy chest	45 - 60
SW5502 R2-D2 toy box	25 - 75
SW5503 Picnic table	45 - 60
SW5504 Bookcase	45 - 60
SW5505 Desk and chair	45 - 60
SW5506 Night stand	35 - 55
SW5507 Table and chairs	30 - 50
SW5515 Wicket Sit 'n Spin	5 - 20

Games

Several board games were produced by Kenner in conjunction with the films. Kenner also manufactured two electronic games.

In 1987, West End Games began a new line of *Star Wars* games. Chief among these was the *Star Wars* Role-Playing Game which produced numerous supplements in addition to the basic rulebooks.

Star Warriors, a starship combat game, was designed to be used on its own or with the role-playing game. Battle for Endor was a solitaire game. The Lightsaber Dueling Pack and Starfighter Battle Book are one-on-one games, containing a book for each player.

SW5625 Adventures of R2-D2	5 - 20
SW5626 Escape From Death Star	5 - 20
SW5627 Destroy Death Star	10 - 30
SW5628 Electronic Laser Battle	50 - 75
SW5629 Electronic Battle Command	30 - 100
SW5630 X-Wing Aces target game	150 - 300
SW5635 Hoth Ice Planet Adventure	5 - 20
SW5636 Yoda	5 - 15
SW5640 Battle at Sarlacc's Pit	10 - 25
SW5645 SW arcade game	500 - 700
SW5646 Similar to SW5645, cockpit style	700 - 1000
SW5647 ESB arcade game	400 - 600
SW5649 ROTJ arcade game	400 - 600
SW5650 ROTJ Play-for-Power Card Game	3 - 10

SW5450

SW5450

SW5627

SW5636	SW5703	SW5650

SW5630	SW5701	SW5702

SW5706	SW5707	SW5708	SW5709
SW5710	SW5735	SW5736	SW5737

176

SW5625

West End Games SW5701-5791 (1987+)
SW5701	Role-playing game	8 - 17
SW5702	Sourcebook	8 - 17
SW5703	Imperial Sourcebook	15 - 20
SW5704	Campaign Pack	8 - 10
SW5705	Rules Companion	10 - 15
SW5706	*Galaxy Guide 1: A New Hope*	10 - 12
SW5707	*Galaxy Guide 2: Yavin and Bespin*	10 - 12
SW5708	*Galaxy Guide 3: The Empire Strikes Back*	10 - 12
SW5709	*Galaxy Guide 4: Alien Races*	10 - 12
SW5710	*Galaxy Guide 5: Return of the Jedi*	10 - 12
SW5711	*Galaxy Guide 6*	10 - 12
SW5735	*Tatooine Manhunt*	8 - 10
SW5736	*Strike Force: Shantipole*	8 - 10
SW5737	*Battle for the Golden Sun*	8 - 10
SW5738	*Starfall*	8 - 10
SW5739	*Otherspace*	8 - 10
SW5740	*Scavenger Hunt*	8 - 10
SW5741	*Riders of the Maelstrom*	8 - 10

SW5705   SW5704   SW5740   SW5742

SW5742	*Crisis on Cloud City*	8 - 10
SW5743	*Rancor Pit*	8 - 10
SW5744	*Black Ice*	8 - 10
SW5775	Star Warriors board game	15 - 20
SW5776	Assault on Hoth board game	20 - 25
SW5777	Battle for Endor board game	20 - 25
SW5778	Escape from the Death Star	20 - 25
SW5790	Lightsaber Dueling Pack	10 - 12
SW5791	Starfighter Battle Book	20 - 25

See also: **Lead Miniatures**

Glasses
Character glasses for each *Star Wars* film were made available by Burger King in conjunction with Coca-Cola.

SW5908   SW5905   SW5907   SW5906

SW5912   SW5910   SW5913   SW5911

SW5915   SW5917   SW5918   SW5916

Star Wars glasses SW5905-5908
SW5905	Luke	6 - 10
SW5906	R2-D2 and C-3PO	6 - 10
SW5907	Chewbacca	6 - 10
SW5908	Darth Vader	6 - 10

ESB glasses SW5910-13
SW5910	Luke	3 - 8
SW5911	R2-D2 and C-3PO	3 - 8
SW5912	Lando Calrissian	3 - 8
SW5913	Darth Vader	3 - 8

ROTJ glasses SW5915-18
SW5915	Jabba the Hutt	2 - 5

177

SW5935

SW6001

SW6003

SW6004   SW6032   SW6045   SW6056

SW6005

SW6011

SW6021

SW6012

SW6160

178

SW6043

SW6029

SW6046 SW6040 SW6041

SW6057 SW6053

SW6120

SW5916	Tatooine Desert	2 - 5
SW5917	Ewok Village	2 - 5
SW5918	Emperor's Throne Room	2 - 5
SW5935	Plastic tumblers, ea	1 - 4

See also: Dixie Cups and Boxes; **Household Goods, Products and Miscellaneous**

Gum Cards, Gum Wrappers and Trading Cards

Five trading card and sticker sets were printed by Topps in 1977-78. Each set included 66 cards and 11 stickers. The numbers on each of the latter sets picked up where the previous one left off, producing a large set of 330 cards and 55 stickers. The boxes the cards were shipped and sold in are also collectible, as are the wrappers. Unopened packs of cards can still be found.

There are two versions of card #207 from the fourth series. The first is the infamous "X-rated" C-3PO, created by a mischievous artist. When the alteration was detected, a corrected version of the card was quickly issued.

At the request of George Lucas, a diabetic, Topps introduced *Star Wars* sugar free bubble gum in 1978. There were four different exterior designs for the paper wrappers, and each had one of 56 movie photos printed on the inside. Another version of sugarless gum was shipped in a foil wrapper depicting C-3PO.

Topps continued to produce trading cards for subsequent films, printing three sets for *The Empire Strikes Back* and two for *Return of the Jedi*. There were 33 stickers in the first Jedi set, but each sticker was printed with red, yellow, green, or purple borders. Stickers from the first series were sometimes packaged with second series cards. As a result, stickers intended for the second set (#34-55) are harder to find.

Two sets of premium cards were also made available. A 16-card set was offered by Wonder Bread, one card per loaf. Burger King marketed a set of 36 cards in 1981 which contained scenes from *Star Wars* and *The Empire Strikes Back*. They came in perforated strips of three.

Topps 1977-83
Star Wars trading cards SW6000-58 (1977)

SW6000	First series cards (blue) #1-66, set	15 - 20
SW6001	Individual 1st series cards, ea	.25 - .50
SW6002	First series stickers #1-11, set	5 - 10
SW6003	Individual 1st series stickers, ea	.50 - 1
SW6004	Box for 1st series	5 - 8
SW6005	Wrappers for 1st series	1 - 2
SW6006	Unopened waxpacks for SW6000	2 - 5
SW6010	Trix stickers, set of 4, ea	2 - 5
SW6011	Lucky Charms stickers, set of 4, ea	2 - 5
SW6012	Monster Cereals stickers, set of 4, ea	2 - 5
SW6013	Cocoa Puffs stickers, set of 4, ea	2 - 5
SW6018	Second series cards (red) #67-132, set	10 - 18
SW6019	Individual 2nd series cards, ea	.25 - .50
SW6020	Second series stickers #12-22, set	4 - 8
SW6021	Individual 2nd series stickers, ea	.30 - .75
SW6022	Box for 2nd series	4 - 7
SW6023	Wrappers for 2nd series	1 - 2
SW6024	Unopened waxpacks for 2nd series	1 - 4
SW6028	Third series cards (yellow) #133-198,

SW6069

SW6010

SW6028

SW6031

SW6013

SW6100 SW6111

SW6126 SW6128 SW6127

180

SW6075

SW6090 SW6101 SW6112

SW6091

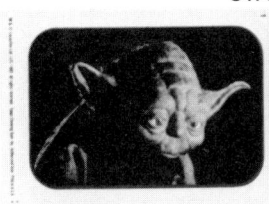

SW6088

SW6140 SW6151

	set	10 - 15
SW6029	Individual 3rd series cards, ea	.25 - .50
SW6030	Third series stickers #23-33, set	3 - 5
SW6031	Individual 3rd series stickers, ea	.25 - .50
SW6032	Box for 3rd series	3 - 5
SW6033	Wrappers, 3rd series	.25 - .50
SW6034	Unopened waxpacks, 3rd series	1 - 2
SW6039	Fourth series cards (green) #199-264, set	12 - 18
SW6040	Individual 4th series cards, ea	.25 - .50
SW6041	Fourth series stickers #34-44, set	3 - 5
SW6042	Individual 4th series stickers, ea	.25 - .50
SW6043	Card #207, "X-rated" version	5 - 15
SW6044	Card #207, redone	3 - 6
SW6045	Box for 4th series	3 - 5
SW6046	Wrappers, 4th series	.25 - .50
SW6047	Unopened waxpacks, 4th series	1 - 2
SW6052	Fifth series cards (orange) #265-330, set	10 - 15
SW6053	Individual 5th series cards, ea	.25 - .50
SW6054	Fifth series stickers #45-55, set	3 - 5
SW6055	Individual 5th series stickers	.25 - .50
SW6056	Box for 5th series	3 - 5
SW6057	Wrappers, 5th series	.25 - .50
SW6058	Unopened waxpacks, 5th series	1 - 2
SW6063	*Star Wars* bread cards, set of 16 (Wonder, 1977)	5 - 8
SW6064	Individual bread cards, ea	.25 - .75
SW6069	Big G trading cards, set of 18 photos and wallet w/SW logo (General Mills, 1978)	15 - 30
SW6070	Individual photos from cereal boxes, ea	.50 - 1
SW6075	Unopened Sugar-Free Bubble Gum pack, paper wrapper, 56 different, ea	1 - 2
SW6076	Unopened Sugar-Free Bubble Gum pack, foil wrapper	5 - 10
SW6077	Bubble Gum wrappers, paper, ea	.50 - 1
SW6078	Bubble Gum wrappers, foil, ea	.50 - 1

ESB trading cards SW6085-6113 (1980)

SW6085	First series cards (red) #1-132, set	8 - 12
SW6086	Individual 1st series cards, ea	.20 - .40
SW6087	First series stickers #1-33, set	3 - 5
SW6088	Individual 1st series stickers, ea	.50 - 1
SW6089	Box for 1st series	2 - 4
SW6090	Wrappers, 1st series	.20 - .40
SW6091	3-pack poly wrapper	1 - 3
SW6092	Unopened waxpacks, 1st series	1 - 2
SW6096	Second series cards (blue) #133-264, set	8 - 12
SW6097	Individual 2nd series cards, ea	.20 - .40
SW6098	Second series stickers #34-66, set	3 - 5
SW6099	Individual 2nd series stickers, ea	.50 - 1
SW6100	Box for 2nd series	2 - 4
SW6101	Wrappers, 2nd series	.20 - .40
SW6102	Unopened waxpacks, 2nd series	1 - 2
SW6107	Third series cards (yellow) #265-352, set	5 - 10
SW6108	Individual 3rd series cards, ea	.20 - .40
SW6109	Third series stickers 67-88, set	2 - 4
SW6110	Individual 3rd series stickers, ea	.50 - 1
SW6111	Box for 3rd series	2 - 4
SW6112	Wrappers, 3rd series	.20 - .40
SW6113	Unopened waxpacks, 3rd series	1 - 2
SW6120	Trading cards, set of 36	

SW6139   SW6150

SW6303

SW6301

SW6308

	(Burger King, 1981)	5 - 15
SW6121	Individual trading cards, ea	.15 - .30
SW6126	Large photo cards, set of 30 (Topps)	10 - 20
SW6127	Display box for SW6126	3 - 5
SW6128	Wrapper for SW6126	1 - 2
SW6129	Unopened pack for SW6126	2 - 4

ROTJ trading cards SW6135-52 (1983)

SW6135	First series cards (red) #1-132, set	6 - 10
SW6136	Individual 1st series cards, ea	.10 - .20
SW6137	First series stickers, #1-33, set	3 - 5
SW6138	Individual 1st series stickers, ea	.10 - .20
SW6139	Box for 1st series	3 - 5
SW6140	Wrappers, 1st series, 4 dif	.10 - .20
SW6141	Unopened waxpacks, 1st series	.50 - 1
SW6146	Second series cards (blue) #133-220, set	5 - 10
SW6147	Individual 2nd series cards, ea	.10 - .20
SW6148	Second series stickers, #34-55, set	6 - 10
SW6149	Individual 2nd series stickers, ea	.50 - 1
SW6150	Box for 2nd series	3 - 5
SW6151	Wrappers, 2nd series, 4 dif	.10 - .20
SW6152	Unopened waxpacks, 2nd series	.50 - 1
SW6160	Sticker/cards, 10 different, (C-3PO's, 1984) ea	1 - 3

See also: **Stickers and Sticker Books**

Guns

The laser pistol was a replica of the gun carried by Han Solo. It was identified as a *Star Wars* item by a sticker bearing the logo of the most recent film. Guns with the original logo are more valued. The 3-position laser rifle had a folding stock and front grip. The biker scout laser pistol was a replica of a gun used in *Return of the Jedi*. All three had a "secret" button in the handle grip which energized the motor for the noisemaker. Guns were manufactured by Kenner. There was also an "action figure" carrying case shaped like a laser rifle.

SW6300	Han Solo Laser Pistol, *Star Wars* sticker (1977)	25 - 40
SW6301	Same as SW6300, but w/ESB or ROTJ sticker	15 - 25
SW6303	3-Position Laser Rifle	35 - 75
SW6305	Electronic Laser Rifle (1980)	20 - 40
SW6308	Biker Scout Laser Pistol	10 - 30

See also: **Action Figure Storage Cases**

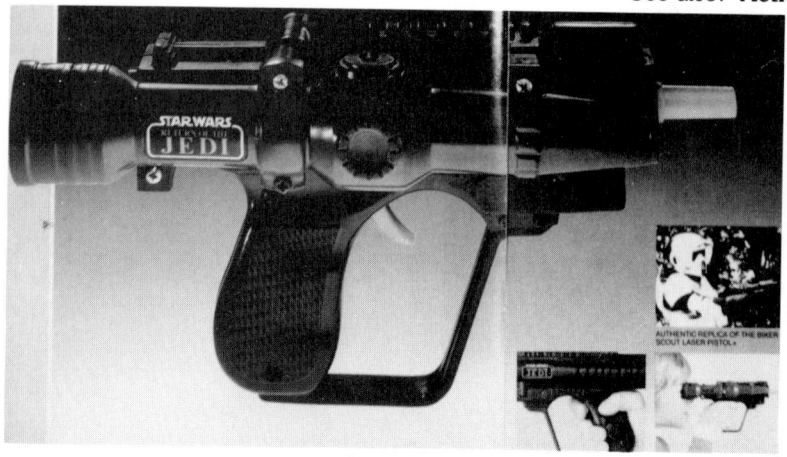

SW6455

182

Hats and Caps

In addition to novelty "baseball" caps, a replica of the cap worn by Imperial officers and a Yoda cap with "ears" were manufactured. Make sure to check for the copyright printed on the cap, however, as fan-produced items of this sort are common.

SW6375	Rebel Forces cap (Thinking Cap Co.)	10 - 20
SW6376	Imperial cap (Thinking Cap Co.)	10 - 20
SW6377	ESB logo cap	5 - 10
SW6378	Yoda cap w/ears	15 - 25
SW6380	ROTJ logo cap (Sales Corp. of America, 1983)	5 - 8
SW6381	Luke and Vader (Sales Corp. of America, 1983)	5 - 8
SW6382	Vader and Imperial Guards (Sales Corp. of America, 1983)	5 - 8
SW6383	Admiral Ackbar (Sales Corp. of America, 1983)	5 - 8
SW6384	ROTJ logo/tassle cap (Sales Corp. of America, 1983)	5 - 8
SW6390	Star Tours logo cap, white	5 - 8
SW6391	Star Tours logo cap, black	5 - 8
SW6392	Star Tours visor	3 - 6

Household Goods, Products and Miscellaneous

This is a catch-all category including household items and other goods not listed elsewhere. If you have an oddball item, this is a good place to start.

SW6450	R2-D2 cake decorating kit (Wilton)	8 - 20
SW6451	Darth Vader cake decorating kit (Wilton)	8 - 20
SW6452	C-3PO cake pan	5 - 15
SW6453	Boba Fett cake pan	10 - 15
SW6455	Puffs boxes, Hoth, Degobah, or Bespin, ea	3 - 6
SW6456	Luke and Tauntaun teapot set	20 - 40
SW6457	ESB centerpiece (Designware)	5 - 10
SW6470-82	**Sigma Ceramic and Household Items**	
SW6469	Yoda backpack box	10 - 20
SW6470	Yoda salt and pepper shakers	10 - 25
SW6471	R2-D2/R5-D4 salt and pepper shakers	15 - 30
SW6472	ESB placemats, set	12 - 20
SW6473	R2-D2 string dispenser w/scissors	20 - 30
SW6474	Yoda vase	15 - 35
SW6475	C-3PO pencil tray	20 - 40
SW6476	C-3PO tape dispenser	20 - 40
SW6477	Yoda tumbler/pencil cup	15 - 35
SW6478	C-3PO picture frame	20 - 30
SW6479	R2-D2 picture frame	25 - 45
SW6480	Darth Vader picture frame	25 - 45
SW6481	Snow speeder toothbrush holder	20 - 40
SW6482	Land speeder soap dish	20 - 40
SW6485	Cookie boxes (Pepperidge Farm)	5 - 15

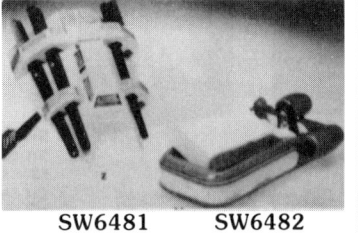

183

Iron-On Appliques and Transfers

Items in this category are best if they have survived their intended use, but may occasionally be found as T-shirts.

SW6650 ESB iron-ons: Boba Fett, Boba Fett (head only), Han Solo, R2-D2, C-3PO, Chewie, Stormtrooper, Darth Vader (only), Darth Vader and Stormtroopers, or Yoda, ea   5 - 10

Jewelry (except rings)

Jewelry was marketed by Weingesoff Industries, Factors Etc. Inc, W. Berrie & Co. Ltd, and Adam Joseph Industries.

SW pendants SW6700-04
SW6700	R2-D2	6 - 14
SW6701	C-3PO	6 - 14
SW6702	Chewbacca	6 - 14
SW6703	Stormtrooper	6 - 14
SW6704	Darth Vader	6 - 14

SW earrings SW6710-12
SW6710	R2-D2	5 - 10
SW6711	C-3PO	5 - 10
SW6712	Darth Vader	5 - 10

SW stickpins SW6720-22
SW6720	R2-D2	3 - 8
SW6721	C-3PO	3 - 8
SW6722	Darth Vader	3 - 8
SW6725	Charm bracelet	8 - 15

ESB Jewelry SW6730-32 (W. Berrie & Co., Inc., 1980)
SW6730	X-Wing medal	4 - 8
SW6731	Chewbacca medal	4 - 8
SW6732	Darth Vader pendant	4 - 8

ROTJ pendants SW6740-44 (Adam Joseph Ind., 1983)
SW6740	Darth VAder	4 - 8
SW6741	Yoda	4 - 8
SW6742	R2-D2	4 - 8
SW6743	Salacious Crumb	4 - 8
SW6744	Imperial Guard	4 - 8
SW6750	Wicket stickpin	3 - 6
SW6751	Princess Kneesa stickpin	3 - 6

Kenner Merchandise Catalogs

Almost all of the Kenner *Star Wars* toys were packaged with a small pamphlet listing available *Star Wars* merchandise and previewing future items. They were also shipped with mail-in premiums or as part of special promotions, and were updated roughly once each year. The 1978 catalog was given out as a Burger Chef premium with an added cover bearing the restaurant's logo. Three different catalog "maps" were printed in 1985.

SW6850	1977, Luke and Leia	4 - 8
SW6851	1978, X-Wing Figher	3 - 5
SW6852	Burger Chef Fun Book (1978 catalog w/extra cover)	3 - 7
SW6853	1979, Death Star Battle Scene	2 - 4
SW6856	1980, Luke and Yoda	1 - 3
SW6858	1982, *Star Wars* Collection w/silver border	1 - 2

184

SW6952   SW6950   SW6951

SW6954   SW6955   SW6956

SW7010   SW7007   SW7006

SW7052

SW6860 1983, ROTJ logo	3 - 5
SW6861 1983, Vader and Emperor's Guards	3 - 5
SW6862 1983, Jabba the Hutt	1 - 2

Planetary maps SW6864-66 (1985)

SW6864 Tatooine, the Planet	4 - 8
SW6865 The Death Stars	4 - 8
SW6866 Endor: The Sanctuary Moon	4 - 8

Keychains and Cases

Adam Joseph Industries produced four metal keychains for *Return of the Jedi*. An enameled keychain was manufactured for Star Tours and sold at the Disney theme parks.

SW6900 Metal keychains): Yoda, *Millennium Falcon*, Darth Vader, Wicket, Kenassa or R2-D2 (Adam Joseph Ind, 1983) ea	5 - 8
SW6920 10th Anniversary	3 - 5
SW6921 Star Tours keychain (1986)	3 - 5

Lamps, Lampshades and Nightlights

SW6950-52 Nightlights: Darth Vader, C-3PO or Yoda, (Adam Joseph, Ind) ea 3 - 6
SW6954-56 Dimensional nightlights: C-3PO, Yoda or R2-D2, (Adam Joseph, Ind) ea 3 - 6
See also: **Switcheroos**

Lead Miniatures

West End Games produced a number of boxed lead miniature sets in conjunction with the *Star Wars* Role-Playing Game. The figures came ten to a box, and included a sheet listing game statistics for each character. These are different from the ones produced for the Kenner Micro-Collection sets.

SW7000 Rebel characters	8 - 10
SW7001 Imperial Forces	8 - 10
SW7002 Stormtroopers	8 - 10
SW7003 Bounty Hunters	8 - 10
SW7004 *A New Hope*	8 - 10
SW7005 *The Empire Strikes Back*	8 - 10
SW7006 *Return of the Jedi*	8 - 10
SW7007 Heroes of the Rebellion	8 - 10
SW7008 Villains of the Empire	8 - 10
SW7009 Cantina Aliens	8 - 10
SW7010 Jabba's Palace	8 - 10
SW7011 The Rancor Pit	8 - 10
SW7012 Rebel Troopers	8 - 10

Lightsabers

The first toy adaptation of the lightsaber was essentially a flashlight connected to an inflatable vinyl "blade". A patch kit was included for repairs. "The Force" lightsaber was a hollow plastic tube molded in yellow or red which whistled when moved. All three were produced by Kenner.

SW7050 Inflatable lightsaber (1977)	50 - 75
SW7051 *Star Wars* lightsaber	25 - 50
SW7052 "The Force" lightsaber (1980)	10 - 25
SW7053 Droids battery-operated lightsaber (1985)	15 - 45

Lunch Boxes

Lunch box collecting is a common cross-over into

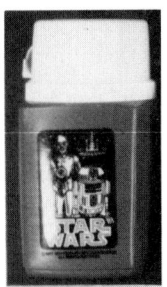

SW7101

SW7107   SW7106

SW7050

SW7111 SW7110

SW7175

SW7206 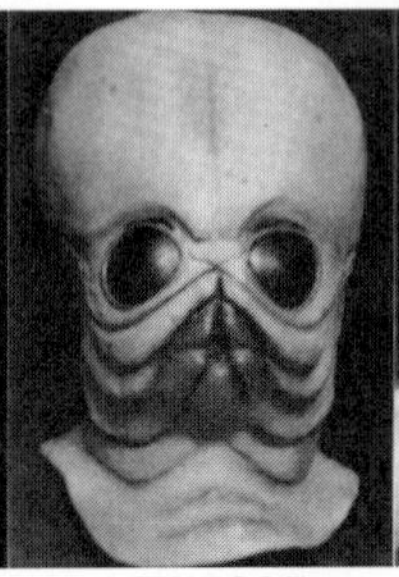 SW7205  SW7203

SW7175

SW7200

SW7207 SW7211 SW7210 SW7208 SW7209

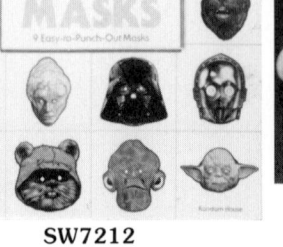

SW7212

SW7201

186

space adventure. The price a buyer is willing to pay for a given lunch box may be influenced by the type of collection the individual is trying to complete. *Star Wars* lunch boxes were produced by King Seeley Thermos.

SW7100 *Star Wars* (1977)	15 - 35
SW7101 Bottle for SW7100	5 - 12
SW7102 *Star Wars* (1978)	12 - 20
SW7103 Bottle for SW7102	3 - 10
SW7104 R2-D2 (1978)	12 - 30
SW7105 Bottle for SW7104	3 - 10
SW7106 *The Empire Strikes Back* (1980)	15 - 35
SW7107 Bottle for SW7106	5 - 10
SW7108 *The Empire Strikes Back* (1981)	15 - 35
SW7109 Bottle for SW7108	5 - 10
SW7110 *Return of the Jedi* (1983)	10 - 20
SW7111 Bottle for SW7110	3 - 9

Magazines and Magazine Articles

Numerous magazine articles have been written about the *Star Wars* saga, including interviews with cast and crew members as well as behind-the-scenes features. Usually the entire magazine is collected, and the values are much higher if *Star Wars* appears on the cover. Several issues of People Magazine containing articles from *The Empire Strikes Back* are among the most common.

SW7175 Magazines w/SW covers	2 - 20
SW7176 Magazines w/SW articles	1 - 2

See also: **Fan Club Kits and Publications**

Masks

Don Post Studios produced a number of masks based on the *Star Wars* saga. The Darth Vader and Stormtrooper helmets were made of plastic, the C-3PO was made of vinyl, and the rest of rubber. The Chewbacca, Wicket, and Yoda masks had natural wool animal hair attached by hand. Methods of manufacturer changed over the many years these masks were produced.

A series of 6 cut-out masks was printed on the back of C-3PO cereal boxes. All prices assume uncut backs or complete boxes.

SW7200 Darth Vader helmet	75 - 125
SW7201 Stormtrooper helmet	50 - 85
SW7202 C-3PO	25 - 40
SW7203 Chewbacca	60 - 120
SW7204 Tuskin Raider	50 - 100
SW7205 Cantina Band Member	50 - 100
SW7206 Yoda	45 - 75
SW7207 Gamorrean Guard	45 - 75
SW7208 Klaatu	45 - 75
SW7209 Weequay	45 - 75
SW7210 Admiral Ackbar	45 - 75
SW7211 Wicket W. Warrick	50 - 85
SW7212 Punch-Out Mask Book	5 - 15

C-3PO Cereal box masks SW7214-19

SW7214 Darth Vader	8 - 15
SW7215 Yoda	8 - 15
SW7216 Chewbacca	8 - 15
SW7217 Luke	8 - 15
SW7218 Stormtrooper	8 - 15

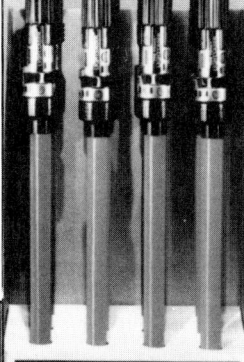

SW7175

SW7279

SW7285

SW7287

SW7219

SW7214

SW7216

SW7217

SW7218

SW7215

SW7281

188

SW7277

SW7282

SW7278

SW7275

SW7276

| SW7219 C-3PO | 8 - 15 |

Ben Cooper soft rubber pull over masks SW7230-34

SW7230 Gamorrean Guard	10 - 12
SW7231 Yoda	10 - 12
SW7232 Klaatu	10 - 12
SW7233 Wicket w/hair	15 - 20
SW7234 Chewbacca w/hair	15 - 20

See also: **Books, Costumes and Play Outfits**

Micro Collection Sets

The Kenner Micro Collection sets consisted of molded plastic settings and die-cast painted metal figures. Each could be purchased individually or several could be bought at once in larger "world" sets. Additional figures were available through mail-in offers. Unpainted figures are known to exist, but were never commercially available.

SW7275 Death Star Escape	15 - 25
SW7276 Death Star Trash Compactor	20 - 30
SW7277 Death Star World (includes SW7275 & SW7276)	35 - 70
SW7278 Hoth Ion Cannon	10 - 20
SW7279 Hoth Turret Defense	8 - 12
SW7280 Hoth Wampa Cave	6 - 10
SW7281 Hoth Generator Attack	25 - 60
SW7282 Hoth World (includes SW7278, SW7279 and SW7280)	30 - 85
SW7283 Bespin Gantry	8 - 20
SW7284 Bespin Freeze Chamber	10 - 30
SW7285 Bespin Control Room	8 - 20
SW7286 Bespin World (includes SW7283, SW7284 and SW7285)	45 - 85
SW7287 Individual Micro-Collection figures	1 - 3
SW7288 Same as ones found in sets SW7275-86, but unpainted	.50 - 2

See also: **Vehicles**

Model Kits

The primary licensee for model kits was Modern Plastics Co. (MPC). The Darth Vader action bust made a raspy "breathing" sound when the head was rocked back and forth on the shoulders. "Structor"

189

SW7332

SW7366

SW7280

SW7330

SW7365

SW7367

SW7304

SW7373

SW7359

190

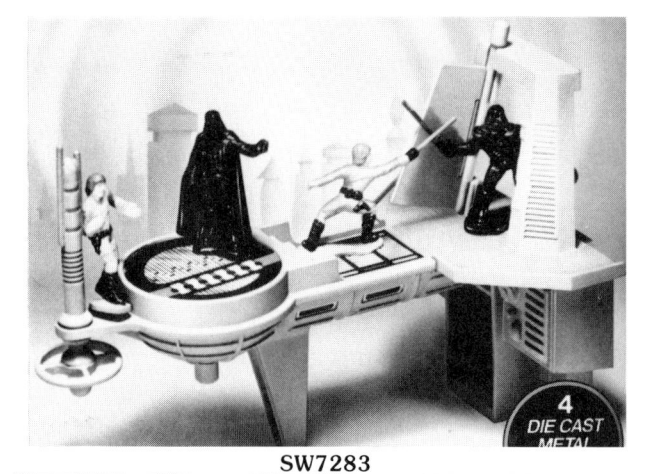

action models of C-3PO, the AT-AT and Scout Walker actually walked after assembly. C-3PO, R2-D2, and several other models were later sold in updated boxes. Some collectors place different values on later issues with a newer film logo. A number of model kits were re-issued in a reprint of the original boxes in 1990. Only the model numbers were different.

SW7300	*Millennium Falcon* w/lights (1977)	35 - 75
SW7302	Darth Vader Action Bust (1977)	15 - 45
SW7304	Darth Vader With Glo Light Saber (1977)	10 - 20
SW7306	Darth Vader TIE Fighter (1977)	10 - 15
SW7308	X-Wing Fighter (1977)	10 - 15
SW7310	C-3PO (1977)	8 - 12
SW7311	Same as SW7310, in ROTJ box (1983)	5 - 10
SW7312	R2-D2 (1977)	8 - 12
SW7313	Same as SW7312, in ROTJ box (1983)	5 - 10
SW7314	R2-D2 Van (snap, 1979)	8 - 25
SW7315	Luke Skywalker Van (snap, 1979)	8 - 25
SW7316	Darth Vader Van (snap, 1979)	8 - 25
SW7330	Degobah (snap)	10 - 30
SW7332	Rebel Base	15 - 35
SW7334	Battle on Ice Planet Hoth	8 - 25
SW7336	Star Destroyer	15 - 30
SW7338	Boba Fett's *Slave I* (1980)	15 - 30
SW7340	AT-AT (1980)	15 - 30
SW7342	Snowspeeder (1980)	15 - 30
SW7350	Jabba's Throne Room (snap)	15 - 30
SW7352	Speeder Bike	10 - 20
SW7354	AT-ST (snap)	5 - 14
SW7356	A-Wing (snap)	5 - 14
SW7357	B-Wing (snap)	5 - 14
SW7358	X-Wing (snap)	5 - 14
SW7359	Y-Wing (snap)	5 - 14
SW7360	TIE Interceptor (snap)	5 - 14

Structor action models SW7365-67

SW7365	AT-AT	8 - 15
SW7366	AT-ST (Scout Walker)	8 - 15
SW7367	C-3PO	8 - 15

1990 Re-release model kits SW7370-75

SW7370	Snowspeeder ESB #8914	8 - 10
SW7371	Star Destroyer ESB #8915	8 - 10
SW7372	Darth Vader's TIE Fighter SW #8916	8 - 10
SW7373	*Millennium Falcon* ROTJ #8917	10 - 15
SW7374	X-Wing ROTJ #8918	8 - 10
SW7375	AT-AT ROTJ #8919	6 - 9

Mugs and Tankards

Ceramic dimensional "toby" mugs were produced in 1977 by California Originals. A plastic mug depicting Luke, Darth Vader and a Stormtrooper was sold as part of a set by Deka in 1980. A *Star Wars* mug collection was offered through the fan club in 1989, with each mug depicting a reprinted scene from various collector's plates. Two different Star Tours mugs were sold at the Disney theme parks.

Tankards SW7400-02 California Originals

SW7400	Darth Vader	20 - 50
SW7401	Obi Wan Kenobi	20 - 50
SW7402	Chewbacca	20 - 50

SW7366

SW7365

SW7314

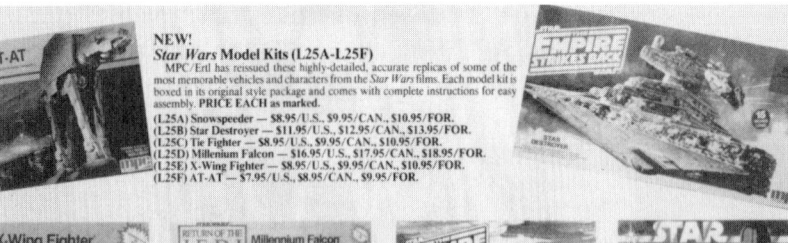

NEW!
Star Wars **Model Kits (L25A-L25F)**
MPC/Ertl has reissued these highly-detailed, accurate replicas of some of the most memorable vehicles and characters from the *Star Wars* films. Each model kit is boxed in its original style package and comes with complete instructions for easy assembly. **PRICE EACH** as marked.

(L25A) Snowspeeder — $8.95/U.S., $9.95/CAN., $10.95/FOR.
(L25B) Star Destroyer — $11.95/U.S., $12.95/CAN., $13.95/FOR.
(L25C) Tie Fighter — $8.95/U.S., $9.95/CAN., $10.95/FOR.
(L25D) Millenium Falcon — $16.95/U.S., $17.95/CAN., $18.95/FOR.
(L25E) X-Wing Fighter — $8.95/U.S., $9.95/CAN., $10.95/FOR.
(L25F) AT-AT — $7.95/U.S., $8.95/CAN., $9.95/FOR.

SW7315

SW7370-75

SW7425-28

SW7602 SW7601 SW7600  SW7665 SW7661 SW7407

SW7607-10

SW7550

192

SW7400 SW7401 SW7402

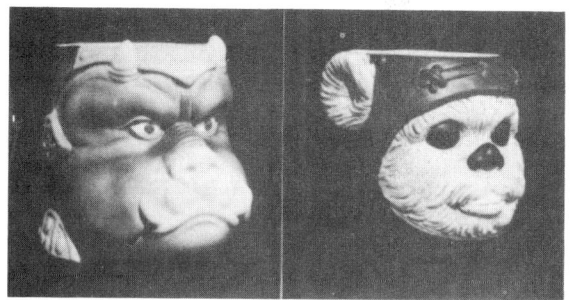

SW7413 SW7416

SW7411 SW7417

SW7414  SW7508

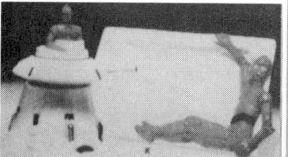

SW7500  SW7660

Ceramic mugs SW7405-14 (Sigma)
SW7405	Luke	15 - 30
SW7406	Leia	15 - 30
SW7407	Han Solo	15 - 30
SW7408	Chewbacca	15 - 30
SW7409	C-3PO	15 - 30
SW7410	Darth Vader	15 - 30
SW7411	Lando Calrissian	15 - 30
SW7412	Yoda	15 - 30
SW7413	Gammorean Guard	15 - 30
SW7414	Klaatu	15 - 30
SW7415	Stormtrooper	15 - 30
SW7416	Wicket	15 - 30
SW7417	Biker Scout	15 - 30
SW7420	Bowl and mug set (Deka, 1980)	8 - 15
SW7425-28	ESB mugs: Heroes, Villains, Robots, or Yoda, ea	5 - 10
SW7435-42	*Star Wars* mug collection, 8 different (1989), ea	3 - 12
SW7445	Star Tours mug, ceramic	5 - 8
SW7446	Star Tours mug, glass	5 - 8

See also: **Dinnerware**

Music Boxes
SW7500	Turret music box w/C-3PO	20 - 45
SW7505	Ewok music box radio	15 - 30
SW7508	Sy Snootles and Rebo Band (Sigma, 1983)	40 - 60
SW7509	Wicket and Kneesa (Sigma)	45 - 65

Newspapers
A *Star Wars* newspaper was printed as a promotion in conjunction with the first film.

SW7550	*Star Wars* newspaper	10 - 20

Party Supplies and Hats
Items in this category are notable because they have survived their intended use. In addition to the usual napkins, invitations, table covers and other items, birthday candles shaped like characters were also produced.

SW7600	R2-D2 birthday candle (Wilton)	3 - 8
SW7601	Darth Vader birthday candle (Wilton)	3 - 8
SW7602	Chewbacca birthday candle (Wilton)	3 - 8
SW7607	Napkins	2 - 5
SW7608	Invitations	2 - 5
SW7609	Table covers	3 - 6
SW7610	Other party supplies	2 - 5

Passports
The *Star Wars* Intergalactic Passport was printed by Ballantine in 1983. It included "visa" stickers allowing passage to various locales in the *Star Wars* universe.

SW7650	Intergalactic Passport w/stickers	5 - 10

Patches
The primary sources of patches were the *Star Wars* and Lucasfilm fan clubs. Most are fairly common, with the exception of the *Revenge of the Jedi* Yoda crew patch. When the third film was re-named, the patch was replaced by a similar patch reading *Return of the*

193

Jedi.

SW7660	Star Wars logo	4 - 10
SW7661	A New Hope	4 - 10
SW7665	ESB logo, red or silver	3 - 8
SW7666	"Vader in Flames" (ESB crew patch)	4 - 10
SW7680	ROTJ logo	3 - 8
SW7681	Yoda/Revenge of the Jedi	15 - 30
SW7682	Yoda/Return of the Jedi	3 - 8
SW7690	Star Wars 10th Anniversary	3 - 8

Patterns

A McCall's pattern set included designs for costumes of Chewbacca, Princess Leia, Yoda, Jawa or Darth Vader. Another set could be used to make apparel from Return of the Jedi.

SW7690	Costume pattern (McCall's)	5 - 15
SW7695	ROTJ pattern	4 - 10

Pens, Pencils and Pencil Cases

Star Wars ballpoint pens, pencils, and plastic pencil cases ere available in stores.

An Empire Strikes Back pencil was included in the Empire fan club kit, and could be purchased as merchandise from the same source. Pencils with character heads at the eraser end were sold with Return of the Jedi.

SW7700	SW pencils and pens, ea	3 - 5
SW7705	ESB pencils and pens, ea	2 - 4
SW7710	ROTJ character pencils, ea	1 - 3
SW7715	ROTJ Pop-a-Point pencils	1 - 2
SW7716	Pencil cases, ea	2 - 10

Photos and Photo Sets

Photos of the cast and scenes from the Star Wars films were regularly offered through the fan club as part of the membership kits. These were process color prints on glossy paper. The Empire Strikes Back "Photobusta" was also a club premium, and included six 12" x 17" photos.

SW7730	SW photos, ea	3 - 6
SW7731	ESB photos, ea	2 - 4
SW7732	ESB Photobusta	5 - 15
SW7733	ROTJ photos, ea	1 - 3

SW7716

SW7880

SW7881

SW7882

Pinback Buttons, Badges and Tabs

Official *Star Wars* buttons were licensed to Adam Joseph Industries. A series of 25 *Star Wars* character buttons were also made available from the fan club. Other button producers have issued unlicensed slogan buttons with comic uses of the word "FORCE" and other film innuendoes.

SW7750	Fan Club membership	5 - 15
SW7751	Fan Club character set of 25	45 - 70
SW7752	May the Force be With You (movie)	1 - 3
SW7755	Darth Vader/Public Radio	3 - 6
SW7775	May the Force Be With You (1977)	4 - 6
SW7776	Darth Vader Lives	4 - 6
SW7777	Droids	4 - 6
SW7778	Darth Vader	4 - 6
SW7779	Darth Vader Lives (stylized)	1 - 3
SW7780-87	*Star Wars* character set, including Ben (Obi-Wan) Kenobi, Chewbacca, Luke Skywalker, Princess Leia Organa, Hans and Chewbacca, C-3PO, R2-D2, and Darth Vader, ea	1 - 3
SW7790-95	ESB character set, including Yoda, Chewbacca, C-3PO and R2-D2, Luke Skywalker, Darth Vader, and Boba Fett, ea	1 - 3

ROTJ buttons SW7800-08 (1983)

SW7800	*Revenge of the Jedi* logo	8 - 12
SW7801-08	*Return of the Jedi* logo, Chewbacca, Gamorrean Guard, Max Rebo, Darth Vader, R2-D2 and C-3PO, Emperor's Personal Guard, or Red Darth Vader Montage, ea	1 - 3

2-1/4" ROTJ buttons SW7810-19 (1983)

SW7810-19	*Return of the Jedi* logo, Heroes in Forest, Chewbacca, Darth Vader, Imperial Guard, R2-D2 and C-3PO, Yoda, Max Rebo Band, Baby Ewok, or Jabba the Hutt, ea	1 - 5
SW7820	10th Anniversary button	5 - 12
SW7825	1" Trilogy Pins: *Star Wars* logo, ESB logo, ROTJ logo, R2-D2, C-3PO, or Darth Vader (1989) ea	5 - 10

Plates

A series of eight plates was produced by The Hamilton Collection. A commemorative plate was also made for the 10th anniversary of *Star Wars*.

SW7850	Han Solo	15 - 30
SW7851	Princess Leia	15 - 30
SW7852	Luke Skywalker	15 - 30
SW7853	Chewbacca	15 - 30
SW7854	Yoda	15 - 30
SW7855	Wicket and R2-D2	15 - 30
SW7856	C-3PO	15 - 30
SW7857	Darth Vader	15 - 30
SW7858	Obi-Wan Kenobi	15 - 30
SW7859	Lightsaber Battle plate	25 - 45
SW7860	Anniversary plate	25 - 45

Play-Doh Sets

A typical set includes a plastic mat printed with a background from one of the films, three hinged molds, a plastic spaceship, three 6-oz cans of Play-Doh, and

SW7901 SW7900

SW7917 SW7918 SW7919 SW7920

SW7908 SW7907 SW7909

SW7905 SW7906

SW7919 SW7920 SW7905

SW7953  SW7962  SW7970  SW7915 SW7916

a plastic trimmer.

SW7880 *Star Wars* action set	15 - 35
SW7881 Ice Planet Hoth	10 - 25
SW7882 Degobah	10 - 25
SW7883 Jabba the Hutt	8 - 15
SW7884 Ewoks	8 - 15

Plush Stuffed Characters

Stuffed versions of R2-D2 and Chewbacca were made by Kenner in 1979. R2 has a built-in squeak mechanism. Plush toys were not seen again until the release of *Return of the Jedi*, when stuffed Ewoks and Woklings were released.

SW7900 R2-D2	8 - 30
SW7901 Chewbacca	15 - 35
SW7905 Wicket	10 - 25
SW7906 Princess Kneesaa	10 - 25
SW7907 Paploo	10 - 25
SW7908 Latara	10 - 25
SW7909 Zephee	10 - 25

Woklings SW7915-20

SW7915 Gwig	5 - 15
SW7916 Malani	5 - 15
SW7917 Wiley	5 - 15
SW7918 Mookiee	5 - 15
SW7919 Leeni	5 - 15
SW7920 Nippet	5 - 15

Posters — Film

There were 21 different film posters produced for the *Star Wars* trilogy. Reprints of the initial release posters were made for video stores and in smaller sizes for retail stores. Japanese half-sheet posters for *Return of the Jedi* were offered through the fan club. Full one-sheet posters measure 27" x 41".

SW7950 SW advance	75 - 175
SW7951 SW advance, second version	75 - 175

SW8106 SW8107

SW8107

SW8037

SW8037

197

SW8107

SW8108   SW8109

SW8119

SW8114   SW8115   SW8190   SW8250

198

SW8008    SW8005

top: SW8006   bottom: SW8007

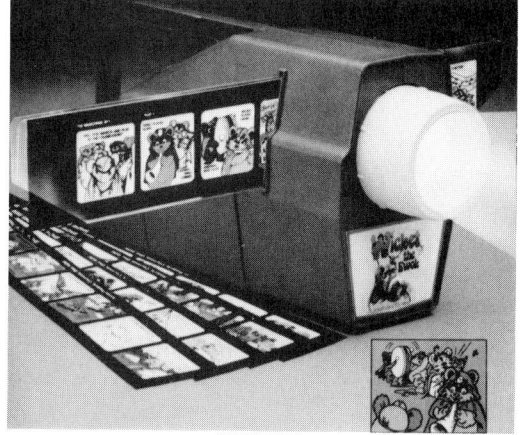

SW8230

SW7952	SW advance, style "B"	75 - 175
SW7953	SW "A"	100 - 200
SW7954	SW "A" w/record promotion	100 - 200
SW7955	SW "C"	75 - 175
SW7956	SW "D"	75 - 175
SW7957	SW Happy Birthday	150 - 250
SW7958	SW 1979 reissue	25 - 70
SW7959	SW 1981 reissue	25 - 70
SW7960	SW 1982 reissue	25 - 70
SW7961	ESB advance	50 - 150
SW7962	ESB "A"	75 - 175
SW7963	ESB "B"	75 - 175
SW7964	ESB 1981 summer re-release	20 - 60
SW7965	ESB 1982 re-release	20 - 60
SW7968	*Revenge of the Jedi*	75 - 175
SW7969	*Revenge of the Jedi*, 2nd version	50 - 150
SW7970	ROTJ "A"	50 - 150
SW7971	ROTJ "B"	50 - 150
SW7972	ROTJ 1985 reissue	25 - 70
SW7975	Movie poster reprints, ea	8 - 10
SW7980	ROTJ Japanese half-sheets	?

Posters — Premium

Premium posters are listed chronologically by sponsor. Display stands, cereal boxes, and other items were produced in conjunction with some of these offers.

Burger Chef SW8000-03 (1978)
SW8000	Luke Skywalker	3 - 6
SW8001	R2-D2	3 - 6
SW8002	Chewbacca	3 - 6
SW8003	Darth Vader	3 - 6

General Mills SW8005-08 (1978)
SW8005	*Star Wars* montage	5 - 10
SW8006	Tie Fighter and X-Wing	5 - 10
SW8007	Star Destroyer	5 - 10
SW8008	R2-D2 and C-3PO	5 - 10

Proctor and Gamble SW8010-12 (1978)
SW8010	Ben Kenobi and Darth Vader	5 - 10
SW8011	R2-D2 and C-3P0	5 - 10
SW8012	Death Star	5 - 10

Nestea SW8018-19 (1980)
SW8018	Luke Skywalker	5 - 10
SW8019	Darth Vader	5 - 10

Burger King SW8020-22 (1980)
SW8020	Hoth	3 - 6
SW8021	Degobah	3 - 6
SW8022	Bespin	3 - 6
SW8025	Coca-Cola ESB montage by Boris Vallejo (1980)	10 - 25

Proctor and Gamble SW8028-31 (1980)
SW8028	Luke Skywalker	2 - 4
SW8029	R2-D2 and C-3PO	2 - 4
SW8030	Darth Vader	2 - 4
SW8031	Bespin Scenes	2 - 4
SW8036	Dixie Cups Story Card poster (1981)	10 - 20
SW8037	HI-C ROTJ poster (double-sided) (1983)	5 - 10
SW8040	Oral-B ROTJ poster (1983)	5 - 10

Posters — Other

The *Star Wars* trilogy created a number of retail posters, and others were included with the *Star Wars*

199

SW8225

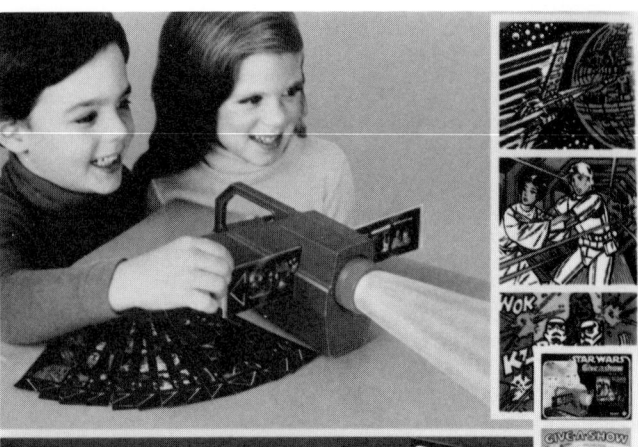

SW8195

SW8205

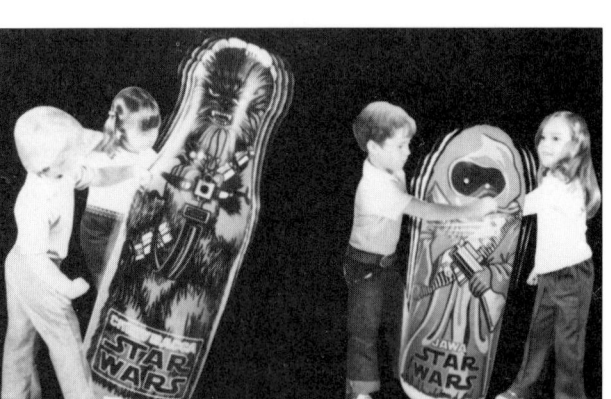

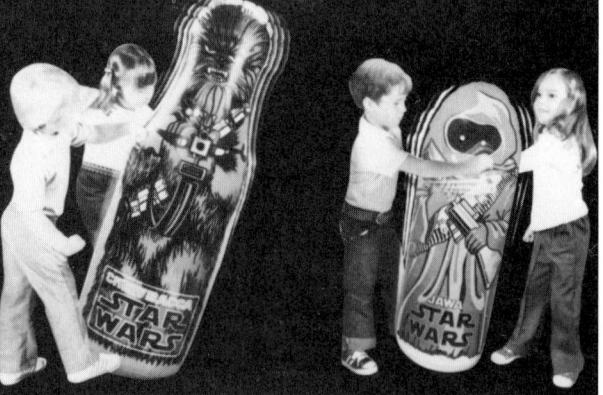

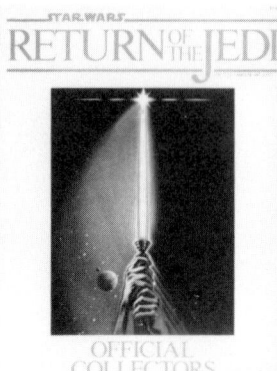

GIVE-A-SHOW
ASSORTMENT
8 STAR WARS
4 SCOOBY DOO
No. 35230
PKD 12, WT 14¾ LB
CUBE 2.63 CU. FT
NO. 35180 STAR WARS
PKD 6, WT 7¼ LBS
CUBE 1.30 CU. FT
NO. 36350 SCOOBY
PKD 6, WT 7¼ LBS
CUBE 1.30 CU. FT

SW8206

SW8264

SW8240

SW8243

SW8241

SW8242

SW8268

SW8308

SW8283

SW8280

200

Fan Club kits. Although the *Empire* poster album is titled "volume 1," no further volumes are known to have been produced. Other items included here were produced in conjunction with the Star Tours exhibit at the Disney theme parks.

SW retail posters SW8100-03
SW8100	Sword montage	15 - 30
SW8101	R2-D2 and C-3PO	15 - 30
SW8102	Luke Skywalker	15 - 30
SW8103	Princess Leia	15 - 30
SW8104	SW concert	25 - 40
SW8105	SW radio program	25 - 40
SW8106	*Star Wars* Official Poster Monthly, issue #1	2 - 6
SW8107	*Star Wars* Official Poster Monthly, #2-?, ea	1 - 4
SW8108	ESB Official Poster Monthly, #1	2 - 6
SW8109	ESB Official Poster Monthly, #2-?, ea	1 - 4

ESB retail posters SW8110-12
SW8110	*Empire Strikes Back*	5 - 8
SW8111	Boba Fett	5 - 8
SW8112	Darth Vader and Stormtroopers	5 - 8
SW8113	ESB montage (fan club)	5 - 10
SW8114	Vehicle scene	2 - 8
SW8115	Darth Vader montage	2 - 10
SW8116	Read and the Force is With You (Yoda)	10 - 20
SW8117	*Empire Strikes Back* poster album, volume 1	5 - 10
SW8118	ESB radio program	10 - 20
SW8119	Darth Vader, life size	5 - 13
SW8125	ROTJ Space Battle (fan club)	5 - 10
SW8126	ROTJ poster album	5 - 10
SW8130	The Ewok Adventure	5 - 10
SW8131	Caravan of Courage "A"	5 - 10
SW8132	Caravan of Courage "B"	5 - 10
SW8135	Star Tours posters: Star Tours, Bespin, Degobah, Endor (2 versions), Hoth, Tatooine or Yavin, ea	2 - 5
SW8145	First Ten Years poster	3 - 7
SW8146	First Ten Years mural poster	5 - 15

See also: **Coloring and Painting Sets**

Press Kits
SW8175	Original SW kit (1977)	20 - 45
SW8176	SW kit (1978)	18 - 40
SW8177	Holiday special kit (1978)	18 - 40
SW8178	NPR Presents kit (1979)	15 - 35
SW8179	ESB kit (1980)	15 - 35
SW8180	Introducing Yoda kit (1980)	15 - 35
SW8181	NPR Playhouse kit (1981)	10 - 30
SW8185	ROTJ kit (1983)	10 - 30

Programs and Official Collector's Editions

The *Star Wars* film program is essentially a listing of the credits for the first film. For the second and third film, this was replaced by the Official Collector's Edition, which is an expanded program including articles about the film.

SW8190	*Star Wars* program	10 - 22
SW8195	ESB Official Collector's Edition (Paradise Press)	8 - 15
SW8205	ROTJ program	
SW8206	ROTJ Official Collector's Edition (Paradise Press)	5 - 10

Projection Equipment

Give-A-Show projectors were marketed by Kenner in 1979 and 1984. It included 16 strips of 7 "slides" which depicted the *Star Wars* story.

SW8225	SW Give-A-Show projector	20 - 40
SW8230	Ewok Give-A-Show projector	15 - 30

Punching Bags

Kenner produced four large inflatable "bop bags" in 1977. When fully inflated, Darth Vader and Chewbacca were 50" tall. The R2-D2 and Jawa bags were 36" tall.

SW8240	Chewbacca	30 - 60
SW8241	Darth Vader	20 - 40
SW8242	R2-D2	20 - 40
SW8243	Jawa	30 - 60

See also: **Lightsabers**

Puppets
SW8250	Yoda hand puppet	7 - 15

Puzzles and Puzzle Sets

Jigsaw puzzles by Kenner were among the earliest *Star Wars* items available. They come in 140-piece, 500-piece, 1000-piece and 1500-piece editions. *Return of the Jedi* and Ewok puzzles were made by Craft Master in 1983.

Kenner jigsaw puzzles SW8260-82
Series #1 SW8260-65
SW8260	Luke #40110, 500 pcs, purple box	5 - 10
SW8261	Luke #40110, 500 pcs, black box	4 - 8
SW8262	Space Battle, 500 pcs, purple box	5 - 10
SW8263	Space Battle, 500 pcs, black box	4 - 8
SW8264	R2-D2 and C-3PO, 140 pcs, black box	3 - 5
SW8265	Han and Chewbacca, 140 pcs, black box	3 - 5

Series #2 SW8266-68
SW8266	Luke and Leia leap for their lives, 500 pcs, black box	4 - 8
SW8267	Trapped in the trash compactor, 140 pcs, black box	3 - 5
SW8268	Darth Vader and Ben Kenobi, lightsaber duel	3 - 5

Series #3 SW8272-75
SW8272	X-Wing Fighters prepare to attack, 500 pcs, black box	4 - 8
SW8273	Victory Celebration, 500 pcs, black box	4 - 8
SW8274	Attack of the Sand People, 140 pcs, black box	3 - 5
SW8275	Stormtroopers stop the Landspeeder, 140 pcs, black box	3 - 5

Series #4 SW8280-83
SW8280	Cantina Band, 500 pcs, black box	4 - 8
SW8281	The Bantha, 140 pcs, black box	3 - 5
SW8282	Jawas Capture R2-D2, 140 pcs, black box	3 - 5
SW8283	The Selling of Droids, 500 pcs, black box	3 - 5

SW8345

SW8272

SW8273

SW8356

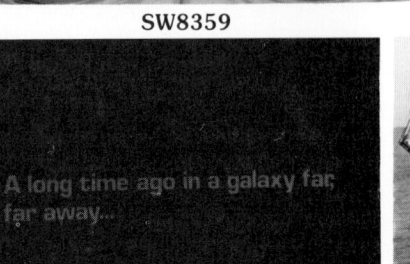

SW8413

SW8359

SW8352

SW8359

SW8357

SW8350

202

SW8274 SW8418

SW8362

SW8373

SW8361

No series number listed SW8286-90
SW8286 *Star Wars* Adventure (movie poster) 1000 pcs, black box	8 - 10
SW8287 Aboard the *Millennium Falcon*, 1000 pcs, black box	8 - 10
SW8288 R2-D2 and C-3PO, 140 pcs, blue box	5 - 10
SW8290 Han and Chewbacca, 140 pcs, blue box	5 - 10

***Return of the Jedi* puzzles SW8295-97** (Craft Master, 1983)
SW8295 Friends of Jabba the Hutt	5 - 10
SW8296 Jabba the Hutt Throne Room	5 - 10
SW8297 Death Star	5 - 10

ROTJ tray puzzles SW8300-05 (Craft Master, 1983)
SW8300 Gammorrean Guard	2 - 5
SW8301 Ewoks on Hang Gliders	2 - 5
SW8302 Wicket and R2-D2	2 - 5
SW8303 Leia and Wicket	2 - 5
SW8304 Ewok Village	2 - 5
SW8305 Darth Vader	2 - 5

9-square tray puzzle SW8308-09
SW8308 *Return of the Jedi*	2 - 5
SW8309 Ewok	2 - 5

Racing Set
SW8345 Star Wars Duel Racing set (Lionel, 1978)	45 - 120

Radios
SW5950 Luke Skywalker AM headset	85 - 250
SW5951 R2-D2 radio	10 - 45

Records, Tapes and Compact Discs

This category includes audio recordings in five possible formats: records, reel-to-reel tape, 8-track tape, cassette tape, and/or compact disc. Although the recordings are the same in most cases, separate number codes have been assigned to each item.

***Star Wars* soundtrack recordings SW8350-54**
SW8350 Record	8 - 15
SW8351 Reel-to-reel	8 - 15
SW8352 8-track, 2 pack	8 - 15
SW8353 Cassette	8 - 15
SW8354 Compact disc	20 - 35

The Story of *Star Wars* SW8356-58
SW8356 Record	6 - 12
SW8357 Reel-to-reel	6 - 12
SW8358 Cassette tape	6 - 12
SW8359 Reel-to-reel boxed set: *Star Wars* soundtrack/Story, includes credits page and color photo book	30 - 75
SW8360 Disney Storyteller Book and Record sets, ea	1 - 4
SW8361 Main title plus Cantina Band	2 - 7
SW8362 Music from *Star Wars*	2 - 6

ESB soundtrack recordings SW8373-75
SW8373 Record	3 - 10
SW8374 Cassette	3 - 10
SW8375 Compact disc	10 - 20

The Story of *The Empire Strikes Back* SW8378-79
SW8378 Record	4 - 8
SW8379 Cassette	4 - 8

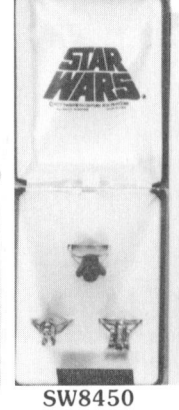

SW8358	SW8379	SW8552
SW8394	SW8404	SW8580
8590	SW8603	SW8580
SW8602	W8551 SW8550	SW8450 SW8601

ROTJ soundtrack recordings SW8390-92
SW8390	Record	2 - 7
SW8391	Cassette	2 - 7
SW8392	Compact disc	10 - 20

The Story of *Return of the Jedi* SW8394-95
SW8394	Record	4 - 8
SW8395	Cassette	4 - 8
SW8397	ROTJ Special Edition Picture disk (Ewok/Luke)	8 - 15
SW8399	Ewoks Original Soundtracks	5 - 10
SW8404	Rebel Mission record or cassette	2 - 5

7-inch records SW8410-20
SW8410	*Star Wars*	2 - 4
SW8413	Planet of the Hoojibs	2 - 4
SW8414	*The Empire Strikes Back*	2 - 4
SW8416	*Return of the Jedi*	2 - 4
SW8418	The Ewoks Join the Fight	2 - 4
SW8420	Droid World, the Further Adventures	2 - 4

See also: **Fan Club Kits and Publications**

Remote-Controlled Toys

The radio-controlled R2-D2 and Sandcrawler were both produced by Kenner. They were operated by a two-channel radio controller with an easily-broken wire. These items cross-over into the field of robot collecting, and bring top prices only if they are in working condition. Of the two, the Sandcrawler is more difficult to find.

SW8425	Radio-controlled R2-D2	40 - 95
SW8426	Radio-controlled Jawa Sandcrawler	75 - 175

Rings
SW8450	Ring set: Vader, R2-D2, and C-3PO	8 - 15
SW8460	Darth Vader (W. Berrie & Co., 1980)	4 - 8
SW8461	X-Wing (W. Berrie & Co., 1980)	4 - 8
SW8462	May the Force Be With You (W. Berrie & Co., 1980)	4 - 8

Rocket Kits
These were made by Estes in 1978-79. A starter kit was required to launch any of the four models available.

SW8500	TIE Fighter	10 - 20
SW8501	X-Wing	15 - 25
SW8502	Flying R2-D2	10 - 20
SW8503	X-Wing w/Maxi-Brutel	18 - 30
SW8504	Starter outfit	10 - 20
SW8505	Proten torpedo	15 - 20
SW8506	Estes catalog w/*Star Wars* cover	2 - 4

Roller Skates
SW8520	Darth Vader and Imperial Guard	5 - 25
SW8521	ROTJ	5 - 10
SW8522	*Star Wars* on Wheels	5 - 10
SW8523	Wicket the Ewok	10 - 20

School Supplies
SW8550	Wookie doodle pad	2 - 5
SW8551	Darth Vader Duty Roster	2 - 5
SW8552	Star Wars portfolio	2 - 6

SW8560	ESB notebooks, ea	3 - 6
SW8580	ROTJ notebooks, ea	2 - 4
SW8590	ROTJ erasers, Gamorrean Guard, Bib Fortuna, Max Rebo, Jabba the Hutt, Darth Vader, Yoda, Wicket, Baby Ewoks or Admiral Ackbar, (Spindex, 1983) ea	2 - 4
SW8600	ROTJ backpack	8 - 12
SW8601	Pencil tablet	3 - 5
SW8602	Doodle pad	2 - 4
SW8603	Color Glue	1 - 4

See also: **Pens, Pencils and Pencil Boxes**

Sheets, Pillows, Bedspreads, Sleeping Bags and Drapes

These items have been produced in conjunction with the films, but like most cloth items, collector interest is low.

SW8640	SW sheets	10 - 15
SW8641	SW blanket	15 - 20
SW8642	SW pillowcase	3 - 5
SW8643	SW sleeping bag	15 - 25
SW8650	ESB sheets	10 - 15
SW8651	ESB pillowcase	3 - 5
SW8652	ESB curtains	10 - 15
SW8653	ESB blanket	15 - 20
SW8654	ESB sleeping bag	15 - 25
SW8655	Yoda sleeping bag	15 - 25
SW8660	Darth Vader pillow (1983)	5 - 10
SW8661	ROTJ curtains	10 - 15

Shoelaces

Although some shoelaces produced are labelled *Star Wars* on the laces themselves, they were produced around the time of *Return of the Jedi*. Four different styles are known.

SW8670	Shoelaces, ROTJ, Darth Vader, *Star Wars*/Droids or Ewoks, (Stride Rite, 1983) ea	1 - 3

Shoes and Slippers

Clarks made dress shoes in 1978. They came in *Star Wars* boxes with wrap-around artwork. When purchased, a special plastic SW bag was provided to carry them home. Stride Rite had a neater spaceship hanger type box in 1982 which came with five cardboard stand-up figures (Lando, Darth Vader, C-3PO, R2-D2 and Luke). Shoes as collectibles aren't near as attractive as the boxes which range from 15-30 each with or without the shoes or sneakers.

Soap, Shampoo and Bubble Bath Products

Soap products were produced after the release of *Return of the Jedi*, although some were designed to represent earlier versions of the characters. Molded soap was produced by Omni Cosmetics. A series of 10 shampoo/bubble bath containers was also made. These were partially wrapped in clear plastic to keep them from leaking (although one collector's experience questions the effectiveness of this method) and had a tag describing the various "benefits" of using the product. Shampoo, cream rinse, and bubble bath also came in non-character plastic bottles packaged as

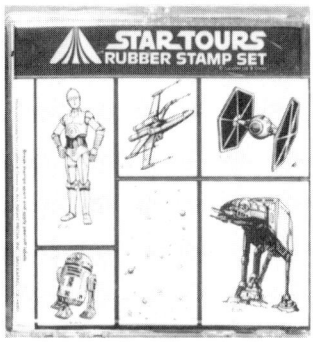

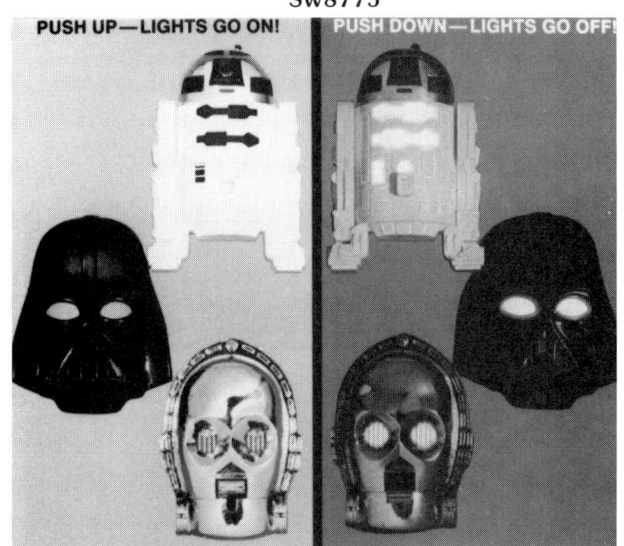

"Princess Leia's Beauty Bag" and "Luke Skywalker's Belt Kit".

SW8720	Character soap, Luke, Leia, Yoda, Darth Vader, Jabba the Hutt, Gammorean Guard, Wicket or other, ea	2 - 5
SW8730	Character soap, set of 4	8 - 12
SW8735	Shampoo, Luke, Yoda, R2-D2, Chewbacca, Gammorean Guard or other, ea	5 - 8
SW8740	Bubble bath, Leia, Darth Vader, Jabba the Hutt or Wicket, ea	5 - 8
SW8742	Princess Leia's Beauty Bag	15 - 20
SW8743	Luke Skywalker's Belt Kit	15 - 20
SW8744	Refueling Station bottles, ea	10 - 18

Stamps, Collector's

A stamp collecting kit was printed in 1977 by H. E. Harris and Company. It included an album, 24 *Star Wars* seals, 35 space exploration postage stamps, a bag of 300 stamp hinges, and a plastic magnifying glass.

SW8775	Stamp kit (H. E. Harris and Co., 1977)	8 - 20

Stamps, Rubber

SW8790	Rubber stamps (1983) Chewbacca, Yoda, *Millennium Falcon*, TIE Fighter, Biker Scout, X-Wing, Darth Vader, Admiral Ackbar, Wicket, Gammorrean Guard, C-3PO or Imperial Guard, ea	2 - 5
SW8805	Wicket, 3 in 1 stamp set	2 - 4
SW8808	Star Tours stamp set	3 - 5

Stickers and Sticker Books

Stickers were produced for all three films. These usually have little value if not in their original packaging.

SW8885	SW Sticker Book (Panini, 1977)	10 - 20
SW8886	Stickers for SW8885, set of 256	20 - 35
SW8889	ESB Sticker Set and Album (Burger King)	6 - 10
SW8891	ROTJ Sticker Album	2 - 5
SW8892	Stickers for SW8891, set of 180	8 - 22
SW8895	3-D Ewok Perk-up sticker sets, ea	1 - 5

See Also: **Decals; Gum Cards, Gum Wrappers and Trading Cards**

Suncatchers
Make It, Bake It kits SW8925- (Fundimensions)

SW8925	R2-D2	2 - 4
SW8926	Darth Vader	2 - 4
SW8927	Gamorrean Guard	2 - 4
SW8928	Jabba and Salacious Crumb	2 - 4
SW8935	Set of 12 (Lee Wards)	8 - 20

Swimming Pools and Accessories

It is usually remarkable for one of these "kiddie pools" to survive intact, but nevertheless they are not in great demand.

SW8940	Kiddie swimming pool	?

SW8889

SW9027

SW9052

SW9000-01

208

SW9035

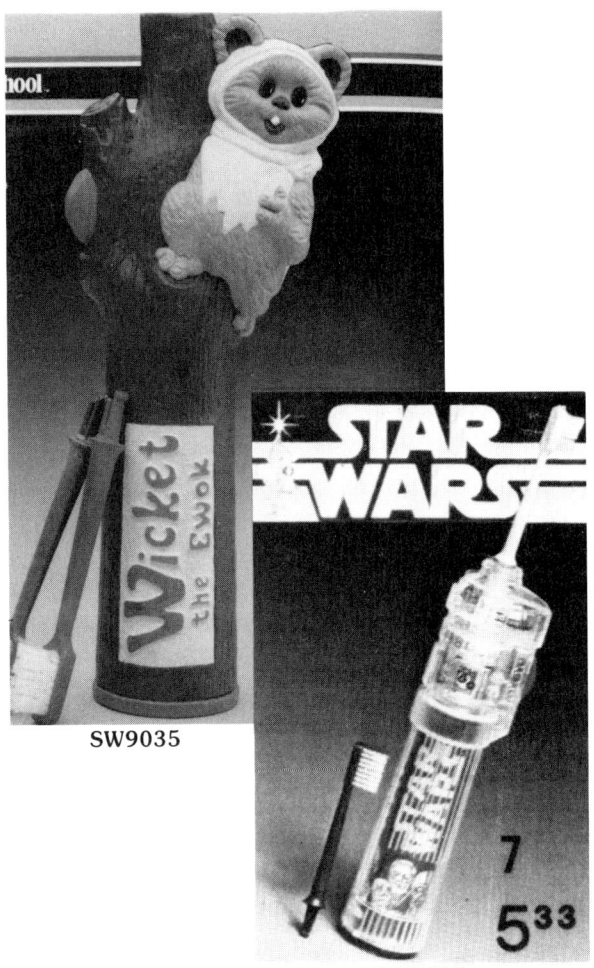

SW9025

SW8877

Switchplate Covers
Switcheroos were dimensional figures of *Star Wars* characters which completely covered a lightswitch fixture. The switch itself fit into the back of the Switcheroo, and was controlled by a moving part of the figure. They were made by Kenner

SW8950 Switcheroos: Darth Vader, R2-D2, or C-3PO, ea   5 - 15

Telephones
SW8975 Darth Vader speakerphone (ATC, 1983)   70 - 110
SW8977 Wicket play phone   15 - 30

Tin Boxes and Containers
A wide variety of tin containers were produced for *The Empire Strikes Back* and *Return of the Jedi*.

SW9000 Tin boxes   5 - 10
SW9001 Tin containers   3 - 5

Toothbrushes
Similar electric toothbrushes were sold by Kenner for both *Star Wars* and *The Empire Strikes Back*. Character toothbrushes were produced by Oral-B for *Return of the Jedi*.

SW9025 SW electric toothbrush (Kenner, 1978)   15 - 25
SW9026 ESB electric toothbrush (Kenner, 1980)   15 - 25
SW9027 ROTJ toothbrushes, Luke, Leia, Chewbacca and Han, C-3PO and R2-D2, Ewoks, Jedi Masters or Darth Vader (Oral-B, 1983), ea   3 - 4
SW9035 Wicket battery-operated toothbrush (1984)   8 - 12

Towels
Towels of various sizes were produced during the time of *Star Wars*, but for the most part these items inspire little collector interest.

SW9050 R2-D2 and C-3PO beach towel   3 - 8
SW9051 Darth Vader beach towel   3 - 8
SW9052 R2-D2 and C-3PO hand towel   2 - 5
SW9053 R2-D2 wash cloth   1 - 4

Vehicles
Numerous spaceships and other vehicles from the *Star Wars* saga were produced in die-cast metal and plastic. The micro-collection X-Wing and TIE Fighter were designed to fall apart on impact, producing a "crash" effect. Perhaps the most incongruous items from this category were the Kenner SSP vans, designed to take advantage of the custom van craze of the '70s. One hundred Speeder Bike play vehicles were prizes in a J. C. Penney contest. A second hundred were awarded in a *Return of the Jedi* movie theater contest sponsored by Coca-Cola. Patrons removed a tab to see if they won the bike or other Kenner ROTJ toy.

SSP vans SW9150-51 (Kenner, 1978)

209

SW9406

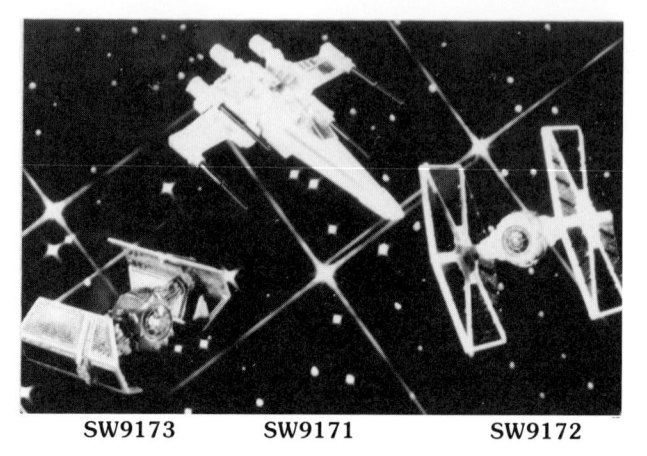

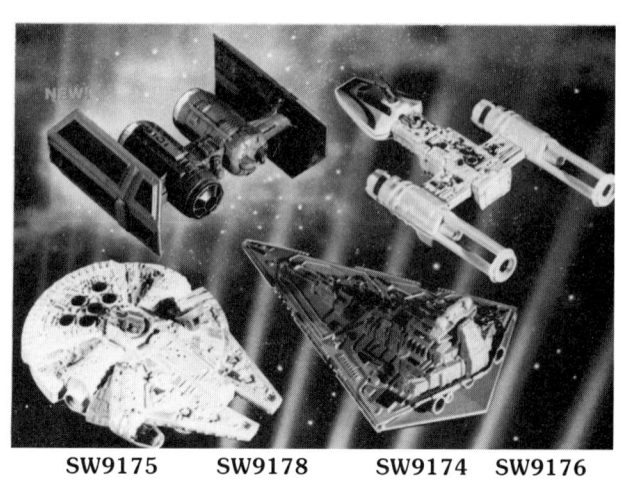

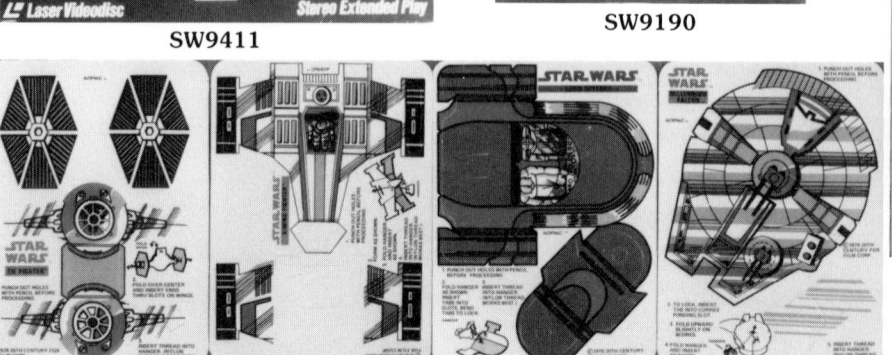

SW9173   SW9171   SW9172

SW9408

SW9175   SW9178   SW9174   SW9176

SW9411

SW9190

SW9195

SW9160

210

SW9150 Darth Vader (black)		8 - 25
SW9151 Luke and heroes (white)		8 - 25
SW9160 Punch-out vehicles: Landspeeder, *Millennium Falcon*, X-Wing or TIE Fighter (General Mills), ea		4 - 10

Diecast vehicles SW9170-80

SW9170 Land Speeder		20 - 40
SW9171 X-Wing Fighter		20 - 40
SW9172 TIE Fighter		15 - 30
SW9173 Darth Vader TIE Fighter		20 - 70
SW9174 Imperial Cruiser		25 - 75
SW9175 *Millennium Falcon* (Sears exclusive)		35 - 100
SW9176 Y-Wing Fighter		25 - 75
SW9177 Snowspeeder		25 - 75
SW9178 Twin TIE Bomber		125 - 400
SW9179 *Slave I*		25 - 65
SW9180 Twin-Pod Cloud Car		25 - 65
SW9190 Micro X-Wing		20 - 50
SW9191 Micro TIE Fighter		20 - 50
SW9195 Speeder Bike pedal vehicle		?

See Also: **Action Figure Playsets, Vehicles and Accessories**

Video Tapes and Discs
***Star Wars* SW9400-01**

SW9400 Video tape		10 - 25
SW9401 Video disc		20 - 40
SW9402 The Making of *Star Wars*, video tape		10 - 25

***The Empire Strikes Back* SW9405-06**

SW9405 Video tape		10 - 25
SW9406 Video disc		20 - 35
SW9407 SP FX: *The Empire Strikes Back*, video tape		10 - 25
SW9408 The Making of *Star Wars*/SP FX, video disc		20 - 35

***Return of the Jedi* SW9410-11**

SW9410 Video tape		10 - 25
SW9411 Video disc		20 - 35
SW9413 *Great Movie Monsters: Return of the Jedi*, video tape		10 - 20

Watches

Star Wars watches were manufactured by Bradley from 1977-83. Watch collecting is also a popular cross-over field. Although collector interest is high, few are interested in watches not in working condition. Watch bands are often replaced or missing, and damage to the face (scratches, dirt, etc.) lessens the value. In addition, some collectors only collect watches in their original packaging. This was usually a box or case, but some later watches were sold on a bubble-pack card.

SW9600 SW logo, digital		50 - 100
SW9602 C-3PO and R2-D2/*Star Wars* digital, rectangular face		50 - 100
SW9604 C-3PO and R2-D2 (drawing), vinyl band		30 - 75
SW9606 C-3PO and R2-D2 (photo), numbers in white border		30 - 75
SW9608 C-3PO and R2-D2 digital, round face		30 - 75
SW9610 C-3PO and R2-D2 (photo),		

SW9191
1 DIE CAST METAL

SW9628 SW9600

SW9645 — BRADLEY

SW9604

SW9632

SW9642

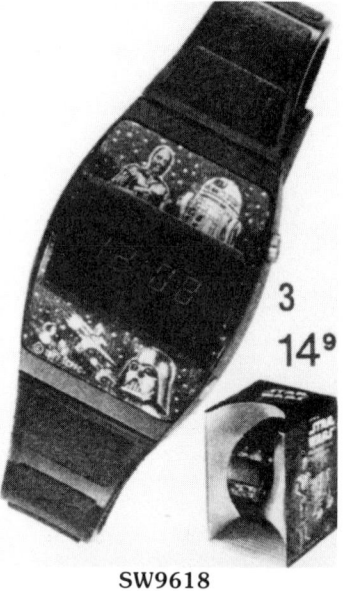

SW9618
3
14.9

SW9800

SW9606   SW9624   SW9622   SW9630   SW9640

SW9602

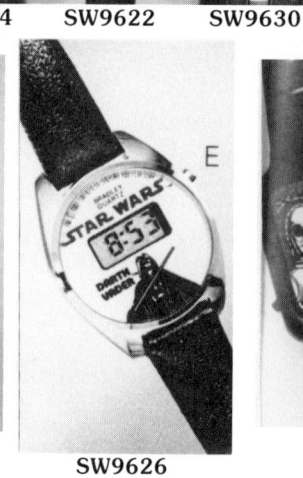

SW9626

SW9616

212

	vinyl band	15 - 45
SW9612	C-3PO and R2-D2 digital, rectangular face	15 - 45
SW9614	C-3PO and R2-D2 digital, round face, musical	75 - 125
SW9616	C-3PO and R2-D2 digital w/TIE fighter, musical	75 - 125
SW9618	C-3PO and R2-D2/Darth Vader digital, rectangular face	50 - 100
SW9620	Darth Vader/*Star Wars* digital, rectangular face	50 - 100
SW9622	Darth Vader, vinyl band	2 - 50
SW9624	Darth Vader, stars and planet on face	30 - 75
SW9626	Darth Vader digital	15 - 45
SW9628	Darth Vader's head, digital	15 - 45
SW9630	Yoda	20 - 50
SW9632	Yoda digital	20 - 50
SW9634	Jabba the Hutt, vinyl band	15 - 45
SW9636	Jabba the Hutt, digital	15 - 45
SW9638	Droids digital	15 - 45
SW9640	Ewoks, vinyl band	15 - 45
SW9642	Ewoks digital	15 - 45
SW9644	Wicket the Ewok, stars and planet on face	15 - 45
SW9645	Radio watch w/headphones (Bradley)	25 - 50

Yoda the Jedi Master

This "fortune telling" device is an old idea forged into a creative new one. A plastic 20-sided "ball" floating in black liquid gives the impression Yoda is answering questions ask of him when he is standing upright. To get his comment on your question, the Jedi Master is turned upside down and the ball floats up to the glass bottom to reveal the message inscribed on the flat side which comes to rest against the glass.

SW9800 Yoda the Jedi Master   15 - 45

TOM CORBETT, SPACE CADET

Tom Corbett, based on Robert Heinlein's novel *Space Cadet*, is a story of growing up in the Space Academy. Students in the Academy are separated into groups of three — a command, power, and radar cadet. Each member of the group has his own set of responsibilities. The series follows the adventures and trials of the Polaris Crew, the best unit in the Academy. The group is led by command cadet Tom Corbett, a natural leader from New Chicago. Accompanying him on the crew are radar expert Roger Manning (the smart alack of the group) and power cadet Astro (an engineering whiz from Venus).

"Tom Corbett" was first broadcast on television on October 2, 1950 by CBS. Like many shows in the early days of television, the cadets came into your living room for 15 minutes, 3 days a week. Scheduling for the show was sporadic, and it appeared on four television networks during its five year span (DuMont was the fourth).

Though primarily seen on television, "Tom Corbett" found its way into almost every other medium except film. Toys and premiums were better than average and may have contributed substantially to the longevity of the show.

T5950	Sunday comic pages, ea	10 - 20
T6000	Space Academy set (Marx Toys)	400 - 800
T6010	Atomic Rifle	50 - 150
T6015	Signal Siren flashlight (Usalite)	40 - 100
T6020	Atomic Pistol flashlight (Marx Toys)	100 - 200
T6025	Lunch box (Aladdin)	20 - 50
T6026	Mug for T6025, red or blue	25 - 60
T6030	2-Way Space Phone (Zimmerman)	75 - 150
T6035	3-Power field glasses, 3 different decals (Herold)	50 - 125
T6040	Wrist watch on card (Ingraham)	200 - 500
T6041	Watch only	75 - 150
T6045	Molding & Coloring set (Model Craft)	50 - 150
T6050	Uniform (Yankiboy)	100 - 225
T6053	Space hat (Lee)	10 - 40
T6055	Cosmic Vision helmet (Practi-Cole)	175 - 250
T6060	View-Master reels, packet of 3	35 - 55
T6063	Space Cadet Song and March (Golden Record, 1951)	10 - 30

T5950

T5950

T6000

T6015

T6010

T6020

T6570 T6179

T6156

T6155

T6161

T6100

T6063

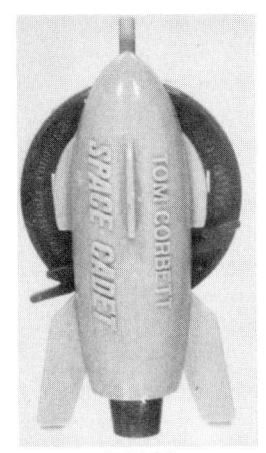

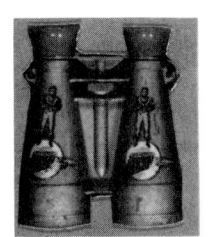

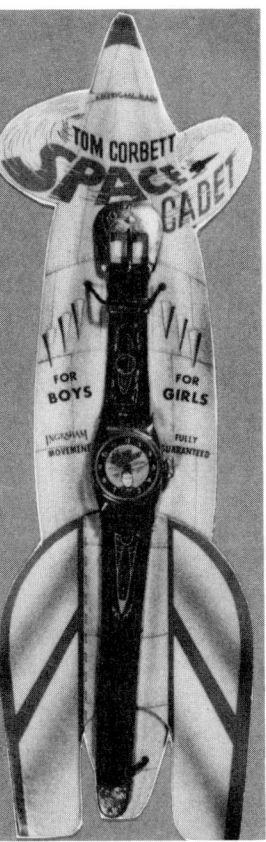

T6065	Illustrated belt	30 - 60
T6070	3-D photo badge	30 - 60
T6075	Wrist compass	25 - 50
T6080	Hair Slickum (Vauntines, Inc.)	25 - 60
T6081	Shampoo (Vauntines, Inc.)	25 - 60
T6085	Belt (on card, w/special metal rocket ship buckle)	55 - 125
T6100	Sparkling Space gun/rifle (Marx)	100 - 200
T6110	Spaceship balloon or Jet-propelled Rocket balloon	25 - 50
T6115	Set of Soap, Rocket Ship & Bubble Bath	25 - 75
T6120	Pin-on Rocket Lite	20 - 55
T6121	Rocket-Lite membership card	5 - 15
T6130	"Space Cadet at Space Academy" record (RCA)	20 - 40
T6140	Tin windup Rocket (Marx)	175 - 325
T6145	Dolls, male or female, ea	95 - 275
T6150	Push-out Book (Saalfield, 1952)	30 - 60
T6155	Coloring book, Corbett cover (Saalfield, 1952)	15 - 50
T6156	Coloring book, cockpit cover (Saalfield, 1952)	25 - 70
T6161-63	Tray puzzles, 3 different (Saalfield, 1952) ea	10 - 35
T6168-78	Comic books (Dell), 11 different, ea	7 - 30
T6179	Face ring	15 - 35
T6180-82	Comic books (Prize), 3 different, ea	10 - 45
T6185	March of Comics #102	15 - 50
T6190	*Wonder Book of Space*	8 - 18
T6191	*Tom Corbett's Trip to the Moon*, reprint of T6190 (1953)	5 - 15
Novels T6192-99 (Grosset & Dunlap)		
T6192	#1 *Stand by for Mars* (1952)	10 - 20
T6193	#2 *Danger in Deep Space* (1953)	8 - 18
T6194	#3 *On the Trail of the Space Pirates* (1953)	8 - 18
T6195	#4 *The Space Pioneers* (1953)	8 - 18
T6196	#5 *The Revolt on Venus* (1954)	8 - 18
T6197	#6 *Treaery in Outer Space* (1955)	8 - 18
T6198	#7 *Sabotage in Space* (1955)	8 - 18
T6199	#8 *The Robot Rocket* (1956)	8 - 18
T6400	Magic Picture Eye, 4 different (Kellogg's) ea	10 - 35
T6450	Cereal boxes	50 - 200

215

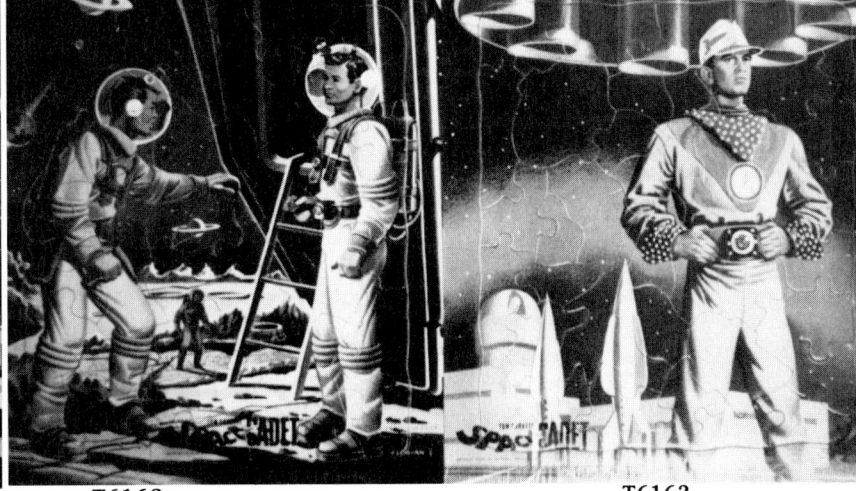

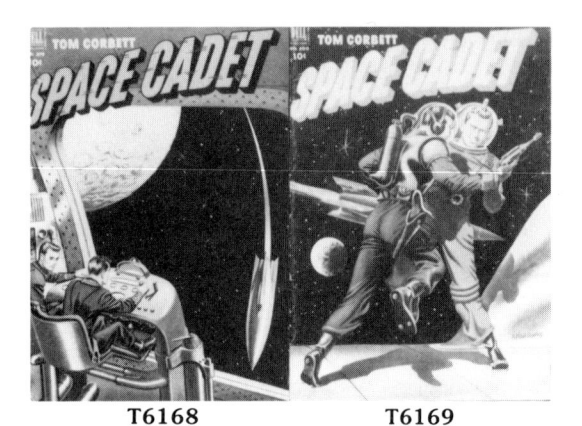

T6168   T6169   T6176   T6177

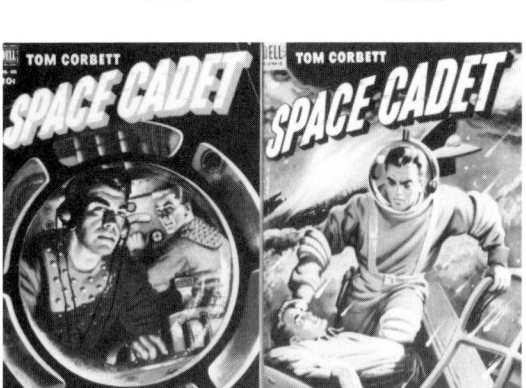

T6170   T6171    T6178    T6520-31

T6172   T6173   T6161   T6162

T6174   T6175    T6510

216

Membership kit T6500-06

T6500	Certificate and mailer	15 - 45
T6501	Badge	20 - 55
T6502	Patch	25 - 65
T6503	Decoder, cardboard	20 - 55
T6504	Photo	15 - 25
T6505	Newspaper	25 - 75
T6506	Membership card	15 - 35

Corn Flakes boxes w/cut-outs T6510-13, complete box

T6510	Visor	40 - 180
T6511	Gauntlets	40 - 180
T6512	Insignia	40 - 180
T6513	Ray Gun	40 - 180

Rings T6520-31 (Kellogg's)

T6520	Space Cruiser	10 - 15
T6521	Rocket Scout	10 - 15
T6522	Space Academy	10 - 15
T6523	Space suit	10 - 15
T6524	Space helmet	10 - 15
T6525	Insignia	15 - 20
T6526	Tom Corbett, Space Cadet	15 - 20
T6527	Space Cadet dress uniform	10 - 15
T6528	Girl's space uniform	10 - 15
T6529	Parallo-Ray gun	10 - 15
T6530	Sound Ray gun	10 - 15
T6531	Strato-Telescope	10 - 15
T6570	Expansion band ring	100 - 225
T6571	Space Cadet figural pin	15 - 45
T6600	Bread end labels, ea	2 - 6
T6605	Album for bread end labels	10 - 35
T7000	Space Cadet paperback	1 - 3

T6505

T6500

T6504

T6501

T6502

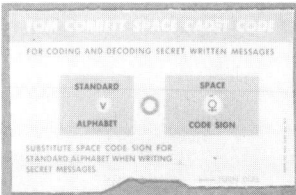

T6503

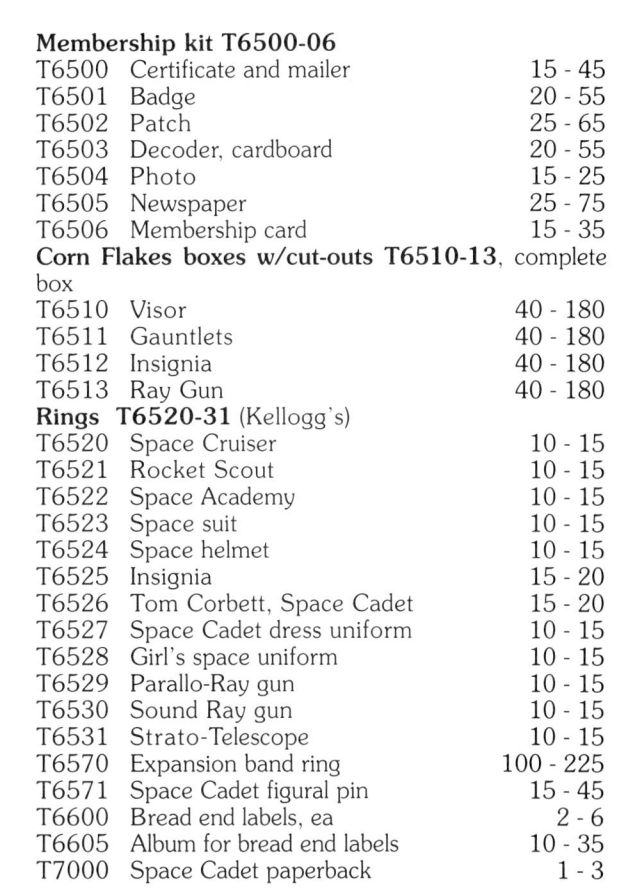

T6450

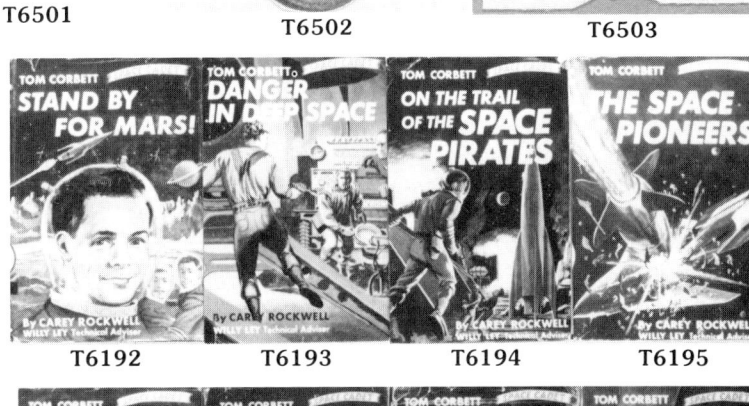

T6192

T6193

T6194

T6195

T6196

T6197

T6198

T6199

217

2001/2010/2061

In 1968, Stanley Kubrick and Arthur C. Clarke collaborated to produce the most highly-acclaimed and debated science fiction film of the time. *2001: A Space Odyssey* was a milestone in special effects, and was one of the first space adventures to take a realistic approach to space travel, rather than a fantastic one. The film and its sequel, *2010: The Year We Make Contact*, related the strange tale of humankind's encounters with the mysterious black monoliths. Clarke wrote novelized versions of both films, as well as *2061: Odyssey Three*.

There are no "heroes" in *2001*, and as such no character merchandise. The most prominent items associated with the films were model kits produced by Aurora.

T9000	*2001* souvenir program	5 - 15
T9005	Button	8 - 20
T9010	Space Clipper model kit	50 - 150
T9015	Space Shuttle *Orion* model kit (reissue of T9010)	25 - 75
T9020	Moon Bus model kit	50 - 150
T9030	*2001* novel, hardcover	2 - 8
T9031	*2001* novel, paperback	1 - 3
T9040	*2001* album	2 - 8
T9045	2001 art print, 24" x 28"	10 - 20
T9050	Graphic novel (Marvel, 1976)	1 - 3
T0960-09	Comic series (Marvel) #1-10, ea	1 - 2
T9080	Jigsaw puzzle	10 - 20
T9200	*2010* souvenir program	3 - 10
T9210	*2010* novel, hardcover	2 - 8
T9211	*2010* novel, paperback	.50 - 2
T9220	*2010* album	1 - 6
T9230	*2010* graphic novel	1 - 3
T9230-31	*2010* comics, #1 or 2, (Marvel, 1985) ea	.50 - 2
T9400	*2061* novel, hardcover	3 - 10
T9401	*2061* novel, paperback	.50 - 2

218

V

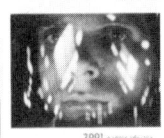

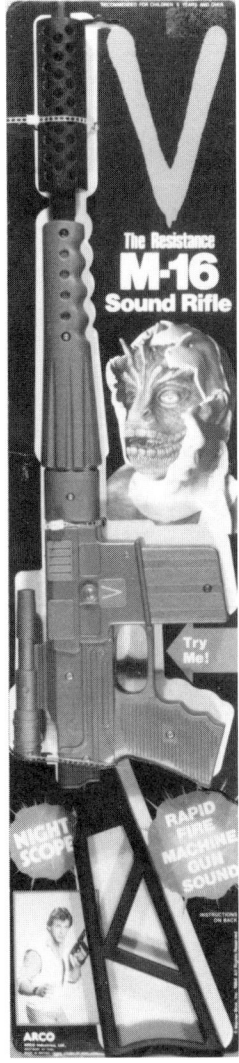

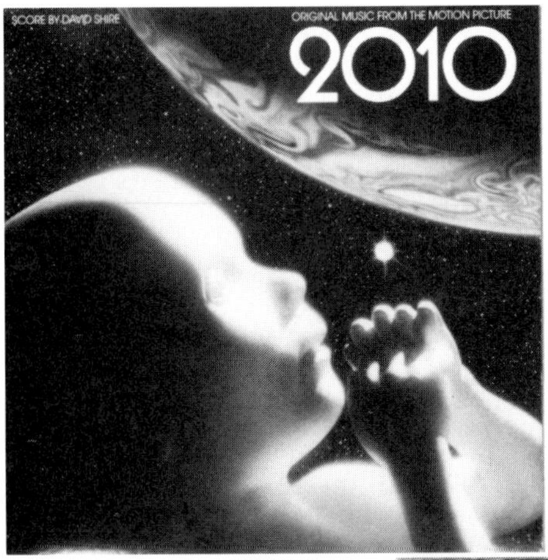

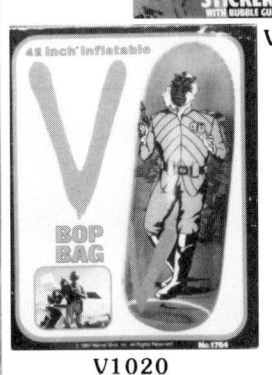

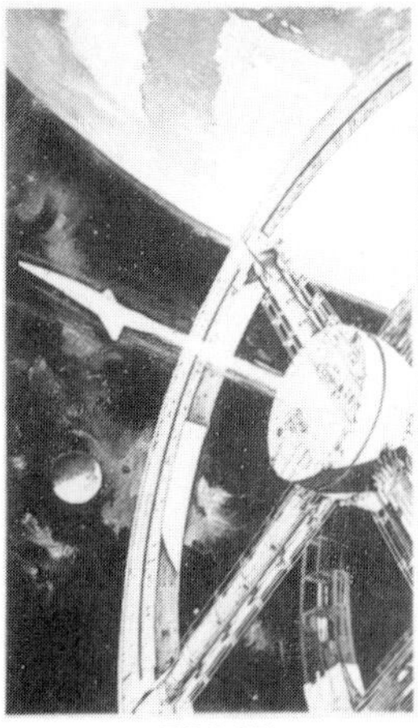

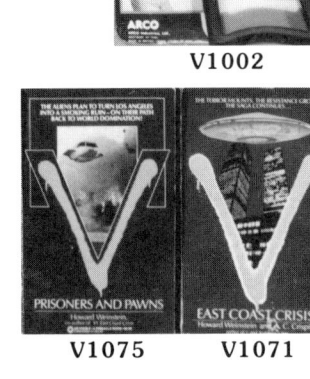

"V" is the story of aliens who come to Earth from a dying planet. The visitors looked human, and claimed to be on a mission of peace. They offered advanced technology in exchange for a small share of Earth's natural resources. It all seemed too good to be true, and it was. The "V" visitors turned out to be cruel reptilian creatures who wanted to enslave the human race. A small group of doubters discovered the truth and struck back. In opposing the visitors, the series commented on humanity's misuse of water, over dependence on mass communication, and commercialization of daily life.

"V" was a 10-hour miniseries in two parts which appeared on NBC in 1984. The story became the basis for a regular television series and a strong merchandising effort which faded with cancellation of the program. Merchandise is harder to come by than most modern space adventures, due to the short life of the series. The lunch box in particular is one of the more widely sought items.

V1000	45'er Action set	30 - 60
V1001	45'er Sound Pistol & holster	18 - 45
V1002	M-16 Sound Rifle	30 - 75
V1005	Walkie-Talkies	20 - 50
V1006	12" V doll w/removable mask (human head) and gun	15 - 25
V1010	Jigsaw puzzles, 4 different, ea	3 - 10
V1020	Bop bag	6 - 18
V1025	Puffy stickers, 3 different, ea	1 - 2
V1030	Trading cards, set of 66	8 - 12
V1031	Individual trading cards, ea	.10 - .25
V1032	Stickers for V1030, set of 22	3 - 6
V1033	Individual stickers, ea	.15 - .25
V1034	Box for V1030	4 - 9
V1035	Wrappers for V1030	1 - 2
V1036	Unopened waxpacks for V1030	1 - 4
V1050	Lunch box (Aladdin)	20 - 50
V1051	Bottle for V1050	15 - 35
V1060	Poster	1 - 3

Paperback novels V1070-79 (Pinnacle, 1984-85)

V1070	*V*	.50 - 2
V1071	*East Coast Crisis*	.50 - 2
V1072	*The Pursuit of Diana*	.50 - 2
V1073	*The Chicago Conversion*	.50 - 2
V1074	*The Florida Project*	.50 - 2
V1075	*Prisoners and Pawns*	.50 - 2
V1076	*The Alien Swordmaster*	.50 - 2
V1077	*The Crivit Experiment*	.50 - 2
V1078	*The New England Resistance*	.50 - 2
V1079	*Death Tide*	.50 - 2

Comic books V1100-17 (DC, 1985-86)

V1100	#1	1 - 2
V1101-17	#2-18, ea	.50 - 1

V1010

V1001

V1005

V1031

V1070

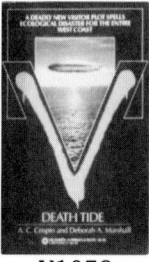

V1000

V1079

V1010

220

INDEX

Alien/Aliens 15
Battlestar Galactica 17
Black Hole, The 23
Buck Rogers 27
   Action Figures 39
   Atomic Pistol 37
   Birthstone Ring 37
   Books 27, 29, 31, 35, 37, 41, 43
   Comic Books 37
   Disintegrator Pistol 31
   Fireworks 35
   Games 29, 43
   Glasses 41
   Gum Cards 30, 34
   Liquid Helium Water Pistol 33
   Pinback Buttons 31
   Ring of Saturn 37
   Rocket Pistol 29, 31
   Rocket Roller Skates 31
   Satellite Pioneers 37
   Solar Scouts 33
   Solar System Map 27
   Sonic Ray Gun 37
   Spaceship Kits 29
   Tootsietoy Rocket Ships 35
   Uniform 29
   Watches 31
Captain Video 43
Close Encounters 45
Dune 45
E.T. 51
Flash Gordon 57
Forbidden Planet 61
John Carter of Mars 62
Planet of the Apes 64
Rocky Jones 77
Space 1999 77
Space Patrol 80
Star Trek 89
   Action Figures 91
   Action Figure Playsets, Vehicles
      and Accessories 93
   Advertisements, Print 95
   Advertising Signs 95
   Animation Cels and Backgrounds .. 95
   Apparel 95
   Banks 95
   Belts and Buckles 95
   Binoculars 95
   Books 95
   Bottles and Decanters 99
   Bumper Stickers 99
   Calculators 100
   Calendars 100
   Candy Boxes 100
   Carded Novelties, Miscellaneous .. 100
   Cereal Boxes 100
   Clocks 100
   Coins 101
   Colorforms 101
   Coloring and Painting Sets 101
   Comic Books 101
   Convention Programs 103
   Costumes and Play Outfits 103
   Dolls 103
   Fan Club Kits and Publications ... 103
   Fanzines 103
   Films, Slides and Viewers 105
   Frisbees 105
   Fun Meal Boxes and Prizes 105
   Games 107
   Glasses 110
   Greeting Cards 111
   Gum Cards, Gum Wrappers and
      Trading Cards 111
   Hats and Caps 113
   Household Goods, Products and
      Miscellaneous 114
   Inflatables 114
   Iron-On Appliques and Transfers . 114
   Jewelry (except rings) 114
   Keychains and Cases 114
   Kites 115
   Lead Miniatures 115
   License Plates 116
   Lunch Boxes 116
   Magazines with Star Trek
      Articles 116
   Maps 117
   Masks 117
   Mobile 117
   Model Kits 117
   Molding Kits 119
   Mugs 119
   Party Supplies and Hats 119
   Patches 120
   Patterns 120
   Phasers, Guns and Other Play
      Weapons 120
   Pinback Buttons, Badges and
      Tabs 120
   Plates 122
   Playing Cards 122
   Playsets 124
   Postcards 124
   Posters — Film 124
   Posters — Other 124
   Press Kits 124
   Programs and Official Collector's
      Editions 125
   Puzzles and Puzzle Sets 125
   Radios, Phonographs, and Tape
      Recorders 125
   Records, Tapes and Compact
      Discs 125
   Rocket Kits 126
   School Supplies 126
   Sheets, Pillows, Bedspreads,
      Sleeping Bags and Drapes 127
   Spock Ears 127
   Stamps, Collector's 127
   Stamps, Rubber 127
   Stickers and Sticker Books 127
   String Art 127
   Towels 127
   Tribbles 127
   Vehicles 128
   Video Tapes and Discs 128
   Walkie-Talkies 130
   Wastebaskets 130
   Watches 130
Star Wars 130
   Action Figures 130
   Action Figure Playsets, Vehicles
      and Accessories 151
   Action Figure Storage Cases 159
   Animation Cels and Backgrounds 159
   Apparel 159
   Art Portfolios 159
   Banks 160
   Belts and Buckles 160
   Book Marks 160
   Book Plates 161
   Bookends 161
   Books 161
   Bumper Stickers 163
   Calendars 163
   Candy Containers 165
   Cereal Boxes 165
   Clocks 165
   Coins 165
   Coloring and Painting Sets 166
   Comic Books 167
   Cookie Jars 169
   Cork Boards 169
   Costumes and Play Outfits 169
   Decals 171
   Dinnerware 171
   Dixie Cups and Boxes 171
   Fan Club Kits and Publications ... 171
   Figures — Other 173
   Films, Slides and Viewers 173
   Furniture 175
   Games 175
   Glasses 177
   Gum Cards, Gum Wrappers and
      Trading Cards 179
   Guns 182
   Hats and Caps 183
   Household Goods, Products and
      Miscellaneous 183
   Iron-On Appliques and Transfers . 184
   Jewelry (except rings) 184
   Kenner Merchandise Catalogs 184
   Keychains and Cases 185
   Lamps, Lampshades and Night-
      lights 185
   Lead Miniatures 185
   Lightsabers 185
   Lunch Boxes 185
   Magazines and Magazine
      Articles 187
   Masks 187
   Micro Collection Sets 189
   Model Kits 189
   Mugs and Tankards 191
   Music Boxes 193
   Newspapers 193
   Party Supplies and Hats 193
   Passports 193
   Patches 193
   Patterns 194
   Pens, Pencils and Pencil Cases ... 194
   Photos and Photo Sets 194
   Pinback Buttons, Badges and
      Tabs 195
   Plates 195
   Play-Doh Sets 195
   Plush Stuffed Characters 197
   Posters — Film 197
   Posters — Premium 199
   Posters — Other 199
   Press Kits 201
   Programs and Official Collector's
      Editions 201
   Projection Equipment 201
   Punching Bags 201
   Puppets 201
   Puzzles and Puzzle Sets 201
   Racing Set 203
   Radios 203
   Records, Tapes and Compact
      Discs 203
   Remote-Controlled Toys 205
   Rings 205
   Rocket Kits 205
   Roller Skates 205
   School Supplies 205
   Sheets, Pillows, Bedspreads,
      Sleeping Bags and Drapes 206
   Shoelaces 206
   Shoes and Slippers 206
   Soap, Shampoo and Bubble Bath
      Products 206
   Stamps, Collector's 207
   Stamps, Rubber 207
   Stickers and Sticker Books 207
   Suncatchers 207
   Swimming Pools and Access-
      ories 207
   Switchplate Covers 209
   Telephones 209
   Tin Boxes and Containers 209
   Toothbrushes 209
   Towels 209
   Vehicles 209
   Video Tapes and Discs 211
   Watches 211
Tom Corbett 213
2001/2010/2061 218
V 219

BIBLIOGRAPHY

Asherman, Allan. *The Star Trek Compendium*. New York: Wallaby Books, 1981.

Asimov, Isaac. *Foundation*. 1951. New York: Ballantine Books, 1983.

—. *Foundation and Empire*.

—. *Second Foundation*.

—. *I, Robot*. Garden City, New York: Doubleday and Co., 1950.

Boulle, Pierre. *Planet of the Apes*. Trans. Xan Fielding. New York: Signet Books, 1963.

Bradbury, Ray. *The Martian Chronicles*. 1950. Biographical sketch and bibliography by William F. Nolan. Garden City, New York: Doubleday and Co., Inc., 1973.

Burroughs, Edgar Rice. *A Princess of Mars*. 1912. New York: Ballantine Books, 1963.

—. *The Gods of Mars*. 1913. New York: Ballantine Books, 1963.

—. *The Warlord of Mars*. 1913-14. New York: Ballantine Books, 1963.

—. *Thuvia, Maid of Mars*. 1916. New York: Ballantine Books, 1963.

—. *The Chessmen of Mars*. 1922. New York: Ballantine Books, 1963.

—. *The Master Mind of Mars*. 1927. New York: Ballantine Books, 1963.

—. *A Fighting Man of Mars*. 1930. New York: Ballantine Books, 1964.

—. *Swords of Mars*. 1934, 1935. New York: Ballantine Books, 1964.

—. *Synthetic Men of Mars*. 1939. New York: Ballantine Books, 1964.

—. *Llana of Gathol*. 1941. New York: Ballantine Books, 1964.

—. *John Carter of Mars*. 1941, 1943. New York: Ballantine Books, 1965.

—. *Pirates of Venus*. 1932. New York: Ace Books, 1963.

Clarke, Arthur C. *2001: A Space Odyssey*. New York: New American Library, 1988.

—. *2010: Odyssey Two*. New York: Del Rey Books, 1982.

—. *2061: Odyssey Three*. New York: Del Rey Books, 1987.

Dunning, John. *Tune in Yesterday*. Englewood Cliffs, New Jersey: Prentice-Hall, Inc., 1976.

Fischer, Stuart. *Kids' TV: The First 25 Years*. New York: Facts On File Publications, 1983.

Foster, Alan Dean. *Alien*. New York: Warner Books, 1979.

—. *Aliens*. New York: Warner Books, 1986.

—. *The Last Starfighter*. New York: Berkley Books, 1984.

—. *Splinter of the Mind's Eye*. New York: Del Rey Books, 1978.

Gent, Donald F. *Star Wars: The Empire Strikes Back*. New York: Del Rey Books, 1983.

Gerrold, David. *Encounter at Farpoint*. New York: Pocket Books, 1987.

—. *The World of Star Trek*. 2nd ed. New York: Bluejay Books, Inc., 1984.

Glut, Donald F. and Jim Harmon. *The Great Television Heroes*. Garden City, New York: Doubleday & Co., Inc., 1975.

Heinlein, Robert A. *Expanded Universe*. 1980. New York: Ace Books, 1982.

—. *Methuselah's Children*. New York: Signet Books, 1958.

—. *Space Cadet*. New York: Charles Scribner's Sons, 1948.

—. *Stranger in a Strange Land*. 1961. New York: Ace Books, 1987.

Herbert, Frank. *Dune*. Philadelphia/New York/London: Chilton Book Co., 1965.

—. *Dune Messiah*. New York: G. P. Putnam's Sons, 1969.

—. *Children of Dune*. New York: G. P. Putnam's Sons, 1976.

—. *God Emperor of Dune*. New York: G. P. Putnam's Sons, 1981.

—. *Heretics of Dune*. New York: G. P. Putnam's Sons, 1984.

—. *Chapterhouse: Dune*. New York: G. P. Putnam's Sons, 1985.

—. *Eye*. New York: Berkley Publishing Corporation, 1985.

Kahn, James. *Star Wars: Return of the Jedi*. New York, Del Rey Books, 1983.

Kaufmann, William J. *Discovering the Universe*. New York: W. H. Freeman and Co., 1987.

Lackmann, Ron. *Remember Television*. New York: G. P. Putnam's Sons, 1971.

Larson, Glen A. and Robert Thurston. *Battlestar Galactica*. New York: Berkley Publishing Corporation, 1978.

Lear, John. *Kepler's Dream*. Trans. Patricia Kirkwood. Berkeley and Los Angeles: University of California Press, 1965.

Lesser, Robert. *A Celebration of Comic Art and Memorabilia*. New York: Hawthorn Books, Inc., 1975.

Lloyd, Ann (ed). *Movies of the Fifties*. Consultant ed. David Robinson. London: Orbis Publishing Ltd., 1982.

Markowski, Carol and Gene. *Tomart's Price Guide to Character & Promotional Glasses*. Dayton, Ohio: Tomart Publications, 1990.

McNelly, Dr. Willis E. comp. *The Dune Encyclopedia*. New York: Berkley Books, 1984.

Menville, Douglas and R. Reginald. *Things to Come: An Illustrated History of the Science Fiction Film*. Introduction by Ray Bradbury. New York: Times Books, 1977.

Naha, Ed. *The Making of Dune*. New York: Berkley Books, 1984.

Overstreet, Robert M. *The Official Overstreet Comic Book Price Guide*. 19th ed. New York: The House of Collectibles, 1989.

Raymond, Alex. *Into the Water World of Mongo*. Introduction by Maurice Horn. New York: Nostalgia Press, 1971.

Scholes, Robert, and Eric Rabkin. *Science Fiction: History, Science, Vision*. New York: Oxford UP, 1977.

Smith, L. Neil. *Lando Calrissian and the Mindharp of Sharu*. New York, Del Rey Books, 1983.

—. *Lando Calrissian and the Flamewind of Oseon*. New York, Del Rey Books, 1983.

—. *Lando Calrissian and the Starcave of Thonboka*. New York, Del Rey Books, 1983.

Spielberg, Steven. *Close Encounters of the Third Kind*. New York: Dell Publishing Co., Inc., 1977.

Tumbusch, Tom [E.]. *Illustrated Radio Premium Catalog and Price Guide*. Dayton, Ohio: Tomart Publications, 1989.

Verne, Jules. *From the Earth to the Moon*. Trans. Walter James Miller. *The Annotated Jules Verne*. New York: Thomas Y. Crowell, Publishers.

Velasco, Raymond L. comp. *A Guide to the Star Wars Universe*. New York: Del Rey Books, 1984.

Weiss, Ken and Ed Goodgold. *To Be Continued...*. New York: Crown Publishers, Inc., 1972.

Wells, H. G. *Collector's Book of Science Fiction*. Secaucus, New Jersey: Castle Books, 1978.

Photography by Pam Lott

ABOUT THE AUTHOR

Tom N. Tumbusch was born six weeks late and has been procrastinating ever since. He first became interested in science fiction when a frazzled, overworked baby-sitter gave him a copy of *Stranger in a Strange Land* to keep him quiet. Since then he has expanded his horizons to include journalism, philosophy, and theatre. In addition to space adventure and science fiction, his hobbies include role-playing games, comic books, loosing at racquetball, speculation on the nature of the universe, singing, juggling (sort of), archery, backgammon, listening to bizarre music and telling bad puns. He is a pursuivant herald in the Society for Creative Anachronism, which has improved his skill in public speaking and dodging crossbow bolts. Please do not confuse him with his father, Tom E. Tumbusch, author of Tomart's Disneyana and Radio Premium guides. This is his first published work.